Explorers of the World

William R. Clark

with paintings by Hans Schwarz

Explorers
of the World

Nature and Science Library: The Earth
published for
The American Museum of Natural History
by

The Natural History Press / Garden City, New York

The Natural History Press, publisher for the
American Museum of Natural History, is a division
of Doubleday & Company, Inc. The Press is
directed by an editorial board made up of
members of the staff of both the Museum and
Doubleday. The Natural History Press has its
editorial offices at The American Museum of
Natural History, Central Park West at 79th Street,
New York 24, New York, and its business offices
at 501 Franklin Avenue, Garden City, New York.

Editorial Adviser	Roy A. Gallant
Editor	Kit Coppard
Designer	Arthur Lockwood
Art Assistant	Brian Lee
Research	Enid Moore
Route Maps	Peter Sullivan

First published in the United States of America in 1964 by
The Natural History Press, Garden City, New York,
in association with Aldus Books Limited

Library of Congress Catalog Card No. 64–10003
© Aldus Books Limited, London, 1964

Printed in Italy by Arnoldo Mondadori, Verona

Contents

1 Explorers of Old

The names of the earliest explorers are lost far back in the mists of time. They lived many thousands of years ago, when men roamed in search of game across land they had not yet learned to cultivate. Later—how many generations we shall never know—other men drifted across the great land masses, populating Europe, Asia, Africa, and the Americas. They traveled overland as wandering tribes, some settling down where the land and climate were to their liking, others pushing ever onward. But these men left no written records of their journeys. The result was that, thousands of years later, when the curtain rose on the prologue of recorded history, the men who became explorers in the modern sense of the word knew only of the peoples and lands that formed their own small world.

This known world—called by the Greeks the Habitable World—surrounded the Mediterranean, which extends for 2000 miles from the fertile coastal fringes of the Middle East to the narrows we call the Strait of Gibraltar (but which the ancients knew as the Pillars of Hercules). Around the eastern end of the Mediterranean, some 5000 years ago, there grew up the civilizations of Egypt and Sumer to be followed, 1000 years or so later, by those of Babylon, Assyria, the Minoans on the island of Crete, and the cities of the Greeks. At the far eastern end of the Mediterranean were a people who flourished for more than 1000 years; and from them came the first real explorers as we use the word today. These men were the Phoenicians.

The Phoenicians Venture for Trade

The Phoenicians lived on the coast of what later became Palestine, and from their rise about 1400 B.C. to their decline about 400 B.C. they were the merchants of the ancient world. Earlier, Egyptians had sent small

Over countless generations tribal groups of the Old Stone Age drifted slowly across the great land masses, some settling where the climate was favorable, others forever on the move. Exploration during this early period arose sometimes from curiosity, but mainly from the constant need to search for food. Chance meetings like this one between members of different settlements must have caused mutual fear and suspicion.

vessels far up the Nile, and their traders had struck southward to the Sudan, which was on the fringe of the known world. The Assyrians had navigated the Tigris and the Euphrates. During the early days of their power, the Phoenicians, in much the same way, gathered further details of the coasts and rivers in the areas. Later they became more ambitious.

Their single-masted ships, many carrying long lines of oarsmen for use when the winds failed, voyaged along the shores of the Mediterranean carrying cargoes of silver and iron, sheep and goats, linen, brasswork, and slaves. These first merchant venturers were constantly looking for new sources of raw materials. When they found such a source, small groups of men, women, and children would be sent to colonize the area.

At a date we do not know (but probably between 900 and 600 B.C.) the Phoenicians began to take their ships out into distant, unexplored waters. First they sailed down the Red Sea, began trading with the tribes that lived at Aden, and then across the Indian Ocean to

Assyrian river craft, about 1000 B.C.

Man's two basic uses for ships have remained constant—the pursuit of trade, and war. In the pre-Christian era, exploration by sea was usually a by-product of one of these. The Assyrians' needs were for simple craft (above) to carry fish or grain up and down river. The more ambitious Egyptians developed larger ships, powered by sail (below), to trade primarily along the Nile. For long voyages across the Mediterranean, however, they often relied on the merchantmen and warships of the Phoenicians (right). It was probably in ships of this type that King Necho of Egypt ordered a Phoenician fleet to sail completely around Africa in about 600 B.C.

Egyptian trading vessel, about 1500 B.C.

Phoenician warships and merchantmen, about 700 B.C.

make contact with the peoples of India. Only the barest details, some recorded by the prophet Ezekiel, are known of these early voyages; and it was not until 600 B.C. that the Phoenicians made a journey of which we have any real record. This bold voyage took them completely around Africa. It was carried out on the orders of the Egyptian king Necho and its importance in the story of exploration is made clear by the Greek historian Herodotus, who recorded it in his *History*.

It appears that this expedition was a large one, but supplies of food, a constant worry to the first seamen, were obtained quite simply; according to Herodotus: "When autumn came they went ashore, wherever they might happen to be and, having sown a tract of land with corn, waited until the grain was fit to cut. Having reaped it they again set sail; and thus it came to pass that two whole years went by, and it was not until the third year that they doubled the Pillars of Hercules, and made good their voyage home."

We know nothing more about this long voyage, and more than a century passed before Phoenicians made a second exploratory venture—this one part-way down the west coast of Africa. This particular voyage was carried out by Hanno of Carthage, the city on the north coast of Africa that had by this time become the most important Phoenician settlement. The object of the voyage was to reinforce the Phoenician colonies on the coast of Morocco and to found new ones farther down the coast of West Africa. Because Hanno left an account of the voyage when he returned to Carthage, we know at least a little of the strange sights that he and his companions saw.

No less than 67 fifty-oared galleys set sail on the expedition, carrying "a multitude of men and women to the number of 30,000, with provisions and other equipments." They passed the Pillars of Hercules, sailed on for two days, and put the first group of colonists ashore. Then they sailed on westward and turned south down the coast of Africa until they came to "a lake not far from the sea, full of reeds, many and large. In it were elephants, and other beasts of all kinds, feeding."

His account reveals the wonder that these first explorers experienced at seeing new sights: "Beyond the Lixiatiae [an unknown race of men] there dwelt the Aethiopians, altogether inhospitable, inhabiting a country abounding in wild beasts and intersected by great mountains, from which they say the River Lixias flows. Round the mountains dwelt, it was said, men of strange shape, called Troglodytes, whom the Lixias asserted to be swifter in running than horses."

After Hanno had taken interpreters on board, he sailed on again south and east, apparently around into what we now call the Gulf of Guinea. "There we found, in the recess of a gulf, a small island, having a circumference of five stadia [the Attic stadium equals 607 feet], which we colonized and named Kerne, after my daughter Kerne, who was the first to land from the 50-oared galley," Hanno wrote.

It was from this point, where they began to sail inland on what he described as a great lake, that their adventures really began. "The lake contained three islands larger than Kerne, from which, accomplishing a day's sail, we came to the end of the lake, beyond which stretch very great mountains, full of wild men, clad in the skins of beasts, who cast stones and drove us off, preventing us from landing," says Hanno. "Sailing thence we came to another large and wide river, full of crocodiles and hippopotami. Here Astraeos, the pilot, was killed by a crocodile, from which circumstances the river received its name."

They returned to Kerne, from where they sailed south for 12 days, "until we came to a great gulf, which interpreters said was called Hesperou Keras [the Horn of the West]. In it was a large island, on which we landed; and by day we saw nothing but woods, but by night we saw many fires burning and heard the sound of flutes and cymbals, and the beating of drums, and an immense shouting. Fear therefore seized us, and the soothsayers bade us [leave]. . . .

"Having speedily set sail, we passed by a burning country, full of incense, and from it huge streams of fire flowed into the sea; and the land was inaccessible because of heat. Being alarmed, we speedily sailed away thence also, and going along four days we saw by night the land full of flame, and in the midst was a lofty fire, greater than the rest, and seeming to touch the stars. This by day appeared a vast mountain, called Theon Ochema [the Chariot of the Gods]. On the third day from this, sailing by fiery streams, we came to a gulf called Notou Keras [the Horn of the South]. In the recess of the gulf was an island, like the former, containing a lake, and in this was an island full of wild men. By far the greater number were women with rough hairy bodies, whom the interpreters called Gorillas. And when we pursued them, we could not catch any of the men, who all escaped our hands, being climbers of precipices, and defending themselves with stones. But we took three women, who bit and scratched those who led them and would not follow. So we killed and flayed them and took their skins to

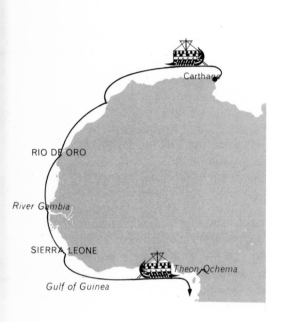

The route of Hanno's remarkable voyage along the West African coast around 450 B.C. is based on records left by him. His fleet of 67 ships carried about 30,000 men and women, many of whom were put ashore en route to colonize the coastal areas.

Karchedon, for we sailed no farther, our provisions running short."

Hanno's voyage was an exceptional example of many journeys made by the Phoenician adventurers. Some, having passed the Pillars of Hercules, turned north instead of south, hugging the Atlantic coast until they crossed the open seas to the Cassiterides, "the Tin Isles," or Scillies, near Britain. From here they brought back the valuable metal to their own country. Yet we have no details of these voyages. And, with the exception of Hanno, we do not know even the names of these adventurous Phoenicians.

Pytheas's Voyage to the North

It was not until the fourth century B.C. that there came on the scene another man who was to enlarge the known world and whose name has been recorded. This was Pytheas of Massilia (the Marseilles of France today), then a Greek colony. An adventurer, astronomer, and scholar, Pytheas set out to discover new lands beyond the Habitable World. According to some of the

In his diary of the voyage, Hanno wrote: "We saw by night the land full of flame, and in the midst was a lofty fire, greater than the rest and seeming to touch the stars. This by day appeared a vast mountain, called Theon Ochema." This must have been Mount Cameroon, a 13,300-foot volcano that last erupted in the year 1922.

authorities, his motive was to find the source of the tin that was reaching European market places by overland routes from the north. According to others, he set out in search of knowledge for its own sake. Whatever his motives, Pytheas was a courageous man. At the time of his voyage the Phoenicians and the Greeks were great trade rivals, and routes to the rich tin and silver markets were jealously guarded by the Phoenicians. To protect their interests the Phoenicians set up a blockade at the Pillars of Hercules.

What we know about Pytheas is not learned from his own account, since this was lost after his return to Massilia, but from second- or third-hand stories, each of which gives only a portion of his tale. Piecing these together, however, we discover that he set out from Massilia about 330 or 325 B.C., passed the Pillars of Hercules, and followed the Atlantic coast around Spain and on to Brittany. He appears to have hugged the coast until he came to the narrows of the English Channel, and then set course for Britain.

Pytheas is said not only to have visited Britain, but according to Polybius, to have "traveled all over it on foot." We have an account from Diodorus Siculus, a Greek historian, based on Pytheas's description of the tin industry he saw in England. "The natives of Britain by the headland of Belerium [most probably Cornwall]

This Greek vase of about 500 B.C. shows a merchantman (left) and a warship. It was probably in a warship very much like this one that the Greek scholar Pytheas made his voyage to northwestern Europe in the fourth century B.C.

Pytheas explored much of Britain and on one occasion described the wicker coracles used by river people. Coracle making still survives in Wales, as this picture shows.

are unusually hospitable, and thanks to their intercourse with foreign traders have grown gentle in their manner. They extract the tin from its bed by a cunning process. . . . Having smelted the tin and refined it, they hammer it into knucklebone shape and convey it to an adjacent island, Ictis [St. Michael's Mount]. They wait until the tide has drained the intervening firth, and then transport whole loads of tin on wagons. The merchants buy the metal from the natives and carry it [from St. Michael's Mount] to Galatia [France]."

Pytheas became the first voyager, of whom we have at least some account, to probe up toward the cold arctic regions, about which men of his day knew nothing. He appears to have reached the Pentland Firth, which separates the north of Scotland from Orkney, and he recorded with wonder the great rise and fall of the spring tides there—so different from the almost tideless Mediterranean. He mentioned more islands—"the sleeping-place of the sun"—six days' voyage farther north, and spoke of hearing tales about places where the sun is above the horizon all day during the summer and below it all day during the winter.

Pytheas may have traveled as far north as Shetland, Norway, or possibly Iceland. In any case he was the first to bring back an account of the frozen sea, and he described the ice as looking like jellyfish. Pytheas's accounts of his voyage staggered the minds of his countrymen, and they tended to doubt his stories. This has often happened when explorers have attempted to explain the new and astounding things they have seen. Pytheas's description of ice looking like jellyfish is a case in point. A flexible film of new ice forming on the sea can easily be broken into pieces by the slightest breeze. These pieces often bump together forming small rounded disks resembling jellyfish.

There are differing accounts of how Pytheas returned to the Mediterranean, but it seems likely that he followed the coastline back from northern France. Like most early seamen he was probably afraid of losing sight of land because of the uncertainty of navigation. Pytheas and the Phoenicians who preceded him were the first real explorers of the seas. They were the forerunners of sea captains who, more than 1000 years later, were to take another great step forward in discovering vast new areas of the world.

Before this new age of exploration was to open, however, the known world was enlarged by a number of men who traveled overland and faced the problems presented by journeys through the barren deserts of the Middle East and central Asia.

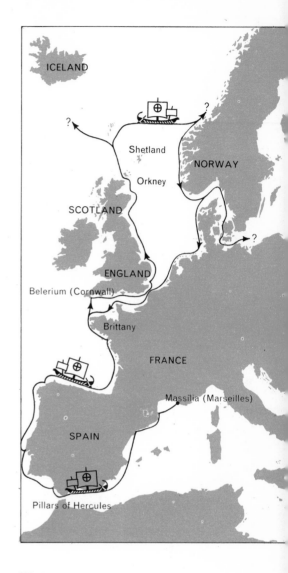

We have only second-hand knowledge of the routes Pytheas followed on his famous voyage. After leaving Britain he sailed to the mysterious "Thule" (possibly Iceland) and became the first Mediterranean explorer to report on conditions near the Arctic Circle.

Exploration by Land

Although the voyages of the Phoenicians were made by traders and colonists, the important land explorations that followed were made by soldiers—by men who led their armies in the wars that were waged in and around the Greek states and the Persian Empire. The world known to European civilizations of this period was still bounded on the east by the hinterland of the eastern Mediterranean—the hills of Asia Minor stretching in brown inhospitable folds northeast toward the Black Sea and the Caspian Sea.

Much of this country, even, was not "known" in the sense that we use the word today—a fact illustrated by one of the great military feats of ancient history: "the March of the Ten Thousand." This took place about 400 B.C., when the Persian prince Cyrus recruited a Greek army to help him force his brother (Artaxerxes II) from the throne.

The army of Greek mercenaries assembled at Sardis in Asia Minor—tall, fair men in armor, willing to fight for whomever paid them. Under Cyrus they marched southeast through the mountains of Cilicia, past Aleppo, and down the Euphrates into Babylon. There, on the plains of Cunaxa, Cyrus himself was killed—and the 10,000 Greeks who survived the battle were left some 1500 miles from home in a country they did not know.

It was then that Xenophon, an Athenian officer, took command of the Ten Thousand. He knew enough geography to realize that if they marched north they must eventually reach the Black Sea, and that from there they would be able to find their way home. As they reached the mountains of Armenia, they passed beyond the territory that even their enemies knew. For days they pushed on northward, passing through narrow gorges where native tribes rolled boulders down on them. Sometimes they marched through driving snow, other times they held to their direction with only the sun as a guide.

After great hardship they finally found a native who claimed that he could lead the army across the final range of mountains ahead. For five more days they pushed on, Xenophon himself marching at the end of the long winding column to see that no stragglers were left behind. On the fifth day the rear guard were puzzled by a great shouting in front. As Xenophon described the scene: "Those who were constantly going forward started running towards the men in front who kept on shouting, and the more there were of them the more shouting there was. . . . Xenophon mounted

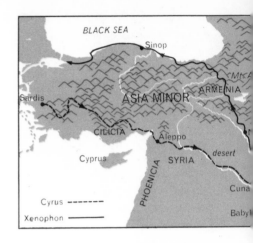

The March of the Ten Thousand (above) under Xenophon began near Babylon about 400 B.C., after their commander, Prince Cyrus, had been killed. This forced march of about 1500 miles was an astounding feat for soldiers so heavily armed (right). The Greeks and Persians knew very little about the lands bordering their empires until Alexander's time, 60 years later.

his horse and, taking Lycus and the cavalry with him, rode forward to give support, and quite soon, they heard the soldiers shouting out 'The sea! The sea!' and passing the word down the column. Then certainly they all began to run, the rear guard and all, and drove the baggage animals and the horses at full speed; and when they had got to the top, the soldiers, with tears in their eyes, embraced each other and their generals and captains."

There before them lay the great expanse of the Black Sea. They realized, at last, that they would soon be reaching country that they knew.

The March of the Ten Thousand shows how little was understood by the Greeks or the Persians about the country that lay on the fringes of their empires. Yet it was less than a century after Xenophon had led his army through the mountains that the first great explorer of the ancient world was to strike out with his troops as far as India itself. His name was Alexander, and while he is renowned as a military leader, his feats as an explorer were equally astonishing.

Alexander's March to India

Alexander was born in 356 B.C. and when he was 14 years old his education was placed under the personal guidance of the Greek philosopher Aristotle. His father, Philip, the king of Macedon (a part of Greece),

Alexander's will to explore and conquer new lands led to his campaigns against the huge armies of the Persian king Darius III. Their battle at Issus, near Antioch, in 333 B.C. (shown below) was one of the most decisive, for it gave Alexander absolute control over Syria and Phoenicia. At the time of this battle Alexander was only 23 years old.

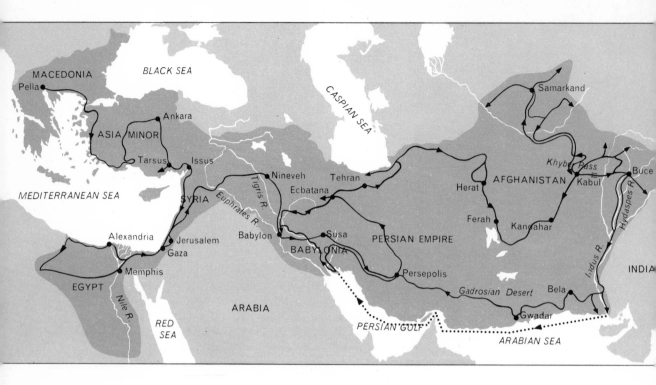

This map shows Alexander's main routes of exploration and his eastern empire (ocher) after his final defeat of the Persian king Darius in 330 B.C. Exploration on such a vast scale did not occur again until the time of the Vikings, more than a thousand years later.

was engaged in the task of uniting the Greek states for an invasion against the Persians. In 336 B.C. Philip was assassinated, and the young Alexander succeeded to the throne. Plutarch, the Greek biographer, describes Alexander as a man of medium height, sturdily built, "of fair complexion and with a tinge of red in his face," with a shock of hair that stood up over his forehead giving the suggestion of a lion, and a certain habit of holding his head on one side.

After first consolidating and establishing his supreme authority in the Greek states, Alexander set out two years later to lead a Greek force against the Persian Empire. In the spring of 334 B.C., with an army of 30,000 men and 5000 horses, Alexander crossed the Hellespont into Asia Minor. The crossing of this narrow stretch of water separating Europe from Asia Minor, known today as the Dardanelles, was the start of an 11-year campaign. Alexander began by leading his armies down through Asia Minor, defeating the Persians and pursuing their leader Darius. Next he marched into Syria, Phoenicia, and Egypt, where he founded the city of Alexandria. In the spring of 331 B.C. he left the Mediterranean and struck deep into the heart of the Persian Empire. He seized Babylonia and finally defeated Darius, who was killed by his own men in the summer of 330 B.C. By this time Alexander was at the foot of the Elburz Mountains (in modern

Direct evidence of Alexander's explorations is to be found in objects like this coin, struck to commemorate his victory over the Indian prince Porus at the Hydaspes River (a tributary of the Indus) in 326 B.C.

Darius's authority over his empire hinged on his control of the royal cities of Persepolis, Susa, and Ecbatana. Alexander destroyed Persepolis (see map) in 331 B.C. This ruined gateway is almost all that remains of Darius's walled palace outside the city.

Persia). At this stage he decided to continue marching northeast instead of turning back toward his homeland, 2000 miles away to the west.

He had by this time conquered all the known world. Now he wanted to know what lay beyond—the constant spur of explorers down the ages. Alexander's "explorers" were for the most part his veteran troops, but he also had with him surveyors, scribes, and men knowledgeable in mining techniques. His supplies were improvised from what he could gather from the land through which his army marched. His only guides were the rumors and reports of the people, and nomadic tribes through whose strange countries he moved. Alexander marched his men to the shores of the Caspian Sea, then through Afghanistan, over the rugged mountains near the Khyber Pass, and, in the spring of 326 B.C., across the Indus River into India.

It was a country whose wonders astounded them. There were great forests in which were elephants and wild peacocks; these were new sights for Alexander's men. And on the upper Indus they had seen crocodiles. The only crocodiles known to Alexander were those of Africa. Was it possible, therefore, that he and his army stood by water that joined the Nile? If they followed the river downstream, might they not eventually come to familiar territory, at the eastern end of the Mediterranean? If we glance at a modern map we will realize how little Alexander and his troops knew of the exciting country through which they now fought their way—traveling almost 1000 miles southward through the Punjab in the Indian subcontinent.

Alexander was continually recruiting new men from the territories he conquered. Now some of his massive army moved on land, along the banks of the Indus, fighting its way past native forces. At the same time other troops advanced in ships that his men had built.

According to the Greek historian Arrian, Alexander's "unquenchable ambition to see the ocean and reach the boundaries of the world made him entrust his own life, and the safety of so many gallant men, to an unknown river, without any guides possessed of the necessary local knowledge. They thus sailed on, ignorant of everything on the way they had to pass. It was entirely left to haphazard and baseless conjecture how far they were from the sea, what tribes dwelt along the banks, whether the river was placid at its mouth, and whether it was thereabout of a depth sufficient for their warships."

Finally there came a day when, as they were passing through a steamy jungle, those on board "began to feel sea-air, and believed the ocean was not far off." At this point in their journey something happened that reveals how little the Greeks knew about any sea other than the Mediterranean, which is virtually tideless. When they began to feel sea air they found that salt water was mingling with the fresh—brought upstream by the rising tide. Not realizing what was happening, they moored their boats on a large island in the middle of the river and went ashore for food. After a while, according to Arrian, "they saw the water continually swelling higher, and overflowing the beach which before was dry. They looked upon this as something supernatural by which the gods signified their wrath against their rash presumption.

"When the vessels were now fairly floated, and the whole squadron scattered in different directions, the men who had gone on shore ran back in consternation to the ships, confounded beyond measure by a calamity of a nature so unexpected. But amid the tumult their haste served only to mar their speed. Some were to be seen pushing the vessels with poles; others had taken their seats to row, but in doing so had meanwhile been preventing the proper adjustment of the oars. Others again, in hastening to sail out into the clear channel, without waiting for the requisite number of sailors and pilots, worked the vessels to little effect, crippled as these were and otherwise difficult to handle. At the same time several other vessels drifted away with the stream before those who were pell-mell crowding into them could all get on board, and in this case the crowding caused as much delay in hurrying off as did the scarcity of hands in the other vessels. From one side were shouted orders to stay, from another to put off, so that amid this confusion of contradictory orders nothing that was of any service could be seen or even heard. In such an emergency the pilots themselves were useless, since their commands could neither be heard for the uproar nor executed by men so distracted with terror."

All this was bad enough. But before order could be regained, the tide began to ebb, leaving the water at a lower level than it had been when the ships had arrived at the island. This caused them to "fall upon their side, and with such violence that the land around them was strewn with baggage, arms, broken oars, and wreckage." As the frightened mariners found themselves marooned on foul-smelling mudflats, there came something else "to add to their terror—monstrous creatures of frightful aspect, which the sea had left behind it, were seen wandering about." Arrian does

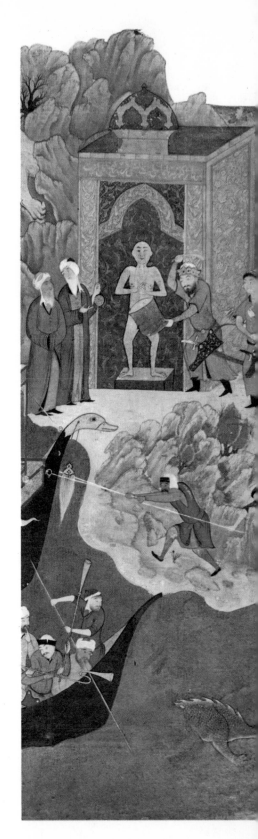

Above: This French painting shows
how the Indus River provided
Alexander and his Mediterranean
sailors with their first, and nearly
disastrous, experience of strong
tidal water. Alexander's men,
according to Arrian, "looked upon
this as something supernatural by
which the gods signified their wrath
against their rash presumption."

Left: This medieval manuscript
shows Alexander destroying "false
idols." Such was the awe inspired
by Alexander that later generations
of Persians adopted him as one of
their own heroes, celebrating him in
poetry and art.

not inform us what these "monstrous creatures" were.

By this time Alexander was very close to the sea.
The ships were repaired, horsemen were sent downstream to give warning of the rise or fall of the tide,
and that night he set sail with an advance party to explore what lay ahead.

On reaching the open sea, according to Arrian, "he
then advanced beyond the mouths of the river Indus
and sailed out into the great main to discover, as he
declared, whether any land lay anywhere in the sea, but
in my opinion, chiefly that it might be said that he had
navigated the great outer seas of India."

When Alexander reassembled his forces at the Indus
delta, he made a decision that reveals him as a true explorer. First he decided to return home along the shores
of the Arabian Sea and the Persian Gulf rather than by
the route on which he had come. This meant the exploration of 1500 miles of unknown land. Dividing his
forces into two groups, he put his stoutest ships under
the command of the Greek admiral Nearchus, who was
ordered to "make himself acquainted with the nature

of the sea" and then to return home via the Persian Gulf. Another party was ordered to travel overland through southern Persia. Alexander himself burned the rest of his vessels and led the second land party on the difficult route along the barren Makran coast. Even today this country is difficult, inhospitable, and dangerous to the traveler.

For about 100 miles Alexander was able to keep contact with his ships at sea. Then he was forced inland, and the desert soon began to take its toll. "The blazing heat and want of water destroyed a great part of the Army," wrote Arrian, "and specially the beasts of burden, which perished from the great depth of the sand, and the heat which scorched like fire, while a great many died of thirst." There were "lofty ridges of deep sand, not hard and compact, but so loose that those who stepped on it sank down as into mud or rather into untrodden snow." They marched by night to escape the heat of the day, but the men would fall asleep on the march. "On awaking afterwards, those who still had some strength left, followed close on the track of the army, and a few out of many saved their lives by overtaking it. The majority perished in the sand like shipwrecked men at sea."

This was the Gadrosian Desert, which long protected the southwestern flanks of India from invasion. As the army marched across it, their numbers diminishing day by day, they were forced to kill their baggage animals for food, and eventually even their horses.

In this barren wilderness almost the only people they saw were the Ichthyophagi, tribes who lived only on fish. They had, it was recorded, "long claw-like nails and long shaggy hair, for they cut the growth of neither. They live in huts constructed of shells and other off-scourings of the sea. Their clothing consists of the skins of wild beasts, and they feed on fish dried in the sun, and the flesh of sea monsters cast on the shore during stormy weather."

The ordeal of Alexander and his surviving men was almost over, for they soon reached "an inhabited region which abounded in all things," a part of the Persian Empire that he had conquered before he set out on his wanderings more than seven years earlier. Plutarch says that "of an army of 120,000 foot and 15,000 horse, he scarcely brought back above a fourth." Alexander rested his men, had them re-equipped, and then marched triumphantly back into provinces and towns where both his name and the exploits of his army had already become famous.

Only the fleet was still missing. Then, at Salmous, in

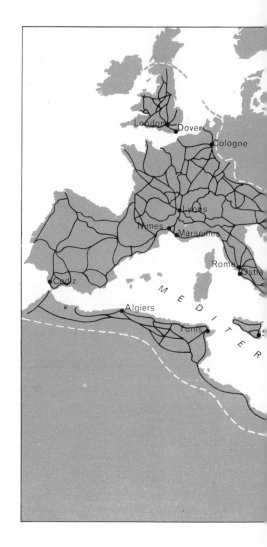

The Romans were colonizers rather than explorers. Their empire in the last two or three hundred years B.C. (above) was smaller although more highly developed than Alexander's. Defense and communications within the empire were greatly strengthened by a vast road network that encircled the Mediterranean and reached as far north as Britain. Roman soldiers, as seen right, served as laborers as well as warriors. In addition to the roads, they built bridges, canals, and forts to guard the frontiers.

what is now Persia, while Alexander was holding a celebration, there came the exciting news that his ships had arrived. Nearchus and his officers appeared with stories of the wonders they had seen on their long voyage through the Arabian Sea and up the Persian Gulf. "The strangest part of their story," wrote Arrian, "was that they had encountered a great many whales, and these of an incredible size. They were in great dread of these monsters, and at first gave up all hope of life, thinking they might at any moment be consigned, boats and all, to destruction; but when, on recovering from their panic, their raised a simultaneous shout, which they increased by rattling their arms and sounding the trumpets, the creatures took alarm at the strange noise, and sank to the depths below."

The men of Alexander's great expedition were reunited after having enlarged the known world; it now included not only the Mediterranean, the northern fringes of Africa, and the coasts of Europe and Britain, but also the huge desert areas of western Asia and parts of India. On a modern map the countries conquered by Alexander or made subject to him include Greece, Bulgaria, Romania, Turkey, Armenia, Persia, Afghanistan, Pakistan, Arabia, Iraq, Syria, Jordan, and Egypt. And, in deciding to split his returning expedition into two groups in order to gain new knowledge, Alexander set an example for mass exploration that has rarely been equaled.

By the spring of 323 B.C., Alexander was again active, this time planning the construction of an immense fleet of ships to open maritime routes from Babylon to Egypt around Arabia. But he was never to see his home again. In June he caught fever and eight days later he died, at the age of 32.

The extent of the known world remained almost unchanged for nearly 1000 years after the death of Alexander. The Romans, who began to build a powerful empire during the middle of the third century B.C., contributed little to exploration. Although the boundaries of Roman military occupation were extended, the geographical information that the Romans acquired was usually of lands already partially known. Rome had enough to do establishing and protecting her frontiers without discovering new lands that she would be unable to control. Her main concern was with administration, and with maintaining a good road network. Merchants plying their trade continued to venture out to the Arabian and Indian coasts, but it was not until many centuries later that explorers began again to set out and discover new lands.

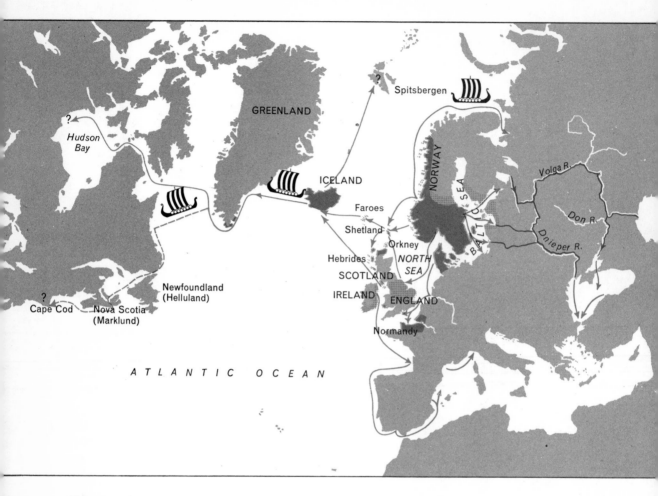

ATLANTIC OCEAN

This map shows the main Viking settlements (blue areas) and routes of exploration (red) from the 8th to 11th centuries. The dotted line traces Leif Ericson's voyage about the year 990. The Vikings were the first sailors who dared strike westward across the Atlantic, and from their colonies in Iceland and Greenland they became the first Europeans to explore the coast of North America.

Vikings Reach the "New World"

These explorers were the Vikings, tall, fair-haired men who lived on the shores of the Baltic Sea and along the Atlantic coast of Scandinavia. While the Mediterranean peoples had been brought up to sail on a semi-enclosed, almost tideless sea, the Vikings learned their seamanship on the great stormy waters that stretch westward from Norway. This, together with the harsher northern climate, made them more conditioned to cold than their Mediterranean predecessors. And, since they were often beyond sight of land, they had more need to learn the art of navigation.

From the middle of the eighth century A.D. the Vikings made many raiding forays in their long galleys to the coasts of England, Scotland, and Ireland, and along the Channel coasts of Europe. In the middle of the ninth century they voyaged northward from Orkney and Shetland, where they had already created colonies, and settled on the coast of Iceland. This bleak, inhospitable country had been visited almost a century earlier by monks from Ireland, but they had not stayed, so it is the Vikings who should receive the credit for settling these desolate shores.

From Iceland there were to start some of the most important voyages in the history of exploration—those to North America. Accounts of these voyages have been handed down—in Icelandic sagas and by word of mouth—for generations, so we know about them in some detail.

About the year 982 a Viking adventurer called Eric the Red sailed west from Iceland. After a few days he came to a land so attractive, by comparison with Iceland, that he called it Greenland. Here, the following year, a number of Vikings settled, and in 985 a long open galley set out from Iceland, its crew also hoping to settle in Greenland.

The captain was Bjarni Herjulfsson and, according to one of the sagas, he "sailed three days, until the land was out of sight, but then the fair wind fell, and north winds and fogs came upon them, and they knew not whither they went." It was many days before the weather cleared. Then they hoisted their large rectangular sail and eventually came to a mild, pleasant land that they could not identify. But, still seeking the Viking settlement, they turned back and finally reached the southern tip of Greenland.

When Herjulfsson eventually returned to Iceland, he described his voyage to the men of the settlement and, as might have been expected, some were determined to discover more about this land, which seemed to be so much more hospitable than Greenland.

The leader of these new adventurers was Leif Ericson, son of Eric the Red, who now bought Herjulfsson's galley and engaged a crew of 35. We have no exact details about this vessel, which was to bring the first settlers to North America, but it was probably little more than 100 feet long. It would have been broader than the fighting galleys that the Vikings used for raids, made of oak and pine, well pitched, and with iron bolts and rivets. It was undoubtedly manned by oarsmen, and had a large rectangular sail that could be hauled up whenever there was a following wind. In

Viking ships were fitted with many oars and a sail. Some of them probably had an awning, as shown here, to shelter the wives and children of the settlers.

Hundreds of Viking memorial stones, like this one on Gotland in the Baltic Sea, have been found in many lands settled by the Norsemen. The stones provide evidence to support the accounts of exploration in the Viking sagas.

addition to other provisions, a number of bulls and cows are believed to have been carried on board.

In this boat Leif and his party sailed southwestward. They came first upon the place that Herjulfsson had last touched before reaching Greenland. This they called Helluland, meaning Flat Rock Land, and there is little doubt that it was what we know today as Newfoundland, on Canada's east coast.

"Then," continues one of the sagas, "they went to the ship and put out to sea and found another country. They again sailed to land, cast anchor, put out a boat, and walked ashore. The country was level and wooded, with white sands in many places where they went, and not steep along the sea. And Leif said: 'This country shall be named according to its qualities Marklund' [woodland]."

This good wooded country was Nova Scotia, but the restless Vikings were not yet satisfied. They still had provisions, and while these lasted they could continue their voyage of exploration. So they set out on the final stage of what was to be the foundation of the first European colony in North America.

According to the sagas, "going down to the ship again as quickly as possible, they sailed seaward with a northeasterly wind for two days until they sighted land. They sailed to the country and came to an island which lay to the north of the mainland, walked ashore there, and looked about in fine weather. They noticed that dew was on the grass, and happening to touch it with their hands and put it into their mouths thought that they had never tasted anything so sweet.

"Then they went to their ship, and sailed into that sound which lay between the island and the ness which jutted out north of the mainland, and steered westward past the ness. Great shallows extended at ebb tide, and then their ship stood aground, and then it appeared far from the vessel to the sea. But so eager were they to go ashore, that they could not wait until the sea should return to their ship, but leaped ashore where a river flowed out of a lake. But when the tide returned to their ship, then they took the boat and rowed to the ship, and it floated up the river and then into the lake.

"There they cast anchor, and carried their leathern hammocks ashore, and made booths [temporary huts] there. Then they decided to dwell there during the winter, and erected a large building. There was no lack of salmon either in the lake or in the river, and greater salmon than they had ever seen. But the quality of the country was so good according to what it seemed to them, that livestock would not need provender for the

The Gokstad ship, shown during excavation in 1880 (above) and after reconstruction (below), is 75 feet long and 17 feet wide. Smaller than most ocean-going longboats, like all Viking "serpents" it has a high bow and stern to improve seaworthiness.

winter. No frosts came there during the winter, and herbage withered there but little. Day and night there were more even than in Greenland or Iceland, for on the shortest day the sun had the place of *eykt* and the place of *dagma*," which means that the sun was above the horizon from breakfast time (about 7:30 A.M.) until the time of the evening meal (about 4:30 P.M.).

The site of this first colony, where Leif Ericson's party wintered, was at some point along the northeast seaboard, and recent excavations suggest the northern tip of Newfoundland as the likeliest spot. Here, at the village of L'Anse aux Meadows, archaeologists have found remains of Viking dwellings of about the year 1000. The Vikings, finding what they called grapes, called the country Vinland ("Vineland"), and it was here that Leif's brother came the following year.

When the Vikings attempted to move inland they were attacked by natives who pursued them to their ships in canoes. These "natives"—the American Indians—were descendants of the original inhabitants of North America, men who had crossed the Bering Strait from Asia some 10,000 to 20,000 years ago and populated the Americas. Eventually, and for reasons we do not know, the Vikings abandoned their camps, settlements, and colonies in the new worlds they had discovered. But by the year 1000, due to their daring and skilled seamanship, the known world stretched westward from Europe via Iceland and Greenland to the east coast of North America.

The Polos' Journey to the Orient

We have seen how the first great wave of exploration was created by the Phoenicians, who sailed to trade and found colonies. The second was made overland by the military conquests of such men as Alexander. And the third was again made on the sea, by the Vikings, who, perhaps more than any men before them, traveled purely for the adventure of discovering new lands. During the early Middle Ages (from about the 10th to the 14th centuries), the emphasis returned to land exploration—to journeys across the great desert areas of Asia.

The reason was that during the 12th century the tribes of central Asia had become united under the Mongols. By the middle of the 13th century these Tartars, as they were called, ruled an empire that stretched from the borders of China to the middle of Europe. In 1245 Pope Innocent IV wished to have news of the Mongols' great leader, Genghis Khan, so he sent a Franciscan friar, John de Carpini, on the 4000-mile journey from Rome to the Khan's encampment at Karakorum, near Lake Baikal in Mongolia. Carpini traveled on horseback with only one companion, a Polish friar, who acted as interpreter, and covered the distance in 100 days' hard riding. After spending more than 16 months at the court of the Khan, he returned to Europe by the same route— through Turkistan, past the northern shores of the Caspian Sea and then through southern Russia.

Carpini was the first European to reach so far into the heart of Asia; soon he was followed by other emissaries to the court of the Great Khan. It was, however, a group of merchants who were to provide the Middle Ages with the greatest of all its explorers. These merchants were Venetians. They built up a great trading empire and became, in some ways, the medieval equivalent of the Phoenicians. By the beginning of the 13th century their galleys had begun to dominate the eastern Mediterranean. And their more adventurous captains were sailing into the Black Sea and beginning to trade with the Russians.

It was a man of this type who became the greatest of all medieval travelers—Marco Polo.

Marco's adventures followed those of his father, Niccolò, and his uncle, Maffeo. In 1260 Niccolò and Maffeo set out from Constantinople to the Crimea on a trading journey. They spent some time at the port of Soldaia on the Black Sea and then, for reasons that are not clear, decided to travel overland eastward with the "store of jewels" that they had brought with them for

Niccolò and Maffeo Polo prepare for their journey to Kublai Khan's court in Peking. The medieval manuscript shows the Polos with Emperor Baldwin in Constantinople (top left); with the Papal Legate Teobaldo, later Pope Gregory X (top right); and setting sail for the Black Sea (bottom).

On their second journey to China in 1271, Maffeo, Niccolò, and his son Marco traveled through northeast Afghanistan and crossed the Badakhshan River (below left), a tributary of the Oxus. Many months later they arrived in Peking and presented papal letters to Kublai Khan (below).

trade. This was the first stage of an astonishing journey, only the barest details of which have come down to us. But we know that they spent a year with a Tartar prince near the banks of the Volga at Sari, and that this prince was, according to Marco Polo, "delighted at the arrival of the Two Brothers, and treated them with great honour; so they presented to him the whole of the jewels that they had brought with them. The prince was highly pleased with these, and accepted the offering most graciously, causing the Brothers to receive at least twice its value."

Fighting between the prince and his neighbors prevented the Polo brothers from returning to the Crimea by the way they had come, so they continued their journey eastward. They rode around the shores of the Caspian Sea, then southeast until they came to the ancient city of Bukhara. It was here, where they remained for three years among races they had never seen before, that the two Polo brothers one day met envoys who said that they were returning to "the Court of the Great Khan, the Lord of all the Tartars in the world"— Kublai Khan, the grandson of Genghis Khan.

From his court at Peking, Kublai Khan governed an empire that stretched from the shores of the Arctic Ocean to the Malacca Strait in the south, and from Korea in the east to the fringes of Asia Minor in the west. It was to the court of this huge empire that the Polo brothers were now invited by the envoys: "The Great Khan has never seen any Latins, and he has a great desire to do so," they were told. "Wherefore, if you will keep us company to his court, you will depend upon it that he will be glad to see you and will treat you with great honour and liberality; whilst in our company you will travel in perfect safety and will be molested by no one."

After riding eastward for a whole year they at last reached the court of the Great Khan at Peking and were questioned by him about the customs of the West and the Christian religion. Eventually they were asked to return to Europe to visit the pope as envoys from the Khan, and to return to Peking with a hundred men of "learning and ability." On returning to Venice, some nine years after they had originally set out, the Polos had accomplished the great feat of twice crossing Asia.

Two years later they set out once again for the East. With them they had gifts from the pope to the Great Khan, two friars, and Niccolò's son, 17-year-old Marco, who in the years to come was to travel tens of thousands of miles throughout the Mongol Empire.

No one today knows exactly what Marco Polo

looked like, but we can imagine him as a well-built, dark lad, and a good horseman. The little group set out for the East in 1271, first sailing to Acre, then traveling overland to the head of the Persian Gulf, where the party expected to take ship eastward. But no ships were available, so the Polos were forced to ride northward along the fringes of what is now Afghanistan.

They passed through the province of Badakhshan in northern Afghanistan, where, according to Marco, "the mountains are so lofty that it is a hard day's work, from morning till evening, to get to the top of them," and where there existed a race of horses "all of whom have from their birth a particular mark on their foreheads, and which were reputed to be descended from Alexander's horse Bucephalus."

Continuing northeast they reached the Pamirs, where, Marco reported, "you get to such a height that it is said to be the highest place in the world. And when you have got to this height you find a great lake between two mountains, and out of it a fine river running through a plain clothed with the finest pasture in the world; so that a lean beast will fatten to your heart's content there in ten days." As a youth Marco appears to have been a hunter, and here he mentions seeing "wild sheep of great size, whose horns are a good six palms in length." This breed of rams was called *Ovis poli* when it was first scientifically described by Europeans some 600 years later.

The party rode on "for twelve days together, finding nothing but a desert without habitations or any green thing so that travellers are obliged to carry with them whatever they have need of. The region is so lofty and cold," Marco continued, "that you do not even see any birds flying. And I must notice also that because of this great cold, fire does not burn so brightly, nor give out so much heat as usual, nor does it cook food so effectually." (This of course was due to the high altitude, not the cold.) It should be mentioned here that somewhere during the journey the two friars became frightened of what lay ahead and turned back, thus ending whatever chances they might have had of converting the Mongols to Christianity.

The Polos finally came down to Kashgar with its "beautiful gardens and vineyards and fine estates" and then, traveling east, they reached the last obstacle across their path to China: the Gobi Desert. "The length of this Desert is so great," wrote Marco, "that it is said that it would take a year and more to ride from one end of it to the other. And here, where its breadth is least, it takes a month to cross. It consists entirely of

This map, constructed in the 19th century by Sir Henry Yule from geographical notes in Marco Polo's journals, shows the Europeans' idea of the world in about 1300. The dark area at the top was known as the Land of Darkness—possibly referring to the long arctic winter nights.

As this map shows, routes to the East had been pioneered by several Europeans before Marco Polo. His fame rests mainly on his detailed descriptions of the peoples and places he saw during his travels through the Mongol Empire. Many of his accounts, however, seemed so strange to his countrymen that Marco was accused of lying.

Lyons

Venice

Constantinople

Soldaia

Sari

BLACK SEA

CASPIAN SEA

L. Baikal

Karakoram

Gobi Desert

Peking

Coiganzu

Acre

Tabriz

Aral

Turkestan

Bukhara

Samarkand

Pamir

Kashgar

Yarkand

Badakhshan

Khotan

CHINA

Hangchow

Baghdad

Basra

Kerman

Hormuz

Changlu

Foochow

Zaitan

Yunnan
(Kunming)

INDIA

Bhamo

Kistna

Andaman Is

Kad

INDIAN OCEAN

Fansun

Marco Polo	1271-95	——————————
colò & Maffeo Polo	1255-69	------------------
Rubruquis	1252-5	– – – – – –
Carpini	1245-7	··················

hills and valleys of sand, and not a thing to eat is to be found on it. But after riding for a day and a night you find fresh water, enough maybe for some fifty or a hundred persons with their beasts, but not for more. And all across .the Desert you will find water in like manner, that is to say, in some twenty-eight places altogether you will find good water, but in no great quantity; and in four places you also find brackish water."

Roughly 600 years later Sir Aurel Stein, the great explorer (who was born in Budapest, but later became a naturalized Briton) testified to Marco's accuracy. For when he crossed the Gobi Desert by the same route he found that the crossing was 380 miles long, and made in 28 stages.

The Polos were now on the fringe of China and near the Great Khan. Told of their coming, the Khan sent out men to meet them. Forty days later the party was escorted into the Khan's great palace in Peking, "the greatest palace that ever was," as Marco called it. It was enclosed by four miles of walls, "a good ten paces in height, white-washed and loop-holed all round. At each angle of the wall there is a very fine and rich palace in which the war-harness of the Emperor is kept, such as bows and quivers, saddles and bridles, and bowstrings, and everything needful for an army. Also midway between every two of these Corner Palaces there is another of the like; so that taking the whole compass of the enclosure you find eight vast palaces stored with the Great Lord's harness of war."

The Moslem city of Hormuz, where the Polos stopped on their journey to Peking, was on an island in the Persian Gulf. It was an important staging post on shipping routes between Europe and Asia. The Indian elephant and North African camel shown in this medieval French painting symbolize the trade link between East and West.

When the Polo brothers presented their letters and credentials, the Khan asked who was the third European in their party.

"My son and your liegeman," replied Niccolò.

From the first, the Khan appears to have taken to the young man, now nearly 21 years old, since their journey had taken them three and a half years. The Polos had been at the court only a short time when the Khan decided to send Marco on a special mission to the ruler of Yunnan, on the borders of Burma. Marco was quick to use his ear for languages, his pleasing manners, and intelligence. When he returned from his six-month journey, he reported to the Khan not only on his mission, but also, as he later described it, "all the novelties and strange things that he had seen and heard."

Niccolò and Maffeo settled down in the great Eastern city of Peking, while Marco began a series of tremendous journeys for the Khan. For nearly 17 years he traveled, first to one distant part of the empire then to another. He was not, in most cases, the first European to visit them; his importance in the story of exploration is that he kept careful records of what he saw. Years later he became the first man to bring stories of distant Asia to the people of Europe.

It was in Yunnan that he saw for the first time "great serpents of such vast size as to strike fear into those who see them, and so hideous that the very account of them must excite the wonder of those who hear it." These great reptiles were 10 paces in length and "in bulk they are equal to a great cask. They have two forelegs near the head, but for foot nothing but a claw like the claw of a hawk or that of a lion. The head is very big, and the eyes are bigger than a great loaf of bread. The mouth is large enough to swallow a man whole and is garnished with great pointed teeth. And in short they are so fierce-looking and so hideously ugly that every man and beast must stand in fear and trembling of them." Thus did crocodiles appear to Marco Polo.

In Hanchung he saw vast numbers of "lions, bears, lynxes, fallow deer, roes, stags and many more." He reported an account from Madagascar (which he did not visit) of giant rocs "like eagles but of the most colossal size . . . with a wing-span of thirty paces and wing-feathers of twelve paces." (This was no fable; it is now believed that these elephant-birds of Madagascar weighed almost half a ton and produced eggs of more than 14 inches in length.) But it was not only of birds and beasts that Marco reported when he, his father,

Paper money, which could be stamped and issued only by officials of the emperor's mint, as shown here, helped to preserve the Khans' economic and political power over their huge empire. Paper money had been used in China for at least 1500 years before Marco Polo's time.

Marco Polo is here seen sampling peppercorns in "Pepperland," the damp, hot region behind the Malabar Coast in western India.

A caravan commanded by Marco Polo sets out on a mission for Kublai Khan in northern China. On such journeys, as the Khan's ambassador, Marco would have been accompanied by mounted body-guards and armed footmen. His pack animals would have carried not only Marco's personal provisions but also gifts for the governors of the provinces he visited. Marco Polo remained in the Khan's service for 17 years, and his journeys took him far and wide over the vast Mongol Empire.

and uncle finally returned to Venice. There was "China in all its wealth and vastness, its mighty rivers, its huge cities, its rich manufactures, its swarming population, the inconceivably vast fleets that quickened its seas and its inland waters."

Its people, Marco Polo reported with wonder, used "a kind of black stone existing in beds in the mountains, which they dig out and burn like firewood. If you supply the fire with them at night, and see that they are well kindled, you will find them still alight in the morning." This was coal. It was almost as much of a wonder to Marco as the paper money he saw, made from the bark of the mulberry tree.

He visited distant Tibet, where the people had "mastiff dogs as big as donkeys, which are capital at seizing wild beasts." And he visited Hangchow, the "City of Heaven" in eastern China, with its 3000 public baths, its 12,000 bridges of stone, for the most

part "so lofty that a great fleet could pass beneath them," and the great lake in its center, bordered by "beautiful palaces and mansions of the richest and most exquisite structure that you can imagine."

All this was part of a great empire of which the Western world knew practically nothing. And for a long time it must have seemed likely that they would never hear of it from the Polos, for the Khan was reluctant to let them leave his court. At last, early in 1292, ambassadors from Persia arrived in Peking seeking a bride for a relative of the Khan, and the Polos persuaded him that they should escort her back to Persia.

They traveled in a fleet of 14 ships built by the Khan, and of the 600 men who set out with the Polos and the princess, only 18 survived the two-year journey, which included a long stay on the coast of Sumatra and in southern India. By the time the group

arrived in Persia, the princess's suitor had died. The Polos traveled on by way of Tabriz, Trebizond, and Constantinople, arriving in Venice at the end of 1295. It is said that their relations failed to recognize them.

Marco had traveled, almost continuously, for nearly a quarter of a century, and when he returned to his native city as a man of 40, he had crossed the whole breadth of Asia. He had become the first Western explorer to see the marvels of China, Burma with its golden pagodas, and the great ranges of the Pamirs and the Karakorams; he had traveled widely in the subcontinent of India, and had visited Java, Sumatra, and Ceylon. And from all these places he brought back detailed stories of strange people, strange animals, and strange customs. Many of his stories, like those of Pytheas, were doubted at the time and only confirmed by men who later followed him.

Marco's fame comes primarily from the journals and notebooks he had kept during his travels. Three years after his return, war broke out between the Venetians and the Genoese, and Marco was taken prisoner. While he was detained he dictated the story of his travels to a fellow prisoner, who happened to be a writer, drawing on the details from material in his notebooks. The book was widely disbelieved at the time. Years later, when he was dying, friends advised him to confess "all the lies he had told." Marco replied: "I have not told half of what I saw."

The Spirit of Exploration Quickens

The information Marco Polo brought back to Venice opened the gates to the East, and during the next century more than one traveler followed in his footsteps. There were John de Monte Corvino, who became Archbishop of Peking, and Friar Odoric, who visited Lhasa in Tibet. More important than either was Ibn Batuta of Tangier. In 1321 he made the pilgrimage to Mecca, and then set out on 24 years of wanderings, during which he covered 75,000 miles and visited almost every country of the Far East.

Ibn Batuta, who died in the last half of the 14th century, brings us to the verge of the great era of discovery.

How far had the oceans, the deserts, the forests and jungles, the mountains of the world, and the polar regions been touched by explorers by this time? As we have seen, seamen had taken their ships around Africa, into the Indian Ocean, and up the coast of China. The Vikings had reached North America by using the stepping stones of Iceland, Greenland, and Newfound-

Marco Polo often mentioned the tales of other travelers in his journals. One such tale concerned the people (above) of the Andaman Islands, in the Bay of Bengal, who were said to be cannibals with heads, eyes, and teeth like those of dogs. There were also many legends about "grotesque marvels" (below) to be found in India.

The invention of printing helped spread the records of exploration and discovery throughout the civilized world. This copy of Marco Polo's journal belonged to Christopher Columbus, whose notes appear in the margin. Columbus was greatly influenced by Marco's accounts of the East.

land. But the great oceans were still virtually unknown.

Of the great deserts, few had been explored. The fringes of the Arabian deserts were known; while caravan routes had crossed the Gobi in Asia and the Sahara in Africa. But beyond such narrow beaten tracks all still lay blank on the maps.

A few of the Vikings are believed to have pressed northward up the coast of Norway beyond the Lofoten Islands, but this was man's only foray into the Arctic; for the south Greenland settlements were on the coast and it is unlikely that the Vikings explored the ice-cap in the island's interior.

The great forests and the jungles, also, had barely been penetrated by the close of the 14th century. Alexander had fought his way down through India, but the vast jungles of Africa and the steamy forests of South America were still known only to the native tribes who inhabited them.

The same was true of most mountain ranges— mainly inhospitable regions in which men kept to the easiest possible passes. Philip of Macedon, Alexander's father, had climbed Mount Haemus in Greece to discover whether he could see from its summit the Adriatic, the Black Sea, the Danube, and the Alps. Hannibal the Carthaginian had taken his army over the Alps in 218 B.C. And throughout the Middle Ages a constant stream of travelers to Rome had crossed the range on their journey from northern Europe. But at the end of the 14th century the mountains of the world were still almost totally unexplored.

By this time, in fact, man had, with few exceptions, struck out across the globe only along the tracks that were the easiest he could find when he wanted to trade with other men or conquer his enemies.

2 Voyages into the Unknown

The long overland explorations of the 13th and 14th centuries were made, as we saw in the first chapter, partly to gather news of the Chinese Empire that had grown up under the Khans. During the 15th and 16th centuries another huge empire was to lead the peoples of Europe into the great age of discovery.

This was the Moorish Empire, which had established itself across the whole of the Middle East, and whose rulers controlled the main land routes to India and the wealth of the East. The kings of this powerful group of states were all Mohammedans. The Europeans who were about to send their small ships on great voyages to distant lands—and to draw the rough outlines of the world we know today—had, therefore, two objectives: They wished to find a sea route to the riches of the Indies; but they wished also to convert the foreign "infidels" to Christianity. These twin aims were responsible for both the circumnavigation of Africa and the discovery of America.

The Portuguese, the Spanish, and the English were the main explorers of these great extensions to the known world, but later the Dutch and the French were to make important discoveries in the Pacific. The man who most encouraged 15th-century sea exploration was the Portuguese Prince Henry the Navigator, a wise

It was in ships like these, often displacing 50 tons or less, that 15th-century Portuguese and Spanish sailors voyaged into unknown seas. Skilled seamen as they were, it was not the oceans they feared but what might lie beyond—regions of perpetual darkness, perhaps, or even the edge of the world.

For long voyages beyond sight of land, explorers needed navigational aids like the cross-staff (above), and astrolabe (below). The latter was invented by the Greeks and developed by the Portuguese from models taken from Arab seamen. Both instruments measured the angle of the sun from the horizon, from which a ship's approximate latitude could be calculated.

and learned man, who set up his court at Sagres, a small town near Cape St. Vincent. Early in the century he became involved in war with the Moors of Africa, who by this time controlled most of its northwest coast. Some of his captains, embroiled with Moorish ships off the coasts of the western bulge of Africa, sailed far south down the continent. Others sailed west into the Atlantic, discovering first Madeira and its outlying islands and then the Azores.

It was after these discoveries that Prince Henry was determined to find a way around Africa to the Indies. He set up a school of navigation at Sagres, and encouraged shipbuilders to strengthen the tiny caravels then used for coastal navigation so that they were sturdy enough to face the great voyages on which he planned to send them.

During the first half of the 15th century his captains navigated their ships farther and farther down the coast of Africa, setting up stone pillars to mark the most distant points they reached, fighting any Moorish ship they met, and landing when they could to capture Negroes and bring them home as slaves. By the time of the prince's death in 1460, Diego Gomez had reached the Gambia River; and, little more than 20 years later, Diego Cam reached the mouth of the Congo River and pressed on another 500 miles south before turning back to Portugal.

In all these early efforts to reach the Indies, the captains had carefully followed the coastline—feeling their way southward toward the cape that marked the southernmost point of the African continent. They

1427 Azores

1418 Porto Santo
1419 Madeira

1434 C. Bojador

1443 C. Blanco

1456 C. Verde Islands

1445 C. Verde
1455 Gambia

1460 Sierra Leone

The map above shows how, in the late 15th century, Portuguese sailors ventured farther and farther down the northwest coast of Africa, exploring and colonizing coastal areas and the neighboring groups of islands. Often, the navigators planted crosses on the mainland coast (below) to mark the most southerly points they reached.

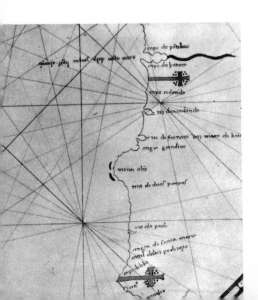

reasoned that if they could round this, the remainder of the voyage to India would give them little difficulty. This same route was followed by Bartholomeu Dias, a Portuguese nobleman who set out from Lisbon in 1487. He sailed far past the last point reached by Cam and was then forced to run before a great storm for 13 days. When the weather cleared Dias tacked back to land—and found to his surprise that the storm had blown him around the cape and that the African coast now lay to the west.

Dias was forced back to Portugal by the near-mutiny of his crew. When he reported to his monarch, King John II, he christened the point he had rounded the Cape of All the Storms. The king, as keen as Henry the Navigator had been to find a sea route to the Indies, insisted that it should be called the Cape of Good Hope, and ordered Dias to plan a new expedition. Several years were to pass before this expedition was ready to sail, and before it did so, the most momentous voyage in the history of exploration had been completed. It resulted in something even more important than the discovery of a sea route to the Indies—nothing less than the opening up of the New World.

The Voyages and Discoveries of Columbus

This discovery was made by Christopher Columbus—mariner, man of letters, scientist, fighter—who was able to write before he set out on his great voyage, "wherever ship has sailed, there have I journeyed." Born in Genoa about 1451, Columbus was the son of a wool comber who sent him to the University of Pavia, where he studied mathematics, the natural sciences, and nautical astronomy. He became a sailor at the age of 15 and for the next few years led an adventurous life, sailing not only to most of the Mediterranean ports, but to far more distant lands as well. On one occasion he wrote that he "sailed a hundred leagues beyond the Isle of Thule. . . . To this island, which is as large as England, the English go with their merchandise. At the time I was there the sea was not frozen, but the tides were so great as to rise and fall twenty-six fathoms." This is almost three times the greatest tidal range known anywhere in the world. Certainly Columbus could not have been referring to Iceland, where tides are not especially great.

In the mid-1400s mariners were usually fighting men. Columbus appears to have taken his part in a long string of semipiratical enterprises, and it was after one desperate battle off Cape St. Vincent that he made his first appearance in Portugal. The sea battle had lasted

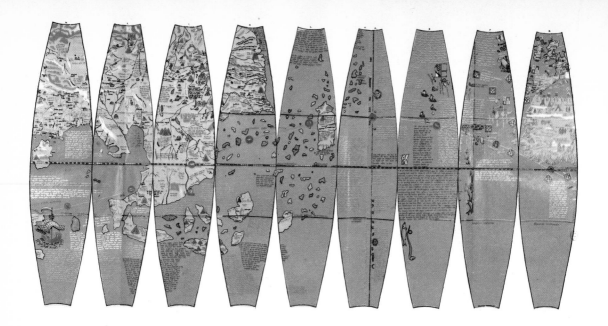

all day, and Columbus's ship, lashed to an enemy with grappling irons, began to sink. According to his son, Columbus, "who was a good swimmer, finding himself at the distance of two leagues from the land, seized an oar, and by its aid succeeded in reaching the shore. Whereupon, learning that he was not far from Lisbon, where he knew he should find many natives of Genoa, he ... took up his abode in the city."

In Lisbon, Columbus married the daughter of a sea captain who had served Henry the Navigator and who later became governor of the island of Porto Santo, off Madeira. And here in Lisbon, Columbus began to brood over his plans for finding a new way to the Indies. Unlike other navigators of his time, he abandoned the idea of sailing eastward around the coast of Africa. Instead, as he studied his father-in-law's maps and charts, a new and bold idea came into his mind.

He had heard stories of how ships, far to the west of Cape St. Vincent, had more than once picked up driftwood coming from farther west still. There were legends of the lost Island of the Seven Cities some hundreds of miles west of the Canaries. And on the coast of the Azores the bodies of two men, "very broad-faced and differing in aspect from Christians," had been found. Columbus may also have known that the ancestors of Icelandic men had found land far to the west. All this suggested that if a captain was courageous enough to sail west, he would eventually reach land. And this, Columbus believed, would be the great land mass of Asia, of which India formed part.

We do not know exactly when Columbus first began to seek support for his expedition. But we do know

The oldest globe of which we have records was made by Martin Behaim in about 1491, just before the discovery of America. It places Japan in mid-Atlantic between Europe and Africa, right, and India and Asia, left, and shows why Columbus was convinced he could reach the Orient by sailing westward from Spain.

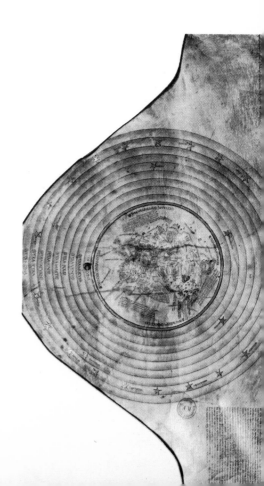

Above: This map, made in France in 1507, was the first to include the name of America, which is printed across what is now Brazil.

Below: Some scholars believe this map of Europe and Africa was drawn by Columbus before he discovered America. On the far left, the earth is shown, wrongly, as the center of the solar system.

that by 1484 his plan had been rejected by the Genoese, the Portuguese, and Henry VII of England.

Columbus next went to Spain and spent the following eight years trying—without success—to interest one Spanish lord after another. Then he wrote to King Ferdinand and Queen Isabella. But the country was involved in a bitter campaign against the Moors; furthermore, astronomers and Church leaders alike were against the idea of trying to reach the East by sailing west. Columbus decided to leave the country.

Then, on almost his last night in Spain, he stopped at the monastery of La Rabida, near the little seaport of Palos in Andalusia. It was here that a meeting with the queen's former confessor led Columbus directly to the king and queen. But Columbus himself nearly wrecked the enterprise. He demanded to be created admiral immediately; to be made vice-ruler of all the lands he discovered; and in addition to have one tenth of all the profit that followed from his voyage. These terms were rejected and Columbus was once again on the point of leaving Spain when he was overtaken by a messenger and asked to return. Finally, on April 17, 1492, an agreement between the king and queen and Columbus was sealed.

The necessary ships were to be provided by the town of Palos. The king and queen had also, as Columbus put it, "bestowed great favours upon me, ennobling me, that henceforward I might style myself Don, appointing me high admiral of the ocean sea, and perpetual viceroy, and governor of all the islands and continents I should discover and gain, and which henceforward· may be discovered and gained in the ocean sea; and that my eldest son should succeed me, and so on, from generation to generation for ever."

When Columbus rode into Palos he found that the royal order to supply ships had struck horror into the inhabitants—who included some of the best and boldest seamen in Europe. They quailed before the prospect of sailing westward—out into the regions of perpetual darkness, or over the edge of the world for all they knew. A second order was necessary and finally, during the last days of July 1492, the little fleet was made ready, if "fleet" is the right word to describe the three diminutive ships that were to sail so far into the unknown.

The largest of the three vessels, the flagship *Santa Maria*, was of only 100 tons, and her crew numbered a mere 50 men. Nevertheless, she almost dwarfed her two sister ships: the 50-ton *Pinta* with her crew of 30; and the 40-ton *Niña* with a crew of 24. Only the flagship was fully decked. Protection for the other two depended partly on their high bows and sterns, which rose well above midships.

By August 2 all was ready. The officers and men took Holy Communion and next day the three ships set off from a little island in front of the town of Huelva. Before they reached the Canaries, however, the rudder of the *Pinta* began to give trouble. Columbus immediately suspected the owners since they had, as he noted in his diary, "been displaying a certain backwardness" in letting the ship make the voyage. They sighted the islands on August 9, then spent nearly a month repairing the broken rudder and taking on supplies.

On September 6 they set sail from the island of Gomera; the great voyage into the unknown had now really begun. There were two days of calm and then, on September 8, the wind rose and the *Santa Maria* "took in much sea over the bows, which retarded progress, and nine leagues were made in that day and night." (A league, in Columbus's usage, corresponded to roughly four nautical miles.) On the days that followed, Columbus recorded in his journal details of the way he managed to deceive his crew. On the 9th, for example, he wrote that "in this day and night [we] made 60 leagues . . . but [I] only counted 48 leagues, that the people might not be alarmed if the voyage should be long."

At first there was no cause for dismay. From day to day various birds were seen, giving the men the illusion that they must still be near land. On the 15th "there fell from heaven into the sea a marvellous flame of fire." On the 16th they "began to see many tufts of grass which were very green, and appeared to have been quite recently torn from the land." From this they judged that they were near some island, but not the mainland.

There was a minor alarm on the 17th when the compass needle did not appear to be pointing true. This was caused by magnetic variation, which Columbus apparently did not understand, but which he explained away to the sailors. The same day they "saw much more weed appearing, like herbs from rivers, in which [they] found a live crab which the Admiral [Columbus] kept. He says that these crabs are certain signs of land. The sea water was found to be less salt than it had been since leaving the Canaries. The breezes were always soft. Everyone was pleased, and the best sailors went ahead to sight the first land."

They were now 11 days out from the Canaries, and

Columbus's seamen prepare to sail across uncharted seas from Palos in 1492. By command of the king and queen of Spain, this small Andalusian seaport provided all three ships and their crews for the historic voyage.

continued seeing more weed. The little ships were, in fact, on the edge of the Sargasso Sea; the weed did not come from the land but is now known to have an independent life in the sea.

There was still no sight of the Indies.

They were slowed by weak winds and a calm that continued for several days. The sailors swam in the sea around the becalmed ships, murmuring that no wind would ever blow them back to Spain. Then, at sunset on the 25th, the captain of the *Pinta* reported land ahead. The ships altered course toward it and sailed on through the night, but by noon the following day Columbus "made out that what had been said to be land was only clouds."

The calm continued, with the sea "like a river, the

The *Santa Maria*, Columbus's flagship, was tiny compared with modern oceangoing vessels. She weighed no more than 100 tons and had a crew of 50. She was less speedy and lower in the water than her two sister ships. In his journal Columbus criticized her as being too cumbersome for voyages of discovery.

air mild," and Columbus wrote that "nothing was wanting but to hear the nightingale."

On October 7 there was another false alarm. The little vessel *Niña*, which had forged ahead, hoisted a flag and fired a gun as the signal that land had been seen. But as the day wore on the crews of the three ships realized that once again they had been deceived by clouds. Three days later, 34 days out from the Canaries, came the first flicker of mutiny. The only details we have are those given in Columbus's journal. "Here," he wrote, "the people could endure no longer. They complained of the length of the voyage. But the Admiral cheered them up in the best way he could, giving them good hopes of the advantages they might gain from it." He added that, "however much they might complain, he had to go on to the Indies, and that he would go on until he found them with the help of our Lord."

That is all that is admitted. But it needs only a little imagination to see the tall figure of an almost fanatical Columbus defying the malcontents, warning them that he would never turn back, and that if they wished to do so they would succeed only by force of arms.

The following day the crews of the *Pinta* and the *Niña* saw signs of land—a floating branch covered with berries, and a pole that appeared to have been worked with iron—and Columbus recorded: "Everyone breathed afresh and rejoiced at these signs." That night he himself watched from the high poop of the *Santa Maria*. At 10 o'clock, he saw through the darkness ahead a glint of light and excitedly called up a courtier sent by Ferdinand and Isabella to see the light "like a wax candle rising and falling." Finally he went below, promising a silk doublet to the first man to sight land. He felt certain that the great voyage was ending. At two in the morning of Friday, October 12, Rodrigo de Triana of the *Niña* saw, eight miles away, faint but unmistakable against the night stars, the dark outline of the New World. The three ships closed up, shortened sail, and hove to, waiting for the sun to rise.

At dawn the Spaniards saw before them a level and beautiful island, covered with trees of great luxuriance. Later they learned that the natives, who came down to the water's edge to stare at the ships as the light increased, called the island *Guanahani*: Columbus named it San Salvador. Although some experts still disagree about which of the Bahamas it really was, there seems little doubt that it was Watlings Island.

The small boats were made ready and Columbus, richly dressed in scarlet, and accompanied by the

Columbus's shrewdness and great determination are well caught in this portrait. There is a legend that his hair turned white at an early age owing to bitter intrigues with rivals at the Spanish court.

The two woodcuts below are from the 1493 edition of Columbus's journal. On the left is a map of the islands he discovered; San Salvador, his first landfall, is in green. On the right is the fort he built on Haiti, where he founded a small colony.

Columbus lands on Haiti, holding the royal spear and planting a cross to symbolize Spain's colonial and missionary ambitions. There was much gold on the island, which the natives were eager to exchange for beads and small bells.

captains of the other two ships, was rowed ashore. The admiral himself carried the flag of Spain, while each of his companions carried banners bearing a green cross beside two embroidered crowns and the letters "F" and "Y," for Fernando and Ysabel. Columbus stepped ashore, went down on one knee, kissed the earth, and claimed the country for Spain.

When the natives drew near, Columbus judged them to be "a people who could be more easily freed and converted to our holy faith by love than by force. [We] gave to some of them red caps, and glass beads to put round their necks, and many other things of little value which gave them great pleasure, and made them so much our friends that it was a marvel to see. They afterward came to the ships' boats where we were, swimming and bringing us parrots, cotton threads in skeins, darts, and many other things; and we exchanged them for other things that we gave them such as . . . small bells."

Columbus realized that he had not reached the "Indies" of the East. What he did not realize was that land farther west, then a vast ocean—the Pacific— hopelessly separated him from his goal. Nevertheless, for three months he searched, first leading his ships southward through a maze of islands, then along the northern shores of what we today know as Cuba.

Wherever the Spaniards went they were astounded by the lush and magnificent scenery. "I know not where first to go," wrote Columbus, "nor are my eyes ever weary of gazing on the beautiful verdure." Of one place, where their water casks were filled from great fresh-water lakes, he wrote that "the groves about them are marvellous, and here and in all the island every thing is green, and herbage as in April in Andalusia. The singing of the birds is such that it seems as if one would never desire to depart thence; there are flocks of parrots which obscure the sun, and other birds, large and small, of so many kinds and so different from ours, that it is wonderful; and beside, there are trees of a thousand species, each having its particular fruit and all of marvellous flavour, so that I am in the greatest trouble in the world not to know them, for I am very certain that they are each of great value."

At one point, so great was the spicy smell from the land, that he thought he might, after all, have found the Indies. Off Cuba he sent two men ashore on a mission to the interior, but the stories they brought back showed that he was nowhere near the great cities of which Marco Polo had written. The men had, however, news of a strange local custom. They had seen "several of the natives going about with firebrands in their hands, and certain dried herbs which they rolled up in a leaf, and lighting one end, put the other in their mouths, and continued exhaling and puffing out the smoke." The Spaniards had never before seen men smoking tobacco.

Still clinging to the hope that he might be somewhere off the coast of Asia, Columbus cruised southeastward until he saw on the horizon the peaks of Haiti, high mountains standing above dark forests.

Here the *Santa Maria* was driven aground and sank. The shipwreck decided Columbus to put some men ashore, protect them with a fort, and then return to Spain with the news of his discoveries. While on the island he found that the natives seemed to have great quantities of gold. What is more, they would trade it for trifles. One native gleefully traded a handful of gold dust for a small bell, then dashed into the woods with his trophy for fear that the Spaniards might regret the bargain.

Columbus now became confident that by the time he came back a ton of gold would have been collected by the men he had left behind and that they would have "discovered mines and spices in [great] quantities."

Columbus discovered the mainland of South America on his third voyage in 1498. Off the coast of what is now Venezuela, he found the natives diving for pearls (above). Columbus never had an opportunity to exploit this new source of wealth, however. He had powerful enemies in Spain and the American colonies, and in the year 1499 he was arrested on the island of Haiti (below) and sent home in disgrace.

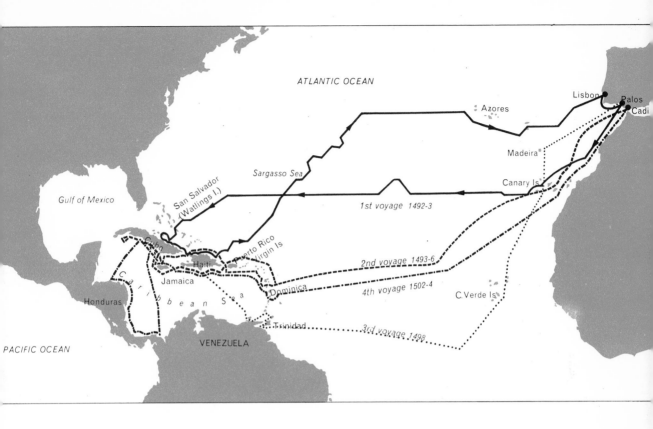

On the map: ATLANTIC OCEAN, Azores, Lisbon, Palos, Cadi, Madeira, Canary Is, San Salvador (Watlings I.), Sargasso Sea, Gulf of Mexico, 1st voyage 1492-3, Puerto Rico, Virgin Is, 2nd voyage 1493-6, Cuba, Haiti, Jamaica, Honduras, Caribbean Sea, Dominica, 4th voyage 1502-4, C. Verde Is, PACIFIC OCEAN, Trinidad, 3rd voyage 1498, VENEZUELA

On January 4, Columbus sailed for home in the *Niña*. At the court in Barcelona he was greeted almost like an ambassador. Seated with the king and queen, he told of his voyage and his discoveries. He exhibited his parrots, the cotton, the gold, the birds, beasts, and plants that he had gathered—also the nine natives whom he had brought to Spain for conversion to Christianity. He impressed on his masters once again the great wealth that lay awaiting them in "the Indies."

All the honors and privileges promised to Columbus were now heaped upon him. On September 24, 1493, he set out again, this time in command of a fleet of three great galleons and 14 caravels, packed with 1500 men, 12 missionaries, and all the materials needed for colonization. On November 3 he sighted land—this time the island of Dominica in the Antilles. After sailing northward and discovering several islands—including the Virgin Islands and Puerto Rico—he finally arrived at the fort he had left at Navidad—only to find it a blackened ruin, destroyed by native attacks, and the colony dispersed.

From this moment, Columbus's luck turned. He found it hard to control his new colony; he quarreled with colonists sent to the new lands by the government;

As this map shows, Columbus made four voyages to the New World. He remained convinced that a way into the Indian Ocean could be found through the maze of islands he discovered—never knowing that the American continent and the Pacific Ocean separated him from his goal.

and he nearly died during a five-month illness. Columbus returned to Spain to find himself discredited. But he was to make two more voyages to the New World—one in 1498 that at last brought him to the mainland of South America; and another in 1502 during which he tried, but failed, to establish a colony on the coast of Honduras. Columbus returned to Spain in 1504, a disappointed man, and died two years later.

By the time that Columbus died, the new world of the Americas was already being opened up. One after another, the galleons of Spain and Portugal began making the voyage that he had shown to be possible; one after another, their captains were staking claims along the eastern coast of South America and in the rich islands of the Caribbean; while other explorers were sailing west across the northern Atlantic.

In the year 1507 Vincente Pinzón, who had set out with Columbus in 1492, sailed with Juan de Solis along the coast of Yucatán to Trujillo. In 1502 Amerigo Vespucci had set out from Europe, reached Rio de Janeiro Bay, and later claimed to have been to what is now South Georgia (latitude 55° s.). In 1497 and the following year John Cabot, who sailed under the English flag, reached south Labrador, visited south Greenland, and sailed down the American coast to Chesapeake Bay. Other explorers—English, Portuguese, Spanish, and Italian—were rapidly adding details to the maps of both the southern and northern coast lines of the vast American continent. Although there were many seamen who were making first attempts to explore the northern Atlantic soon after the turn of the 16th century, we will not mention their voyages in detail here. Their story, one of struggles against the ice and bitter cold, is better told in the chapter on polar exploration.

The prospects opened up by the New World were so great that there seemed to be enough land and wealth for everyone. However, to lessen rivalry between Portugal and Spain, the reigning pope, the Spaniard Alexander VI, "divided" the prospects between the two countries. This was done by the Treaty of Tordesillas. Signed in 1494, it "gave" all new countries west of a line from the south of Greenland to the mouth of the Amazon to Spain; all to the east to Portugal. Thus the discoveries by Columbus made on behalf of Spain were confirmed. However, he had not, as he had hoped, discovered a new route to the Indies. That great prize had gone to a Portuguese, some five years after Columbus's lookout had sighted the New World. The name of this Portuguese sea captain was

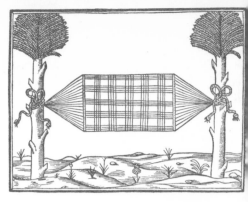

Hammocks, iguanas, and pineapples were among New World discoveries made by the early colonizers.

Part of Cantino's world map of 1502 shows the Tordesillas Line running from Greenland to the mouth of the Amazon. The 1494 Treaty of Tordesillas was intended to lessen the bitter colonial rivalry between Spain and Portugal. It "gave" all new lands to the east of this line to Portugal, and all those to the west of it to Spain.

Vasco da Gama. It was this tall, black-bearded sailor who in 1497 set out on the epoch-making voyage that was to provide Europe's first great sea link with the Orient.

Da Gama's Voyage to the East

Vasco was born about 1460, the year Prince Henry the Navigator died. In many ways his career was a direct continuation of the exploration that had been started by Prince Henry. We know little about Vasco's early life except that he was born in the little seaport of Sines on the Alentejo coast; that his father was civil governor of the town; and that he grew up in a community where there was always talk of the sea, ships, and navigation. And no doubt there was talk of how one day men would carry on Bartholomeu Dias's work, and eventually find a sea route to the Indies.

King John, in whose reign Dias had first rounded the Cape of Good Hope, died in 1495. One of the first acts of his successor, King Emmanuel, was to plan another expedition. Vasco da Gama's father was at first chosen to lead the four vessels fitted out for the voyage, but he died while preparations were still being made. It was Vasco who in the summer of 1497 was summoned by the king and asked to lead the expedition. At the same time he was presented with a huge silken banner bearing the Cross of the Order of Christ. With his companions he rode to Lisbon—and from the heights above the town looked down on his four small ships riding quietly on the waters of the Tagus.

These vessels, which were to voyage half-way around the world and back, were astonishingly small judged by modern standards. Just how small we do not know, for the experts give very different estimates of their tonnage. Both Vasco da Gama's flagship, the *San Gabriel*, and her sister ship, the *San Raphael*, were probably between 100 and 200 tons and less than 100 feet long. The ships were built from the plans of Dias, who designed his vessels to face the hazards he knew they would have to endure. They were of small draught, which enabled them to sail up the shallow waters of estuaries. Their square rigs made them slower than the usual Portuguese caravel, but more stable and better suited to long voyages. Both fore and aft were stout wooden "castles" from which the crew could fight hand-to-hand if the vessels were boarded by an enemy.

In addition to these two main vessels there was a store ship of roughly the same size, and the *Berrio*, about half the size of the other three.

By the beginning of July 1497 all was ready. The night before they set sail, Vasco and his three captains —one of whom was his brother Pedro—went to the small chapel that had been built on the banks of the Tagus by Henry the Navigator. There they remained all night; then just after dawn they led a procession of priests to the landing stage. Along the river bank, thousands of spectators had gathered to see the expedition off. A priest heard confessions and gave absolution to all who might die on the voyage. Then the four captains rowed out to their ships. A light wind filled the sails and slowly the ships began to move down the Tagus toward the open sea.

Although Vasco himself left no record of the great adventure that was about to begin, one of his crew did. From his diary of the voyage we can learn something of the problems faced by the crew numbering less than 150 men in all.

At first all went well. There was fair weather as far as the Canaries. Then fog suddenly appeared and for nine days the ships lost touch with the *San Gabriel* as they sailed on south toward the Cape Verde Islands. Then, on July 26, when they were 18 days out of Lisbon, the little fleet was reunited. "At about 10 o'clock on that day we sighted the captain-major, about five leagues ahead of us," wrote the unknown sailor, "and having got speech with him in the evening, we gave expression to our joy by many times firing off our bombards and sounding the trumpets."

These "bombards"—used for firing stone shot— formed part of the armament of 20 guns. Both the *San Gabriel* and the *San Raphael* carried them and frequently used them for signaling.

In the Cape Verde Islands the ships took on water, food, and wood. The crew made final adjustments to the sails and the yards, and in other ways prepared themselves for what they knew was to be a crucial "leg" of the voyage. Vasco had no intention of creeping down the African coast. Instead, he planned to sail straight across the southern Atlantic and make a landfall near the Cape of Good Hope itself—a voyage of some 4000 miles. During the entire course he would be out of sight of land.

On August 3, the four ships weighed anchor and sailed from the bay of Santa Maria in San Tiago, the largest of the Cape Verde Islands. Fifteen days out the main yard of the *San Gabriel* broke and the other three ships had to heave to for 48 hours while it was repaired.

They sailed throughout the rest of August and on

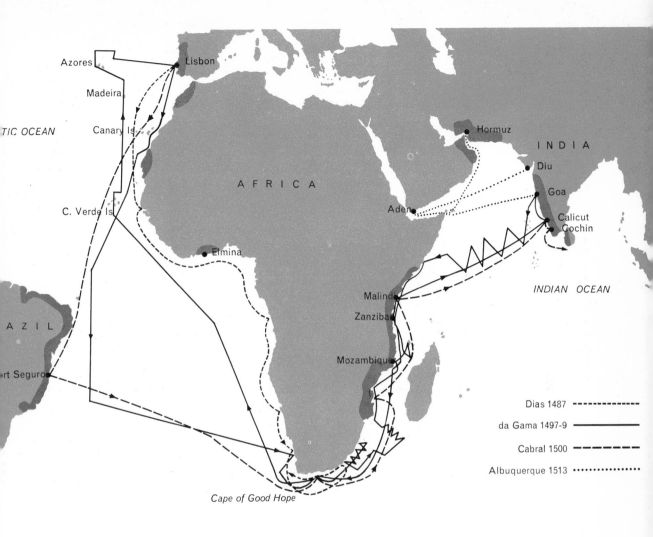

Azores
Madeira
Canary Is
C. Verde Is
TIC OCEAN
Lisbon
AFRICA
Elmina
AZIL
rt Seguro
Hormuz
Diu
I N D I A
Aden
Goa
Calicut
Cochin
INDIAN OCEAN
Malindi
Zanzibar
Mozambique

Dias 1487 ----------
da Gama 1497-9 ————
Cabral 1500 -- -- --
Albuquerque 1513 ············

Cape of Good Hope

The bustling quayside at Lisbon (above left) was the starting point for many Portuguese voyages of discovery. The pioneers of trade with the Indies were Bartholomeu Dias, Vasco da Gama, Pedro Cabral, and Alphonso d'Albuquerque, whose routes appear on the map above. Great wealth and honor could be won by the colonizers; Da Gama (left) made a fortune in the East and, like Albuquerque, was appointed a viceroy of India.

through the whole of September, their vessels butting their way south. The long days were broken only by the occasional sight of a whale, of seals, or of porpoises. They sailed on through October, cramped in their narrow quarters and limited to daily rations of one and a half pounds of biscuits, a pound of beef or half a pound of pork, two and a half pints of water, and one and a quarter pints of wine. There was also oil, vinegar, and on days of abstinence rice, fish, or cheese instead of meat.

More than 10 weeks after setting out, on November 1, All Saints' Day, they "saw many indications of the nearness of land, including gulf-weed which grows along the coast." Then, three days later, the unknown diarist recorded the news for which everyone had been waiting:

"On Saturday, the 4th of the same month, a couple of hours before break of day, we had soundings in 110

On his first voyage to India in 1497, Vasco da Gama put ashore on the east coast of Africa to careen his ships. This involved sailing them on to a beach, waiting until the tide ebbed, and then hauling the ships onto their sides so that their underwater planking could be cleaned and repaired.

fathoms [about 650 feet, since the depth was measured in Portuguese fathoms] and at nine o'clock we sighted the land. We then drew near to each other, and having put on our gala clothes, we saluted the captain-major by firing our bombards, and dressed the ships with flags and standards."

The little fleet then tacked down the African coast and three days later anchored in a sheltered bay which Vasco called the Bay of Santa Helena (on the coast of what is now Cape Province). During the eight days they spent mending sails, making minor repairs, and taking on fresh stocks of fuel, they were visited by tawny-colored natives. The food of these people, they found, was "confined to the flesh of seals, whales and gazelles, and the roots of herbs. They are armed with poles of olive-wood to which a horn, browned in the fire, is attached. Their numerous dogs resemble those of Portugal and bark like them."

These men were Hottentots. Vasco went ashore to discover whether any of the goods that the little fleet had brought were known to them. "This merchandise," it was reported, "included cinnamon, cloves, seed-pearls, gold, and many other things, but it was evident that they had no knowledge whatever of such articles, and they were consequently given round bells and tin rings."

After a few days the Portuguese put out to sea again and continued south. Then on Saturday, November 18, they saw in the distance the bluff outlines of the Cape of Good Hope, with the great plateau of Table Mountain rising behind it.

They had still to turn the Cape, however, and the task lasted four days until, on November 22, a following wind took them round, and the four ships began to tack up the east coast of Africa.

After rounding the Cape, Vasco led his ships north-

Many of the perils and excitements of exploration were caught in the melodramatic engravings of the 16th-century German artist Theodor de Bry, several of whose pictures illustrate this chapter. Above, sailors shipwrecked on the coast of India repair their ship while their comrades beat off an attack by giant crabs.

ward for five months. They passed Natal—so named because it was reached on Christmas Day—Mozambique, Zanzibar, and Mombasa. At places they saw animals unknown to them, such as those on an island a short distance north of the Cape, which they thought to be seals. Some were "as big as bears," wrote the unknown diarist, "very formidable, with large tusks. These attack man, and no spear, whatever the force with which it is thrown, can wound them. There are others much smaller and others quite small. And whilst the big ones roar like lions, the little ones cry like goats. One day, when we approached this island for our amusement, we counted, among large and small ones, three thousand, and fired among them with our bombards from the sea. On the same island there are birds as big as ducks, but they cannot fly, because they have no feathers on their wings. These birds, of whom we killed as many as we chose, are called Fotylicayos, and they bray like asses."

The birds were Cape Penguins, and near the island where they were seen, Vasco and his men set up a stone pillar bearing the arms of Portugal and a cross made from a mizzen mast of one of the ships. Then, before they were out of sight, they watched a dozen of the natives appear from the brushwood and dismantle both pillar and cross.

At more than one place along Africa's east coast they had to land for supplies and fresh water. South of Mozambique they put ashore to "careen" the ships. This meant sailing them up on to a beach, waiting until the tide ebbed, then hauling the ships over on to their sides so that their planking could be cleaned. It was near Mozambique that the Portuguese first experienced scurvy (caused by a lack of vitamin C). "Many of our men fell ill here, their feet and hands swelling, and their gums growing over their teeth so that they could not eat."

Farther up the coast, at Mozambique itself, Vasco and his men found the first of several Arab settlements at which they were to call. Arab ships, they found, had planks that were held together by cords rather than by nails, and had sails of palm matting. Their seamen used the mariner's compass, and the Arab merchants appeared to be rich. "They all wear toucas [robes] with borders of silk embroidered in gold. They have transactions with white Moors, four of whose vessels were at the time in port, laden with gold, silver, cloves, pepper, ginger, and silver rings, as also with quantities of pearls, jewels, and rubies, all of which articles are used by the people of this country."

Sudden death at sea claimed many
of those seeking to exploit the riches
of the Indies. The battered wrecks
of ships like these littered many
an African and Indian coast
in the 15th and 16th centuries.
On land, too, the early colonizers
faced death—as here, at the hands
of Arabs and Turks of the Moorish
Empire, whose stranglehold on trade
with India was threatened by the
arrival of the Portuguese.

The Arabs, in fact, "ran" the trade of the Indian Ocean and resented Portuguese interference. The result was a series of minor skirmishes when the Europeans landed for fresh water.

It was from Malindi, on the coast of modern Kenya, that Vasco and his four ships set out on the final stage of their voyage to India. Their Hindu pilot guaranteed that he would bring them to a landfall near the town of Calicut. More than three weeks after leaving Africa, on Sunday, May 20, they first sighted the mountains rising behind the town. Here, at last, was the goal they had been seeking for nearly a year. The Portuguese had finally completed the task that Henry the Navigator had begun nearly a century before. They had found a sea route to the Indies by which the vast riches of the East could be brought back to Europe. Vasco now made every attempt to open trade negotiations with the local ruler. But this angered rival Moorish traders already in Calicut, and they turned the Indian ruler against the Portuguese. In the end Vasco and his group had to fight their way out of harbor.

By September 1499 Vasco and his men had returned home by following roughly the route by which they had come. He himself was made a noble and granted great honors, and almost immediately a fleet of 13 ships was sent to reopen negotiations with the Indians. This expedition, led by Pedro Cabral, took an interesting turn. By accident—or possibly deliberately—the ships sailed too far west across the South Atlantic and reached the coast of Brazil. Cabral claimed this new land for his country. From Brazil they sailed across to Africa and rounded the Cape of Good Hope, but it was here that tragedy struck the expedition. As they were rounding the Cape a storm sent three of the ships to the bottom; on board one of them was Bartholomeu Dias. In spite of its losses the expedition sailed on and eventually reached Calicut, where the Portuguese established a small colony on Indian soil. Then its members were massacred. Back home, Vasco knew that a powerful fleet of warships would be sent to avenge the killings and pleaded to be put in charge of it. As he wrote to his master, "the king of Calicut [once] arrested me and treated me with contumely, and because I did not return to avenge myself of that injury he has again committed a greater one, on which account I feel in my heart a great desire and inclination to go and make great havoc of him."

Vasco was given the task. In 1502 he led an expedition bent on plunder and destruction, culminating in the bombardment of Calicut. After savagely treating the inhabitants (as did the Spanish in the West Indies), he next moved on to Cochin "doing all harme he could on the way to all that he found at sea." He returned to Lisbon in 1503, having laid the foundation for Portuguese trade with the East, and then went into rich retirement.

Throughout the last part of Vasco's life merchants and mariners were busy reaping in India and the islands of southeast Asia the rich harvest that he had prepared for them. Meanwhile the Spanish were doing the same on the Spanish Main and benefiting from the discoveries of Columbus. Both the Indian and the Atlantic oceans thus became better known and less dangerous. But one great puzzle remained: It was still not clear whether the Americas were joined to Asia. For no man had yet sailed round the world, or explored the vast Pacific Ocean.

In fact, no mariner had yet proved that one could, as some of the ancients had believed, reach the Indies by sailing west. This great exploit was carried out by another Portuguese—Ferdinand Magellan.

Magellan's Voyage around the World

Navigator, soldier, and gentleman of fortune, Magellan had sailed to the Indies at the beginning of the 16th century. He had helped found a Portuguese colony in the Moluccas, or Spice Islands as they were then called, and was later wounded while fighting the Moors in Morocco. After this incident Magellan, then a man of about 40, returned to Portugal, but he failed to receive the compensation he demanded. In disgust, he left the country and proposed an ambitious plan of conquest to Emperor Charles V. Magellan claimed he could reach the Spice Islands by sailing west. In doing so he would seize for the king of Spain all the newly discovered lands that lay on the "Spanish" side of the famous line laid down by the pope in 1494. On September 20, 1519, Magellan set out from San Lucar. Under his command was a "fleet" of five tiny ships—the *Victoria*, 85 tons; the *Conception*, 90 tons; the *San Antonio*, 120 tons; the *Trinity*, 110 tons; and the 75-ton *Santiago*.

The Portuguese, jealous of any success the Spanish might win, were anxious to see the voyage fail. The Portuguese ambassador in Spain, writing to his king, said of the ships: "[They] are very old and patched up. I saw them when they were beached for repairs. It is eleven months since they were repaired, and they are now afloat and they are caulking them in the water. I

Vasco da Gama visited Calicut (above) in 1498 and four years later devastated it to avenge the destruction of the colony founded there by Pedro Cabral in 1500. The word "calico" comes from the town's fame as a cotton-weaving center.

Hormuz (below) was a key trading center in the Moorish Empire—a great prize to the Portuguese. It was taken by Albuquerque in 1514, soon after he had captured Goa in India, and Malacca in Malaya.

went on board of them a few times and I assure your Highness that I should be ill inclined to sail in them for the Canaries because their knees are of touchwood. The artillery which they all carry are eighty guns, of a very small size: only in the largest ship, in which Magellan is, there are four very good iron cannon. All the crews they take, in all the five vessels, are 230 men, and they carry provisions for two years."

Much of this was wishful thinking. Whatever shortcomings there may have been in the small fleet that now sailed down past Tenerife to the Cape Verde Islands were more than balanced by the skill of their commander.

Like Da Gama, Magellan himself did not keep a diary, but two of his officers wrote accounts of the amazing voyage. From one of them, Antonio Pigafetta, we are given a strikingly vivid picture "of the very great and awful things of the Ocean."

Like many mariners of his day, Magellan concealed from his sailors the true nature of the coming voyage, "so that his men should not from amazement and fear be unwilling to accompany him on so long a voyage."

The little fleet reached the Cape Verde Islands without incident, and on October 3 Magellan struck southwest for the coast of South America. So that his ships would not lose touch with one another at night, the leading ship, commanded by Magellan, burned torches as signals: two lights meant that he was about to turn on a new tack; three formed a signal for the other ships to reduce the amount of sail they were carrying; several

Vasco da Gama saw many small Indian boats of this kind off the Malabar coast near Calicut. The Indians rarely sailed beyond coastal waters, relying on the dhows of the Arab seamen for trade with other lands.

In this allegorical portrait by De Bry, Ferdinand Magellan calmly plots his position as the *Victoria* sails around the southernmost tip of South America. Ahead of him lies the vast Pacific Ocean, which no European had crossed before.

lights accompanied by the firing of guns meant that land had been sighted. For more than eight weeks his ships sailed on. At times the weather was calm and "there came large fishes near the ships which they called Tiburónes [sharks], which have teeth of a terrible kind and eat people when they find them in the sea either dead or alive."

At times there were great storms during which glowing balls of static electricity clung to the mast top. (This was a common occurrence at sea, and the "fire," which Pigafetta described as "Saint Anselme," is known as *Saint Elmo's fire*.) "During these storms the body of St. Anselme appeared to us several times; amongst others, one night that it was very dark on account of the bad weather, the said saint appeared in the form of a fire lighted at the summit of the mainmast, and remained there near two hours and a half, which comforted us greatly, for we were in tears, only expecting the hour of perishing; and when that light was going away from us it gave out so great a brilliancy in the eyes of each, that we were near a quarter-of-an-hour like people blinded, and calling out for mercy."

In mid-December they at last sighted land, reaching it in the neighborhood of Rio de Janeiro. The natives they met lived in long, low houses, each containing about 100 people. They used sharp stones to hollow out trees into canoes that would carry up to 40 oarsmen. After tribal wars they ate their captives, cutting up the bodies into small pieces "which they set to dry in the chimney, and every day they cut a small piece, and ate it in memory of their enemies."

Magellan's plan was now to sail down the east coast of South America and to turn it in much the same way that Dias and Vasco da Gama had turned the Cape of Good Hope. Alternatively, he might be able to find a passage that would lead him to open sea on the other side of the continent. (He had argued correctly that the great mass of South America narrowed to a point, as did Africa.) For months he and his men sailed south. At one place they discovered an island full of "geese" (actually penguins) and of "sea wolves" (probably sea lions). "These latter were of many colours, and of the size and thickness of a calf, and have a head like that of a calf, and the ears small and round. They have large teeth, and have no legs, but feet joining close on to the body, which resemble a human hand; they have small nails to their feet, and skin between the fingers like geese. If these animals could run," wrote Pigafetta, "they would be very bad and cruel, but they do not stir from the water, and swim and live upon fish."

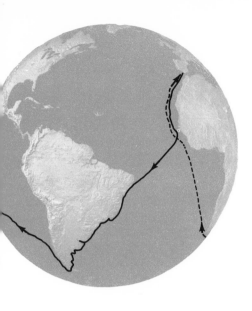

These two globes show the route of Magellan's voyage, which began in 1519. By this time, Portugal's right to the eastern route to the Indies—provided by the Treaty of Tordesillas—had been confirmed in practice by Da Gama, Cabral, and many others. The importance to Spain of Magellan's voyage was not that he sailed around the world but that he found an alternative trade route to the Indies.

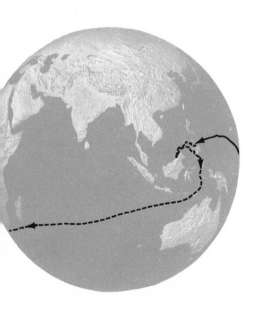

Eventually the ships reached what is now Puerto San Julian on the coast of Patagonia, and here they stopped for five months. The country appeared to be deserted until one day, "without anyone expecting it, we saw a giant, who was on the shore of the sea, quite naked, and was dancing and leaping, and singing, and whilst singing he put the sand and dust on his head. Our captain sent one of his men towards him, whom he charged to sing and leap like the other to reassure him and show him friendship. This he did, and immediately the sailor led this giant to a little island where the captain was waiting for him; and when he was before us he began to be astonished, and to be afraid, and he raised one finger on high, thinking that we had come from heaven."

Magellan was now farther south than any explorer had been before, and he had been six months at sea. Fear, uncertainty about the future, cold, and hunger (the men were now on short rations) began to make the crew grumble. Magellan was soon facing that problem second only to the scourge of scurvy—mutiny by many of his senior officers and crew.

"Three of the ships rose up against the Captain-major," wrote the other diarist who kept an account of the voyage. "Their captains [said] that they intended to take [Magellan back] to Castile in arrest, as he was taking them all to destruction." Magellan had been brought up in too tough a school to be defeated by this particular mutiny. One of the captains was, we are told, "killed with stabs of a dagger" by a messenger sent by Magellan. The second "had his head cut off, and afterwards was cut in quarters." The third, who had been personally appointed by Charles V, was landed on the desolate coast with a priest.

Meanwhile, the *Santiago* had run aground during a reconnaissance farther south, but all her men were picked up. Before leaving San Julian the company "set up at the top of the highest mountain which was there a very large cross, as a sign that this country belonged to the king of Spain."

With the return of warmer weather the remaining ships set sail once again. On October 21, the feast day of Saint Ursula, the leading ship came to a cape which they called the Cape of the Eleven Thousand Virgins. And only a few miles farther on they reached "an opening like unto a bay." Three separate channels, in fact, led westward, and the *San Antonio* and the *Conception* both went forward to reconnoiter. It was at this stage that the crew of the *San Antonio* mutinied, put their commander in chains, and turned back east

Many of the "very great and awful things of the Ocean" were described by Antonio Pigafetta, one of Magellan's officers, who kept a diary. Harmless but surprising were these flying fish, whose ability to skim over the waves was greatly exaggerated by De Bry in this engraving.

for home. The *Conception*, floundering in the darkness, was found with difficulty by Magellan.

Many men would now have given up at this stage. With two of his original five ships lost, Magellan pressed on into the unknown—sailing by day, anchoring by night, cautiously feeling his way through a channel only half a league wide at times, and bordered by high, inhospitable, snow-covered mountains. At places small boats were sent out in advance to explore one channel or another. This happened one day during the last week of November, and from this sortie the men came back with the "news that there was an outlet, for they already saw the great sea on the other side." When Magellan heard this news he "ordered much artillery to be fired for rejoicing."

On November 28, 1520, the ships drew westward out of the channel (which Magellan had named All Saints' Strait) and into the vast expanses of an unknown, unsailed sea, so calm that Magellan christened it the Pacific Ocean.

Although he could not be certain of it at the time, Magellan was on the verge of proving his point: that the Americas did not form an impassable barrier separating Europe from the East. And they were not, as Columbus had mistakenly supposed, the eastern part of the continent of Asia. Yet in some ways Magellan's troubles were only beginning. The whole of the vast Pacific, covering half the surface of the globe, now lay before him. His route, moreover, took him beyond sight of the countless islands that dot that great ocean.

The three remaining ships making the first circumnavigation of the globe sailed on for three months and 20 days without taking on food or water. "We ate only old biscuit reduced to powder and full of grubs, and stinking from the dirt which the rats had made on it," Pigafetta reported, "and we drank water that was yellow and stinking. We also ate the ox hides which were under the mainyard. They were very hard on account of the sun, rain, and wind, and we left them for four or five days in the sea, and then we put them a little on the embers, and so ate them. [We also ate] the sawdust of wood, and rats at half-a-crown each."

As Magellan and his men worked their way across the wide Pacific they saw that "the antarctic pole is not so covered with stars as the arctic, for there are to be seen there many small stars congregated together, which are like to two clouds, a little separated from one another, and a little dimmed." These are the Magellanic Clouds, as they are called by astronomers today. They also saw the constellation of the Southern Cross, familiar to everyone south of the Tropic of Cancer.

As the voyage continued there were fewer and fewer to record such sights. First one man, then another, and finally a total of 19, died of scurvy. "Besides those who died," wrote Pigafetta, "twenty-five or thirty fell ill of divers sickness, both in the arms and legs, and other places, in such a manner that very few remained healthy."

Eventually, on January 24, Magellan made a landfall in the Tuamotu group, then sailed on to the Marianas, named by him Ladrones (Thieves) Islands, as the inhabitants stole from the seamen anything they could lay their hands on. Finally, in April, the three ships reached the Philippines. On Cebu, Magellan began to organize trade with the local population and to baptize into the Christian faith several local chiefs.

For a while all went well. Then Magellan made a fatal mistake. He was so eager to convert other

On the coast of Patagonia, where he stopped for two months, Magellan found a giant who was, wrote Pigafetta, "quite naked, and was dancing and leaping, and singing," and thought the explorers had descended from heaven.

islanders to Christianity and to win the support of the raja of the spice-rich island of Cebu, that when he learned that the raja was planning an attack on the neighboring island of Mactan, Magellan offered to fight the battle instead. On April 27 he landed on Mactan with a force of 48 companions, but "found the islanders, fifteen hundred in number, drawn up in three squadrons," wrote Pigafetta.

Most men would have turned back in the face of such overwhelming odds. Magellan went on. Almost immediately his troops were forced back toward the water. "We went thither, retreating little by little, and still fighting . . . the islanders following and picking up again the spears which they had already cast, and they threw the same spear five or six times. As they knew the captain, they aimed specially at him, and twice they knocked the helmet off his head. He, with a few of us, like a good knight, remained at his post without choosing to retreat further. Thus we fought for more than an hour, until an Indian succeeded in thrusting a cane lance into the captain's face. He then, being irritated, pierced the Indian's breast with his lance, and left it in his body, and trying to draw his sword was unable to draw it more than half-way, on account of a javelin wound which he had received in the right arm. The

Watched by 1500 hostile islanders, Magellan lands with 48 companions on Mactan in the Philippines. He had rashly offered to invade Mactan as a favor to the raja of Cebu, a neighboring island, and was killed by the natives soon after he stepped ashore. His death was a senseless and ignoble end to one of the great voyages of discovery.

PACIFIC OCEAN

Sulu Sea

Celebes Sea

MOLUCCAS

Sulu Islands

CELEBES

Banda Sea

TIMOR

PHILIPPINES

Cebu

Bohol (Mactan)

Magellan had crossed the Pacific and reached the Philippines in April 1521. On his death, the rest of his party sailed to northern Borneo, then down through the Moluccas, past Timor, and out into the Indian Ocean. Only 13 of the original party of 230 reached home, three years after they set out.

enemies seeing this all rushed against him, and one of them with a great sword, like a great scimitar, gave him a great blow on the left leg, which brought the captain down on his face, then the Indians threw themselves upon him, and ran him through with lances and scimitars, and all the other arms which they had, so that they deprived of life our mirror, light, comfort and true guide."

Their leader dead, the remainder of the expedition decided to sail on. But before they left the Philippines there was another battle, and only 115 men were left to continue the voyage. With such a small crew, the *Conception* had to be destroyed: This left only two of the original five ships—the *Trinity* and *Victoria*. On November 8 the ships reached the Moluccas and filled their holds with spices, but the *Trinity* developed a leak and was left behind to return home whenever she could. Later she was captured by the Portuguese and only a few of her crew managed to return home many years later.

The *Victoria* sailed on alone. With a crew of only 47 Europeans and a few natives, she set out to cross the Indian Ocean, round the Cape of Good Hope, and make for Spain. But before the Cape was reached scurvy had claimed the lives of 25 men; then when they called at the Cape Verde Islands a number of the survivors were arrested. Of Magellan's full complement, only 13 Europeans anchored off Seville in September 1522, three years after he had set out to sail around the world.

While these seamen of the Iberian peninsula had been searching for new routes to the Indies, the British had not been idle. As early as 1497, ships under the command of John Cabot, a Venetian pilot settled in England, had sailed from the port of Bristol. Like Columbus, he was searching for a western route to the Indies, but at this time in the history of exploration the waters of the northern Atlantic and hundreds of islands in and around the Arctic were unknown, and Cabot was stopped somewhere around Nova Scotia. So it was a British venture, supported by Henry VII, that *rediscovered* the "Vinland" of the Vikings and now brought the mainland of North America into history once again. During the years of the 1500s several sea explorers set out in search of a northwest passage to the East; their voyages will be described in the chapter dealing with the polar regions. We mention them here only to show that some men were sailing the northern waters of the Atlantic in the early 1500s, although most sea exploration was in more southerly areas.

67

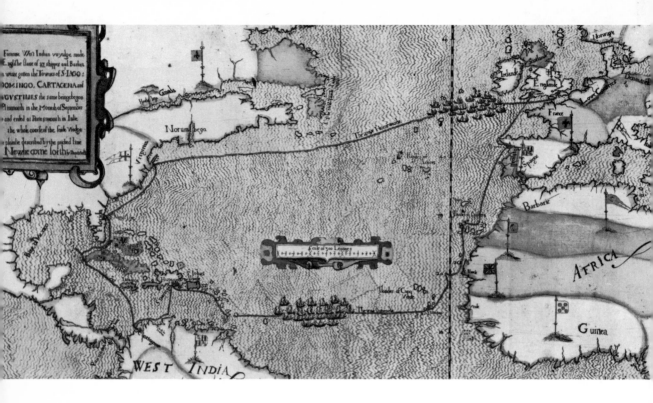

As the century rolled on, with war flickering more brightly between the Spaniards and the English, more adventurers sailed out from Britain in search of Spanish galleons. They pursued them wherever they could, and made inroads on the colonies that Spain was setting up in the Caribbean and along the coasts of South America.

The most famous of these adventurers was Francis (later Sir Francis) Drake, who was born about 1540. He served his apprenticeship in coastal vessels and sailed to the West Indies at the age of 30 on the first of many expeditions of privateering against the Spaniards. Two years later he burned the Spanish settlement of Portobello (in what is now Panama) and then traveled across the narrow isthmus. From its highest point he looked down on the Pacific, excited by what he saw. Here he "besought Almighty God of His goodness to give [him] life and leave to sail in an English ship in that sea."

Five years later he was to have his wish. In 1577 he sailed from England with five ships: the 100-ton *Pelican* (later renamed the *Golden Hind*); the 80-ton *Elizabeth*; and three smaller vessels. He sailed south across the Atlantic to the Americas, and on his arrival in San Julian he tried and executed Thomas Doughty, a mutineer, whose case later became famous. After this he worked his way through the Strait of Magellan in

This old map shows the route of Francis Drake's expedition in 1583 against the Spanish settlements in Hispaniola (Haiti), Cartagena, and St. Augustine, Florida. Although he sailed around the world, Drake (whose portrait is below) was more pirate than explorer, and spent most of his life plundering Spanish ships and colonies.

16 days. Once in the Pacific, Drake lived off the Spaniards, taking loot whenever he could. Eventually he sailed past Java, crossed the Indian Ocean, and rounded the Cape of Good Hope. Like Magellan's men, he had sailed around the world, but unlike Magellan himself, Drake survived to tell the tale and to take the honor. For Queen Elizabeth, at first cautious in view of Spanish protests, finally visited his ship at Deptford, and knighted him on deck.

The successors of Magellan and Drake in the 16th and early 17th centuries crossed the northern and southern Atlantic in increasing numbers. With each voyage the charts of the great oceans began to be drawn with greater accuracy and more detail. Yet there remained one great area about which little was known. This was the Pacific Ocean.

Many seamen had crossed it by now, but its sheer vastness forced them to keep to known and tested routes. Only in this way could they be certain of finding landfalls where they could take on fresh water and food. Spaniards sailing from their colonies in Peru discovered several of the many groups of islands that dot the great ocean—the Marquesas, the northern New Hebrides, and the Solomon Islands. The English discovered others. Abel Tasman, from Holland, sailing across the Indian Ocean from the west, discovered

Drake's tactical skill was well demonstrated in his capture of San Domingo, on Hispaniola, in 1584. As this picture shows, the colony was strongly defended to seaward, so Drake placed most of his fleet in the bay to divert attention. He then landed a little way along the coast (see ships at left), marched inland, and attacked the town from the rear.

what he called Van Diemen's Land (Tasmania). Then he sailed along the western coast of New Zealand.

Nearly all these explorers sailed with the intention of staking claims for their countries in foreign lands and with the hope of finding gold or other precious metals. But the Spanish and English had an additional motive—they were in search of new bases from which they could carry on their war. Few of them made more scientific observations than they had to in order to go about their business. They were not, in fact, geographers. The result was that well into the 18th century there lingered the theory of a "great southern continent." Bounded by the Pacific, it was thought to stretch up from the South Pole and "balance" the great land mass of Asia.

Above: This typical medieval map, with Jerusalem at its center, has little relation to reality.
Below: A more recognizable world map of 1596 stresses the old belief in a "great southern continent." As new navigational instruments were developed, seamen were able to plot the size and shape of the great land masses and oceans with ever-increasing precision. In turn, reliable maps of known territories helped in exploration of unmapped areas.

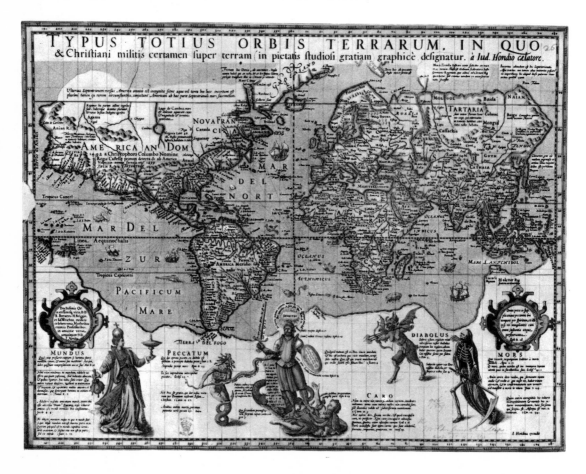

Cook Explores the Pacific

One man was to destroy this illusion, to *re*discover Australia, and leave a vastly more accurate map of the great Pacific Ocean. His name was James Cook and he rose from the lower levels of society to become Captain James Cook in the stern school of the British navy. Cook was typical of the new kind of seaman whose chief aim was discovery, not of gold, but of knowledge.

Cook was born in 1728 in a small Yorkshire village. The son of a laborer, he was apprenticed at the age of 13 to a draper and grocer in a small fishing village on the Yorkshire coast. After a year of apprenticeship he ran away to sea; then for 15 years he learned the business of his craft, sailing in small ships on the North Sea. To this day no one knows quite how Cook managed to develop a knowledge not only of navigation, but of surveying.

In 1755 he joined the British navy and was soon making an accurate survey of the St. Lawrence River; this survey later helped General Wolfe to capture Quebec from the French. Three years later Cook was carrying out survey work for the governor of Newfoundland. Then, in 1768, came his great opportunity.

In 1769 the planet Venus was to cross the Sun's disk. Scientists of England's Royal Society wanted the "transit" carefully observed, for they hoped that this would give them a more accurate measurement of the sun's distance from the earth. The best place for the observations would be the central Pacific, and the Royal Society asked King George III that a ship be sent to make them. The king agreed and command was given to James Cook, who was specially commissioned for the task. This in itself was a great tribute to the man, since it was rare for a master—as Cook then was—to be transferred to the executive ranks of the British navy. Even rarer was it for a newly created lieutenant, as he now became, to be given control of such an important scientific expedition.

Cook chose his own vessel, the 370-ton *Endeavour*, a stoutly built collier with a draft of only 13 feet 6 inches. When she sailed for the South Seas on August 26, 1768, she had on board, as Cook recorded in his journal: "94 persons including officers, seamen, Gentlemen and their servants, near 18 months' provisions, 10 carriage guns, 12 swivels, with good store of ammunition and stores of all kinds." Of the "Gentlemen," the most important was Joseph (later Sir Joseph) Banks. He was a wealthy botanist who later became President of the Royal Society, and accompanied Cook with his

James Cook was interested more in scientific knowledge than empire building, and his skilful navigating and surveying added greatly to geographical knowledge of deep southern latitudes.

own staff of assistants and artists who helped him observe the transit of Venus.

To prevent outbreaks of scurvy, which had killed so many men on so many previous voyages, they took supplies of a special malt. Each day it was made freshly into "wort," which was taken by all the crew. But this was only one of the many dietetic precautions. Others are described in a report issued by Mr. Perry, the Surgeon's Mate. "Sour krout, mustard, vinegar, wheat, orange and lemon juices, saloup, portable soup, sugar, molasses, vegetables (at all times when they could be got) were, some in constant, others in occasional use," he wrote. "Cold bathing was encouraged and enforced by example; the allowance of salt beef and pork was abridged from nearly the beginning of the voyage, and the sailors' usual custom of mixing the salt beef fat with their flour, etc., was strictly forbad.... At Tierra del Fuego [at the southern tip of South America] we collected wild celery, and every morning our breakfast was made with this herb, with ground wheat and soup."

It was not only in their safeguards against scurvy that Cook and his men illustrated the new scientific approach to seafaring. "No people ever went to sea better fitted out for the purpose of Natural History, nor more elegantly," wrote John Ellis, a Fellow of the Royal Society. "They have a fine library of Natural History: they have all sorts of machines for catching and preserving insects; all kinds of nets, trawls, drags and hooks for coral fishing: they have even a curious contrivance of a telescope, by which, put into the water, you can see the bottom at a great depth, where it is clear. They have many cases of bottles with ground stoppers, of several sizes, to preserve animals in spirits. ... Solander [one of Banks's assistants] assured me that this expedition would cost Mr. Banks £10,000."

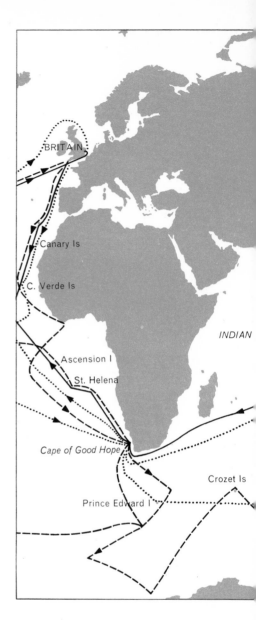

Walruses off the North American coast

This map shows the routes of Cook's three voyages. On his first, he observed the transit of Venus from Tahiti, then went on to explore New Zealand. On his second, he sailed around Antarctica and reduced the "great southern continent" to its proper size. On his third, he explored the northern Pacific near Bering Strait, then sailed south to Hawaii, where he was killed by natives. At left and right are three of the sights he witnessed on his voyages.

1st voyage ———

2nd voyage — — —

3rd voyage ··········

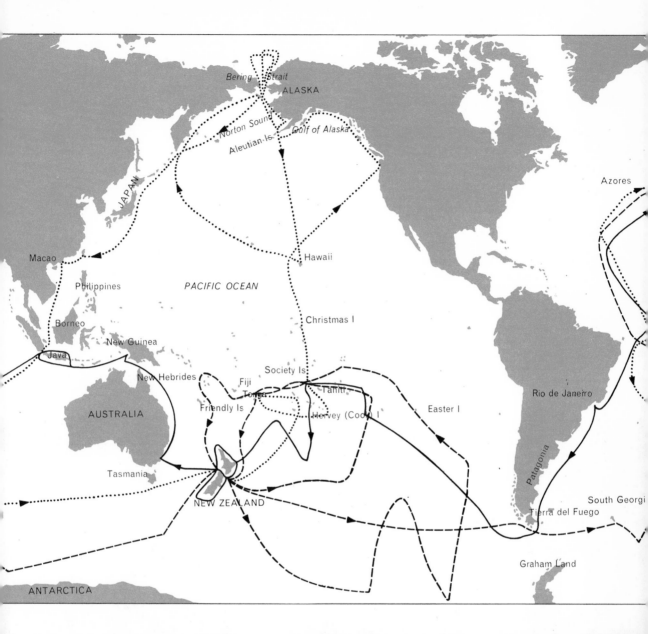

Bering Strait

ALASKA

Norton Sound

Gulf of Alaska

Aleutian Is.

JAPAN

Macao

Philippines

Borneo

New Guinea

Java

New Hebrides

AUSTRALIA

Tasmania

ANTARCTICA

PACIFIC OCEAN

Hawaii

Christmas I

Society Is.

Fiji

Tonga

Tahiti

Friendly Is

Hervey (Cook) I

NEW ZEALAND

Easter I

Azores

Rio de Janeiro

Patagonia

South Georgi

Tierra del Fuego

Graham Land

South American Indians at Tierra del Fuego

Native dancers on the Tonga Islands

Cook's ship, the *Endeavour*, was better equipped for scientific investigations than any previous expedition. Here in his cabin Cook examines a sextant, used to calculate latitude by measuring the angle of the sun from the horizon; at the other end of the table is a microscope. On the right, front, is a dip circle for measuring terrestrial magnetism. Behind it, in the box, is a ship's compass with sights for taking bearings. In front of the celestial globe is a theodolite, used in surveying.

Equipped better than any ship that had sailed before, the *Endeavour* reached the Cape Verde Islands, crossed the southern Atlantic to Rio de Janeiro, and by New Year's Day was off Patagonia and making for Cape Horn. At Patagonia, Banks went ashore and collected many natural history specimens, which his artists later drew. Toward the end of January the expedition sailed for the cape, "the wind foul; but our keeping boxes being full of new plants," Banks wrote, "we little regarded any wind, provided it was but moderate enough to let the [artists] work who, to do them justice, are now so used to the sea that it must blow a gale of wind before they leave off."

Cook turned the cape safely and then sailed northwest into the Pacific, navigating toward the Society Islands. It was here that the group was to make observation of the transit of Venus. Unlike so many earlier voyages, everything went according to plan. The crew was virtually free of scurvy and the weather was good. On the morning of April 13, eight months after setting out, the *Endeavour* anchored off the island that Cook named Otaheite, and which we know today as Tahiti.

"Before the anchor was down," Banks wrote, "we were surrounded by large numbers of canoes, the people trading very quietly and civilly, chiefly for beads, in exchange for which they gave coconuts, breadfruit both roasted and raw, some small fish and apples. They had one pig with them which they refused to sell for nails upon any account, but repeatedly offered it for a hatchet; of these we had very few on board, so thought it better to let the pig go than to give one of them in exchange, knowing on the authority of those who had been here before, that if we did so they would never lower their price."

Cook's repeated message to his crew was that the islanders should be treated kindly and fairly in all ways. We should try by "every fair means," he said, "to Cultivate a Friendship with the Natives, and to treat them with all imaginable Humanity." This insistence that the islanders should be treated properly sets Cook apart from most earlier seamen. Yet he was in no way a soft commander. He maintained stern discipline on his ship. At one point he "punished Richard Hutchins, seaman, with 12 lashes for disobeying commands."

The observations of the transit of Venus were to be made on June 1. To prepare for them, Cook set up a fort that could easily be defended against any possible attack. The islanders' habit of stealing everything they could—in spite of their continuing friendliness—was one of Cook's major problems. Even with the safeguards of the fort, things were stolen—for one, a navigational instrument that was recovered only after a chase by Banks. A wooden cask was also taken from inside the fort, and "so immediately under the eye of the sentry that we could hardly believe the possibility of such a thing having happened," Banks wrote.

During the days before the transit of Venus, Cook and the scientists studied the Tahitians and their customs, the way they buried their dead, their wrestling matches, and their surf riding. On Thursday, June 1, observations were begun, but they were not so successful as the scientists had hoped. In his diary Cook wrote: "We very distinctly saw an Atmosphere or Dusky shade round the body of the planet, which very much disturbed the times of the Contact, particularly the two internal ones. Dr. Solander observed as well as Mr. Green and myself, and we differ'd from one another in Observing the time of the Contact much more than could be expected."

The first object of the expedition had now been attained. But for Cook, this was only the beginning. He next began to explore and map the Society Islands to

This breadfruit was painted by one of Sir Joseph Banks's botanical artists aboard the *Endeavour*. A staple food of South Pacific islanders, breadfruit was introduced into the West Indies, at Cook's suggestion, to feed the slaves.

This chart of Matavai Bay, Tahiti, was drawn by Cook. Venus Point is seen at top left.

For his observations of the transit of Venus in June 1769, Cook built a small station at Venus Point in Tahiti. He fortified it against the natives, who were quick to steal anything they could lay hands on.

the west of Tahiti, islands that had never before been visited. Then he turned south toward the "great southern continent." Unlike most other geographers, Cook did not believe in the existence of the great land mass. As they continued south Cook studded his diary with such entries as "Fresh Gales and Hazey Weather," or "Strong Gales with much rain, Thunder and Lightning." Onward they sailed, but still without signs of the southern continent. On August 31 Banks recorded in his diary that they had seen some seaweed float "by the ship, but as it was a very small piece, our hopes are not very sanguine on that head." Three days later, having traveled some 1500 miles south, Cook decided to turn back. He had proved that no great southern continent existed—or at least one was not visible from lat. 40°22's.

Turning course first northwestward and then southwestward, the *Endeavour* reached Poverty Bay on the east coast of North Island, New Zealand, on October 7. During the next six months Cook and his men circumnavigated both North Island and South Island, charting much of their coasts. He proved that they are two separate islands by sailing between them through what is today Cook Strait. Abel Tasman, who had sighted rather than discovered New Zealand in 1642, thought that the two islands were one, mistaking Cook Strait for a bay. Tasman also thought that the west coast of the islands marked the westward extension of the "great southern continent." By sailing completely around the islands, Cook delivered another blow to the idea of a mythical continent. Still not satisfied, he now sailed west again, making this time for "New Holland" (Australia) and the uncharted coast of what is now New South Wales.

The *Endeavour* reached the Australian coast on Saturday, April 28. The following morning Cook, Banks, and Solander landed at a place they first called Sting Ray Bay. It was renamed Botany Bay because of the large collection of plants made there by Banks. For the next four months the *Endeavour* tacked slowly up the east coast of Australia. Cook claimed the country in the name of Great Britain and made a careful survey of the entire coast. When necessary, he went ashore for water or other supplies and made what contact he could with the natives.

Until the middle of June all went well. Then there

was a near-disaster that might have put an end to the whole expedition. The *Endeavour* was off Queensland, near what is now the port of Cooktown. It was a clear moonlit night with the ship moving slowly along the coast. The linesman, regularly taking soundings, was calling out depths of from 14 to 21 fathoms. Then, a few minutes before 11 o'clock, the linesman called 17 fathoms and "before the Man at the Lead could heave another cast, the Ship Struck and stuck fast." She had gone aground on a sharp coral reef.

Cook immediately took charge, ordering the sails to be taken in and the boats lowered. He was rowed round the *Endeavour* only to find that she was firmly grounded, "upon which," he wrote, "we went to work to lighten her as fast as possible, which seemed to be the only means we had left to get her off. . . . [We] threw overboard our Guns, Iron and Stone Ballast, Casks, Hoop Staves, Oil Jarrs, decay'd Stores etc. . . ." But even this failed to free the ship. It was not until the following day that "I resolved to risk us all, and heave her off . . . and accordingly turn'd as many hands to the Capstan and Windlass as could be spared from the Pumps. About 20 minutes past 10 o'clock the Ship floated, and we hove her into Deep Water, having at this time 3 feet 9 Inches Water in the hold."

Cook now beached the ship and repaired the damage near the mouth of the Endeavour River. In July the voyage up Australia's northeast coast was continued, but before heading for home, Cook was to make one more addition to the world map. On reaching the northernmost tip of Australia, the *Endeavour* sailed westward through what is now Torres Strait, proving for the first time that Australia and New Guinea were not linked.

Cook's mission had by this time been fulfilled. His instructions from the Admiralty had ordered him to proceed ". . . southward in order to make discovery of the [great southern] continent abovementioned until you arrive in latitude of 40°." Next he was to proceed to "the eastern side of the land discovered by Tasman and now called New Zealand." He was instructed to ". . . carefully observe the latitude and longitude in which that land is situated and explore as much of the coast as the condition of the bark, the help of her crew and state of her provisions will admit of." This accomplished, it was Cook's choice to return to England or to continue surveying and charting unknown coasts. He chose the former.

This was just as well, for according to Banks most of the crew were by this time "pretty far gone with the

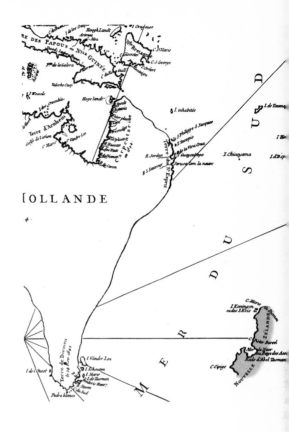

Above: This French map of 1756, used by Cook on his first voyage, shows New Zealand as a peninsula, for many thought it was part of the "southern continent." In 1769 and 1770 Cook sailed around New Zealand and proved that it was two islands separated by what is now Cook Strait. He drew the chart below from his careful plotting of the islands' coast lines.

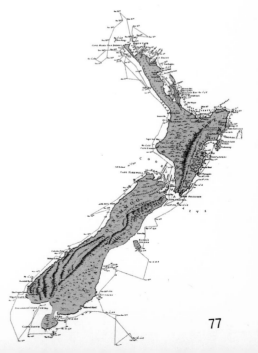

Cook visited Easter Island in the southeast Pacific in 1774, when this picture was painted by the ship's artist William Hodges. The stone monuments, which are of great archaeological interest, were investigated by Thor Heyerdahl, the Norwegian anthropologist, in 1955.

longing for home which the physicians have gone so far as to esteem a disease under the name of Nostalgia." There were still many thousands of miles to go, and it was not until July of 1771 that the *Endeavour* had passed Java and Batavia, crossed the Indian Ocean, rounded the Cape of Good Hope, and come to safe anchorage in the English Channel.

Cook's great voyage was the first to be undertaken for a purely scientific purpose, and to be carried out by officers whose chief aim was fresh discoveries about the natural world in which they lived. Its success was due not only to Cook's seamanship, but to the confidence that he inspired both in his crew and in the civilian scientists who sailed with him. And to Cook there justly came promotion to the rank of commander.

The following year he was put in charge of the *Resolution* and the *Adventure*, two ships whose mission it was to discover how far northward the antarctic ice stretched. Once again Cook was away for three years —years during which he explored much more of the southern Pacific, and sailed completely round the outskirts of the antarctic ice. The completion of this voyage once and for all settled the "great southern continent" myth. There was, to be sure, a southern continent, but not the giant land mass imagined by early geographers. Even though Cook never saw Antarctica, he was able to visualize its appearance from his position outside the icepack. He was "well satisfied no continent was to be found in this ocean but must be so far south as to be wholly inaccessible on account of ice. ... Yet I think that there must be some land behind this ice, but if there is it can afford no better retreat for birds or any other animals than the ice itself, with which it must be wholly covered."

When he returned to England he was sent on yet another expedition. This time his mission was to discover a route from the northern Pacific around the north coast of America—a northwest passage linking East and West. He set out in 1776 by sailing around the Cape of Good Hope, then crossed the Indian Ocean to Tasmania. From here he cruised north through the Pacific to the Bering Strait, but a wall of ice finally forced him to turn back south.

He visited the extreme northeast of Siberia, then crossed over to America, exploring Norton Sound north of the Yukon. From here he sailed to Hawaii, arriving in 1779. The crews of the *Resolution* and her sister ship the *Discovery* traded with the natives and at first all went well. But then the islanders stole a boat, and on February 14 Cook landed with a party to retrieve it. Exactly what happened next we do not know. There was a long parley with the local chief, then Cook was threatened and eventually forced to fire a warning shot. Stones were thrown at the seven marines who accompanied him, and one of the chiefs tried to stab Lieutenant Phillips, one of the *Resolution*'s officers. Cook fired again, as did a marine sergeant. The reply was a volley of stones. The marines fired back, were rushed by the natives, and forced back with Cook to the water's edge. Cook now turned to give orders to the boat's crew. As he did so, he was hit on the head and stabbed in the back. He fell and was now set upon by the rest of the natives who had already killed four of the marines. Several days later the islanders returned to the British the hacked remains of the commander's body, which were buried in Hawaii.

Thus died James Cook, whose achievements had helped shape the rough outline of the world as we now know it. In the three centuries and more that had passed since the days of Prince Henry the Navigator, men had crossed the northern and southern Atlantic oceans to discover the New World. They had opened up the Indian Ocean, sailed around the world, and discovered that the vast spaces of the Pacific lay between the Americas and "the Indies." The positions and sizes of the continents and of the oceans that separated them were more accurately known than ever before.

With the exception of the oceans in the far north and south, the sea routes of the world were open at last. Many men now began to turn their attention to the interiors of the new lands that had been discovered.

Cook was killed by Hawaiians in February 1779, when he landed with a party to retrieve a boat that had been stolen by the islanders.

3 Jungles and Forests

By the time Captain Cook had proved that the Antarctic continent did not stretch northward into temperate latitudes, the position of the world's major land masses was known. Although the Antarctic and Arctic were yet to be explored in detail, men were now able to draw fairly accurately the shapes of Africa, North and South America (linked by the narrow isthmus of Panama), and the huge tracts of Asia and Europe.

But in many places their knowledge extended only a short distance inland from the coasts. Such areas included the great steamy jungles of South America, the rolling prairies and forests of North America, and the mysterious depths of Africa from which the four great rivers of the Nile, Congo, Niger, and Zambezi wound their serpentine ways. These regions were only then becoming known to Europeans, and their later exploration was made possible by the great age of oceanic exploration that had started with the voyages inspired by Henry the Navigator and that reached a climax with Cook and his scientists.

Exploration of the jungles of South America and Africa, and of the forests of North America, presented problems that were very different from those faced by sea explorers. The first of these was the sheer difficulty of forcing a track through the dense network of trees, creepers, and tangled undergrowth. In this thick carpeting of greenery, which covered the earth for thousands of square miles, men often found it impossible to force a way without laboriously hacking a path step by step. And with the stars frequently concealed by the unbroken canopy of foliage overhead, it was often impossible to determine the way, or to keep to it once it had been found. To avoid the physical difficulty of carving a way through the jungle, many explorers used the great rivers as highways. Yet the rivers pre-

Seeking gold, spices, and new lands to colonize, Spanish conquistadors first penetrated the vast tropical rain forests of South America in the mid-16th century. Some were able to use the rivers as highways; others, as here, had to hack their way step by step through dense undergrowth and swamps, often under attack from local tribesmen. Much of these jungles remains unexplored by Europeans even today.

sented problems of their own; currents that helped to carry an expedition in one direction sometimes made its return by the same route impossible.

There were also dangers from native tribes, since many of the rain forests were inhabited by savage peoples who did not understand, or who feared, the intrusion of white men, whom they had never seen before. Another hazard was the climate of the jungles themselves, a steamy heat in which men's clothes quickly rotted away, which induced the spread of disease, and which sapped men's strength.

All of these dangers and difficulties had to be weighed carefully against the great attractions that the jungles offered to explorers. From many jungle areas—particularly South America—there seeped legends of a fabulous El Dorado, a city of gold. To this was added the desire for conquest and the building of empires, as well as conversion of the natives to Christianity. All these motives were to play their parts in the conquest of the jungles that began with the establishment of the Spaniards in the New World.

Following the discoveries of Columbus, a host of tough adventurers—the *conquistadors*—sailed west from Spain. Part soldiers and part sailors these men claimed vast areas for Spain and vast loot for themselves. At the same time they tried to convert the native peoples to Christianity, by persuasion when possible, but by force if necessary. Sometimes brutal but always courageous, the conquistadors succeeded in winning territory in both central and southern America. Among the most splendid of them all was Hernando Cortes, who in November 1518 sailed from a base in Cuba to conquer the great Aztec Empire of Mexico. With him was an army of about 600 Spaniards, about 200 Indians, and 16 horses.

Cortes landed in Yucatán on the shores of the Gulf of Mexico, defeated the Indians, who thought that his cavalrymen were centaurs, and marched westward to found what is now the city of Veracruz. With this as a base, he next marched on Tenochtitlan (now Mexico City), the Aztec capital, having burned his fleet when some of his followers pleaded to return to Cuba.

Outside the capital, which stood in a great lake and was approached by causeways, rose the volcano of Popocatepetl, then in eruption. Cortes' men, who had never before seen a volcano and were curious about this one, climbed up to the crater to look inside; this astonished the natives who, through a mixture of superstition and common sense, never approached it during eruption.

This medallion with its profile of Hernando Cortes was struck in Spain or Italy about 1530.

Cortes, with Doña Marina, his Mexican companion and interpreter, meets the Aztec emperor Montezuma. Believing the Spaniard to be the incarnation of a pale-skinned Aztec god, Montezuma made little attempt to defend his capital, Tenochtitlan, against Cortes' small army.

Tenochtitlan.

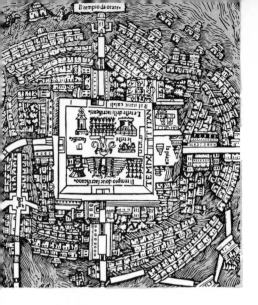

This map of Tenochtitlan, which was on the site of the present Mexico City, is thought to be based on a sketch by Cortes. It shows the city surrounded by a lake and intersected by canals. In the center is the temple enclosure, used for human sacrifices.

Besieged by Aztec forces, Cortes withdrew his troops from the city in July 1520. His retreat across one of the city's causeways was discovered. The Aztecs, in canoes, destroyed the causeway and killed many Spaniards.

"When we saw so many cities and villages built in the water, and other great towns on dry land, we were amazed, and said that it was like the enchantments they tell us of in the legend of Amadis," wrote Bernal Diaz, the historian of the party. "And some of our soldiers even asked whether the things were not a dream."

Then Cortes, with 400 men, captured Tenochtitlan with its 300,000 inhabitants. Although there were reverses of fortune, the Spaniards eventually occupied Mexico; and from it during the 16th century they sent out expeditions that gradually opened up the southwestern parts of what is now the United States. One party, which set out in 1528 under Cabeza de Vaca, spent eight years exploring what is now Florida, crossed the Mississippi, marched overland to the Colorado River, and finally made its way back to Mexico. By the time they returned there were only four survivors.

About this time Hernando de Soto was working his way up through Florida. In 1539 he landed at Tampa Bay with 600 men, 20 officers, and 24 priests, and began a march into the interior that took him through what is now Georgia, Alabama, Mississippi, and Arkansas. Steadily losing men in battles with the Indians, the group reached the Mississippi River in 1541, crossed it, and spent their third winter on the Wichita River. Only then did they give up hope of finding the great wealth for which they had come. De Soto himself died the following year (probably some-

Tolteca acalotl ypan õcãmicovac.

where near present-day Memphis) and only about 300 men finally returned to Spanish-held territory—by sailing down the Mississippi and eventually reaching the town of Pánuco in Mexico.

Meanwhile, the tide of exploration was surging down the western coast of South America. As early as 1510 Vasco Nuñez de Balboa had become second-in-command of an expedition to Darien on the isthmus of Panama. Three years later, investigating reports of a great western ocean, he succeeded in crossing the isthmus and from a little peak caught sight of the rolling expanses of the Pacific.

In 1540 another group, commanded by Francisco de Coronado, set out and reached the Grand Canyon, although Coronado himself did not participate in this part of the expedition. They were almost certainly the first Europeans to look down into that immense chasm and see the silver trickle of the river far below.

Other conquistadors were soon traveling across the narrow isthmus of Panama and down the coast of South America. Among the most brilliant of them was Francisco Pizarro, an illiterate soldier, who first sailed to Panama in 1508. By 1526 he had risen high enough in rank to take command of a ship and, at the age of about 50, went with two others down the coast to South America. Their task was to collect details of the empire of the Incas. During the previous five centuries the Incas had developed a great civilization along the western seaboard of the continent, and their territories stretched inland to the peaks of the Andes, which run like a narrow spine down the western side of South America.

After great difficulties—a near-mutiny and then opposition from the Spanish authorities in Panama—Pizarro reached the Peruvian port of Tumbes, returned to Panama with information about the Incas, and then sailed for Spain. His object was to gain permission to try to conquer Peru. In 1529 that permission was granted by Queen Juana of Spain, and the following year Pizarro sailed for Panama. Then on December 28, 1531, with three ships, carrying about 180 men and 27 horses, he sailed from Panama to conquer a great empire.

Pizarro succeeded, and his conquest was one of the great military feats of history. It was marred, however, by his treachery in killing the Inca. He offered to spare the emperor Atahualpa in return for a roomful of gold; but even though he was given the gold, he murdered the emperor.

Pizarro and his small band of companions were

The manuscript at right shows an Aztec conception of the universe, centered on a Great God. In the Aztec drawing below, the missionary zeal of the Spanish is represented by a conquistador carrying the cross. Catholic ritual attracted many American Indians away from their native religions.

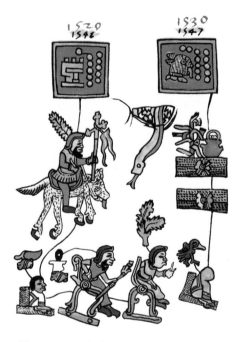

The drawing below is an Inca's impression of a Spanish galleon sailing to Peru. Many Spanish colonists were lured to South America by reports of gold.

This gold llama—a traditional beast of burden in South America—demonstrates the skill of Inca goldsmiths, who used the metal entirely for decorative purposes.

followed by other emigrants from Spain who, during the 1530s, colonized the long strip of Peru that lies between the Pacific Ocean and the Andes. In 1535 one of their leaders, Diego de Almagro, who had taken part in the conquest of Peru with Pizarro, rode south with a small band of soldiers to occupy what is now Chile. Unsuccessful, he nevertheless paved the way for the colonization of that country by other Spaniards a few years later.

The Crossing of South America

In 1539 Pizarro's brother Gonzalo was sent on a hazardous expedition eastward. The journey was to take him across the high barrier of the Andes and result in a fantastic voyage down the 4000-mile course of the Amazon River.

There had been reports that beyond Quito, east of what we know today as Ecuador, there was a country rich in cinnamon. Gonzalo eagerly accepted the offer to explore the region, since he regarded it as an "op-

ANDAS DEL INGA
PILLCORAUPA

Rival commanders are carried into battle on litters: an Inca chief (above) and a Spanish general (below) as seen by a 16th-century Peruvian artist. The wheel was unknown to the indigenous peoples of North and South America.

COMENDERO
Q̃ ELCOMENDERO

portunity of proving his valour." This was the comment of the Inca Garcilaso de la Vega, a man who left the only surviving account of the astonishing venture.

The expedition was fitted out in the city of Quito, where Gonzalo recruited 150 cavalrymen and 190 infantry. To support this group were 4000 natives, "laden with arms, supplies, and all things requisite for the service, such as iron, hatchets, knives, ropes, hempen cords, and large nails." To augment the food supplies that they hoped to gather en route they took nearly 4000 pigs in addition to a herd of llamas, which they used as pack animals. Thus equipped, the expedition set out from the city of Quito on Christmas Day 1539. As one of his lieutenants, Gonzalo had a man named Francisco de Orellana, a spirited adventurer, who was to play a leading role in the expedition.

At first all went well. The company marched northeastward until they reached what their chronicler called "the limits of the ancient Empire of the Incas." Soon after this "many warlike Indians sallied forth . . . but when they beheld the multitude of the Spaniards and horses, they quickly retired."

A few days later Gonzalo and his men faced the first of their troubles—an earthquake, thunder, lightning, and torrential rain that lasted for many days. All of this took place, it appears, on the western slopes of the Andes near the volcano of Pichincha. With the arrival of better weather the Spaniards next set about crossing the main chain.

We know little about the difficulties they now had to face, except that they pushed their way through heavy snowstorms, and that many Indians died of the cold. At one point the Spaniards decided to abandon their pigs and certain other provisions so that they might reach the shelter of native villages more quickly. Once over the Andes—the crossing of this range, which here reaches 10,000 feet, was an achievement in itself—they came to a large stretch of uninhabited country and, beyond it, the rain belt. Garcilaso wrote that "during [the two months they spent in this region] it did not cease to rain for a single day; so that the Spaniards received great injury, and much of their clothing became rotten."

Gonzalo had now arrived in the province of Sumaco, where he found vast areas of the wild cinnamon trees he had heard about. But they were not so good as cultivated trees and he decided to continue eastward in search of greater riches, into the great forests that now spread out before and below him. At this stage he set out ahead of the main party, taking only the most active

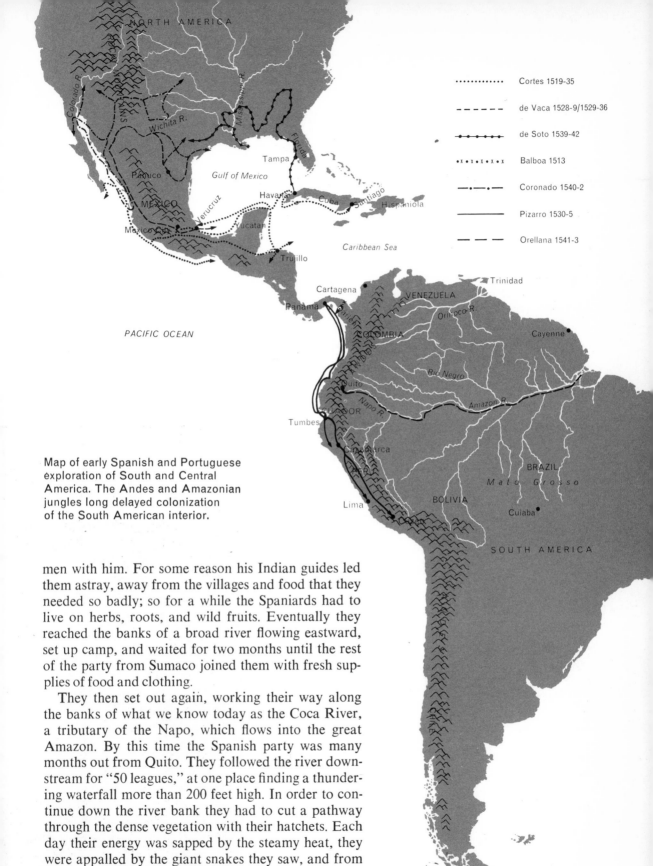

Map of early Spanish and Portuguese exploration of South and Central America. The Andes and Amazonian jungles long delayed colonization of the South American interior.

men with him. For some reason his Indian guides led them astray, away from the villages and food that they needed so badly; so for a while the Spaniards had to live on herbs, roots, and wild fruits. Eventually they reached the banks of a broad river flowing eastward, set up camp, and waited for two months until the rest of the party from Sumaco joined them with fresh supplies of food and clothing.

They then set out again, working their way along the banks of what we know today as the Coca River, a tributary of the Napo, which flows into the great Amazon. By this time the Spanish party was many months out from Quito. They followed the river downstream for "50 leagues," at one place finding a thundering waterfall more than 200 feet high. In order to continue down the river bank they had to cut a pathway through the dense vegetation with their hatchets. Each day their energy was sapped by the steamy heat, they were appalled by the giant snakes they saw, and from time to time they caught glimpses of natives who would peer out at them through the leaves and then disappear into the depths of the jungle.

Eventually the forest thinned out and Gonzalo's men found themselves among natives who wore cotton clothes and grew maize. These people were altogether more civilized than the jungle dwellers Gonzalo had seen earlier. He decided to camp here and sent out men to reconnoiter the country. But as each one returned he had the same story to tell—ahead lay lagoons, swamps, and more dense jungle.

Gonzalo now decided to build a ship, and the way he did it proved him a man of ingenuity. According to Garcilaso, he "set up a forge for making nails, and burnt charcoal with great trouble, because the heavy rains prevented the tinder from taking fire. They also made roofed huts to burn the wood in, and defend it from the rain. Some of the nails were made from the shoes of horses, which had been killed as food for the sick, and the rest of the iron they had brought with them. They now found it more valuable than gold."

When they had built their ship, the Spaniards loaded it with gold they had been carrying with them, as well as their forge, and everything else of value. They then put their sick men on board and set off down the river in two parties, the one on land hacking its way along the river bank. Thus they continued eastward for two months until finally they met natives who said that only 10 days away lay a country where they would find gold, food, and provisions.

At this stage of the journey more than half of the 4000 men who had set out from Quito a year earlier had already died; and others were dying each day of disease and starvation. Gonzalo now decided to send the ship on ahead with orders to return to the main party with supplies as soon as they could be gathered. Orellana was put in charge of the small group, and within three days the strong current had carried the ship downstream to its junction with the Napo River. Here the expedition took a dramatic turn. According to some, Orellana deserted; but according to others, the strong current prevented him from working his way back up the river to rejoin Gonzalo. For whatever reason, he continued down river on what was to be the fantastic first voyage down the Amazon to its mouth.

After restlessly awaiting Orellana's return, Gonzalo finally decided to set out after him. When the group reached the junction of the two rivers they found Hernan Sanchez de Vargas, who had been put ashore by Orellana and who now told Gonzalo what had happened. Shocked by the story, the Spaniards pur-

To speed progress on his expedition across South America in 1539, Gonzalo and his men built a boat from local materials in the Amazonian jungle. It was aboard this boat that Orellana and 50 companions made part of their journey to the mouth of the Amazon.

sued Orellana down river in hopes of overtaking him. By the time they had traveled "100 leagues" many men had fallen along the way; there were now only 1000 of the 4000 Indians who had left Quito. Of the 150 horses, only 80 were left, and only a few of the 900 dogs. The only things Gonzalo's men could find to eat were "herbs and roots and wild fruits, frogs and serpents and other wretched food."

Gonzalo now realized that the only hope of survival lay in going back. Once again they were forced to test their endurance against the jungle and endless marshes. The sick were carried on the shoulders of the able men, and "on account of the constant waters from above and below, they were always wet; and their clothes rotted, so that they had to go naked." They were attacked by scurvy. They ate their dogs and then their horses, and when they finally emerged from the forests near the foothills of the Andes, the remaining 1000 Indians had died. So had 210 of the 340 Spaniards who had left Quito nearly three years earlier. The tiny band

of men who eventually reached home were a sorry lot. Undernourished, "some began to eat with such will that it was necessary to stop them. Others were of a different constitution, and could not eat what they wished because their stomachs, used to fasting and abstinence, would not receive what was given to them."

Everyone was anxious to have news of the expedition and was saddened by the account of it. There were many tears but, says the chronicler, "they consoled each other in thinking that there was no remedy for the past, and that tears availed little."

All this time Orellana and his little band of 50 men had continued sailing downstream, but they, too, were meeting with their own problems of finding food and keeping themselves alive. "They had nothing to eat but the skins which formed their girdles, and the leather of their shoes, boiled with a few herbs." One by one the emaciated men began to die. By January 8, 1541, about eight had collapsed and the rest were now "all expecting their deaths."

At this stage in their journey they heard the sound of native drums in the distance. As the small ship rounded a bend in the river, the Spaniards saw in front of them a village, but by the time they reached it the natives had fled. Orellana's men lost no time eating the rough provisions that they found in the village, then they awaited the return of the natives. Soon they came in their canoes, parleyed with Orellana, and agreed to bring as much food as his men wanted—"abundance of turkeys, partridges, fish, and other things." The next day, several chiefs arrived, "with plumes of feathers and gold ornaments. Orellana spoke to them with great courtesy, requested them to be obedient to the crown of Castile, and took possession of the country."

The Spaniards now decided to build a stouter ship and follow the great river all the way to the sea; but how long would the journey take? They could only guess. "Having commenced building the brigantine, they found no difficulty except in getting nails," wrote the chronicler of this part of the expedition, Antonio de Herrera, "but it pleased God that two men should make that which they had never been taught to make. . . . Timber [for the ship] had been cut and prepared with great labour, which the men endured with much willingness, and in thirty-five days she was launched, caulked with cotton, and the seams [filled] with pitch which was given them by the Indians."

On April 4 all was ready and the party set sail. For more than a month they passed through uninhabited country, the jungle reaching to the river banks and the

Portuguese explorers defend a stockaded village they have captured from Indian cannibals on the coast of Brazil, about 1549.

While serving as a gunner with the Portuguese forces on the Brazilian island of Amaro, Hans Staden (the bearded figure at center) is captured by Indians.

Staden, taken by his captors to their camp near modern Rio de Janeiro, is subjected to ritual torture by Indian women. Later he was rescued by French seamen.

current so strong that they were unable to stop and fish. Then one morning the Spaniards saw paddling toward them "a number of canoes, full of warlike Indians, with large shields made of the skins of lizards and dantas [tapirs] beating drums and shouting, with threats that they would eat the Christians." Because their powder had become damp the Spaniards had to rely on their crossbows, and waged a desperate running fight which continued for many miles down the Amazon. At one point Orellana sent 12 men ashore in hopes of capturing provisions from a village. Although the party managed to collect some supplies, the men suddenly found themselves being pressed back to the river by a force of 2000 natives. Hurriedly Orellana took on what provisions he could, then gave the order to sail. By this time even more natives had gathered along the shore and began following the boat downstream. "In this way the whole night was passed until dawn, when they saw many villages," wrote their diarist. "The Spaniards, fatigued by so bad a night, determined to go and take refreshment on an uninhabited island, on which, however, they were unable to get any rest from the crowds of Indians who landed and attacked them."

Once again the Spaniards were chased downstream. For two days and two nights they managed to keep the natives at bay and eventually left the exhausted canoers far behind. From now on the tribes Orellana and his men saw, and the country through which they passed, varied considerably. At some places the natives were of the most primitive sort; at others they appeared to be civilized. At one place the Spaniards found "a country house containing very good jars of earthenware, vases, and goblets of glass enamelled with many bright colours, resembling drawings and paintings. The Indians at this place said that these things came from the interior, together with much gold and silver. They also found idols worked from palm wood in a very curious fashion . . . with wheels in the fleshy part of the arms. The Spaniards found in this village, gold and silver; but as they only thought of discovery and of saving their lives, they did not care for anything else."

Orellana and his men had by this time become more cautious. They sailed in midstream to give themselves as much warning as possible against surprise attack. And whenever they went ashore they were careful to be back on their ship before dark, since, as their chronicler put it, "In a country so well peopled, it was not advisable to remain on shore during the night." At one place they passed a great river flowing into the main

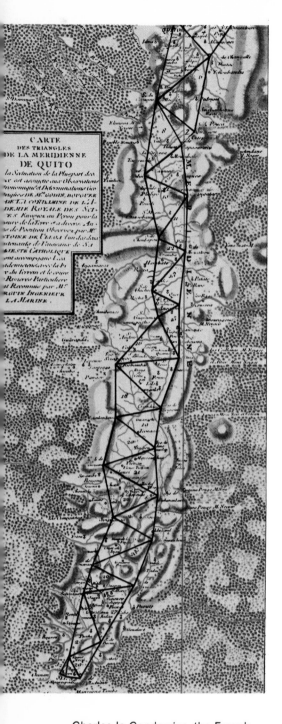

CARTE
DES TRIANGLES
DE LA MERIDIENNE
DE QUITO

Charles la Condamine, the French geographer and mathematician, was one of the earliest scientific explorers of South America. This map of part of Peru was drawn in the 1730s when he was making measurements to determine the true shape of the earth.

stream from the north, the Rio Negro, "with waters as black as ink, the force of which was so great that, for more than twenty leagues, its waters flowed separately, without mingling with the Amazon river."

At some places the natives had "gentle dispositions," yet at others they attacked the Spaniards whenever they could. And at more than one place there were the "Amazons," a tribe of women warriors after whom Orellana named the great river. These women were described as being "very tall, robust, fair, with long hair twisted over their head, skins round their loins, and bows and arrows in their hands, with which they killed seven or eight Spaniards." Soon after this encounter Orellana and his men saw the sight for which they had been waiting so long—the flow of the tide, which showed that they were at last approaching the sea. At this point the river was so broad that the Spaniards were unable to see from one bank to the other. Cautiously they felt their way among the islands that dot the great estuary of the river and found themselves on the open sea.

By this time Orellana had sailed nearly 4000 miles. He and his small band had made the first crossing of South America at its widest part, passing through territories where no European had been before and where few have been since. Orellana brought to the world the first news of the tribes and country of the huge Amazon basin. They had been traveling for more than seven months before they at last sailed out from the mouth of the great river, here some "50 leagues across" (now known to be over 100 miles across).

Orellana now sailed northward to Trinidad, refitted, and then crossed the Atlantic to report his great achievement to his masters in Spain. He insisted that he had not deserted Pizarro but had been forced by circumstances to continue his journey down the river. In Spain, Orellana was treated as a successful explorer. He was ordered to return and occupy for Spain the lands through which he had sailed, but he died on the voyage out, and the opening-up of the great Amazon basin was left to others.

Portuguese, French, and Dutch settlements sprang up along the northeast coast of South America in the years that followed. The Portuguese founded Pará in 1616 largely through fear of the Dutch and French settlers near the mouth of the Amazon. In 1639 the Portuguese Pedro Texeira led an expedition up the Amazon to its source, making a rough survey of the river and its tributaries. He spent 10 months on the journey, which eventually took him over the moun-

Alexander von Humboldt used this
barge on the Guayaquil River in
Ecuador during his expedition to
South America, 1799–1804. Below
is a sketch of one of the thousands
of new plant species he identified.

tains and to Quito. He was followed by others, notably
Father Samuel Fritz, a Jesuit priest from Bohemia,
who spent over 40 years in the Amazon basin and
added much to geographical knowledge of the area.

In 1735 the French geographer and mathematician
Charles la Condamine was sent to Peru by the French
Academy of Sciences to make measurements to help
determine how nearly the earth came to being a true
sphere. During this expedition he traveled from Quito
down the Amazon, eventually reaching the east coast
at Cayenne in what is now French Guiana. La Condamine's was the first scientific exploration of the
Amazon. In 1799 the famous German naturalist Alexander von Humboldt set off on a five-year expedition
to South America, during which he explored what is
now Venezuela, Colombia, Ecuador, and Peru. Like
La Condamine, his interests were of a scientific nature.
He carried out meteorological and climatic observations in addition to a study of magnetism.

In spite of such expeditions, vast forest tracts of
what is now Brazil remained unknown until well into
the present century. The opening-up of the interior of
South America was to be a slow and challenging effort.

During the first half of the present century one of the men engaged in filling in blanks on the map of this huge territory was the American explorer Dr. Hamilton Rice, who began a systematic examination of the Amazon basin in 1907. One of the most important modern scientific explorers of South America, he was among the first to make use of seaplanes for survey work, and he helped to trace in detail many of the tributaries of the main river. In 1912-13 he explored the upper tributaries of the Orinoco, and seven years later used both airplanes and radio in further work.

An Englishman, Colonel P. H. Fawcett, became the central figure in one of the great unsolved mysteries of exploration. Fawcett first went to South America in 1906, when he helped to settle the boundary between Brazil and Bolivia, after Bolivia had granted some 70,000 square miles to her neighbor. This was the first of several remarkable journeys during which Fawcett explored the virtually unknown jungle country south of the Amazon, traveling among hostile and sometimes cannibal tribes. In 1925 he set off on one more journey from Cuiabá in the Mato Grosso area of the frontier, but he failed to return. A search made three years later by G. M. Dyott suggested that Fawcett had almost certainly been killed by natives. But the legend that he was still alive persisted for years.

Even now there are many areas of South America that have not been mapped in detail, most of them in the Amazon basin; and primitive tribes like those seen by Orellana are still discovered from time to time.

Orellana named the Amazon River after legendary female warriors such as these pictured on a Greek frieze of about 350 B.C. Several of his men were killed by tribeswomen on his journey down the Amazon.

As this photograph shows, the huge Amazonian jungles remain today as dense and inhospitable as in the early years of Spanish exploration.

The Crossing of North America

As the Spanish and Portuguese had established themselves in South America (the Spanish in Central America as well), the French, British, and Dutch began to look north and colonize North America. Jamestown, Virginia, was founded by the English in 1607; the Pilgrim Fathers settled at New Plymouth in 1620; the Dutch, trading on Manhattan Island from 1610, founded New Amsterdam in 1626; and the Puritans founded Salem in 1628, and Boston in 1630.

The first steps in opening-up the North American continent since the travels of the conquistadors came early in the 17th century. In 1609 Henry Hudson sailed on a fruitless expedition in an attempt to find a sea route from Europe to the East around the top of America. Finding himself forced southward along the coast of what is today the United States, he reached the entrance of the river now named after him, and sailed up it for 150 miles before returning to Europe. The following year he went north once again, discovered the immense Hudson Bay, and wintered there, intending to explore farther during the spring. Then his men mutinied and cast him and his young son adrift in an open boat. Only a few of the mutineers survived attacks from Indians and finally succeeded in returning to England, where they told of the discoveries that Hudson had made.

Farther south it was the French who were the pioneers. Jacques Cartier, searching like many men of his time for a route to the Spice Islands, had sailed into the mouth of the St. Lawrence as early as 1534. Now, in the early 17th century, he was followed by Samuel de Champlain, who in 1608 founded Quebec and began a long series of explorations into the interior. Between 1608 and 1621 a companion of Champlain, named Étienne Brulé, reached and explored the Great Lakes—Huron in 1611, Ontario in 1615, and Superior in 1621.

These and other French explorers continued to hear Indian accounts of a great sea to the west, stories that convinced them that it must be possible to travel overland to the Pacific coast. Those who tried to do so included Jean Nicolet, who reached the watershed between the St. Lawrence and the Mississippi, and Sieur René de la Salle who in 1681 reached the Mississippi itself. He then sailed down that great river to the Gulf of Mexico and claimed the country for the French, naming it Louisiana after King Louis XIV.

La Salle was accompanied on some of his journeys by the Belgian friar Louis de Hennepin, who visited

During the 17th century many explorers were attracted to North America by the fortunes to be made from fur trading with the Indians.

Fur-trading stations formed the nucleus of many of the smaller colonial settlements in Canada in the 18th and early 19th centuries. Fort Garry, seen here in the 1820s, was on the site of the present city of Winnipeg, capital of Manitoba.

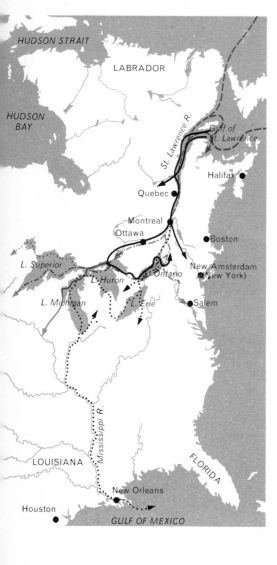

--- — 1535 Jacques Cartier

——— 1603 Samuel de Champlair

-·-·- 1608 Étienne Brulé

——— 1634 Nicolet

········· 1669 René de la Salle

········· 1728 Vérendrye

As this route map shows, the Gulf of St. Lawrence and the mouth of the Mississippi provided the gateways to North America for early explorers.

the upper Mississippi in 1679 and pushed the frontier farther westward—an expansion that was to be continued during the 1720s and 1730s by Sieur de la Vérendrye and his four sons. This family of fur traders traveled northwest into what is now Saskatchewan and were possibly the first European settlers to see the Rocky Mountains from the east.

By the latter part of the 18th century most of the country south and east of a line running from the Great Lakes to the Gulf of California was known in varying degrees of detail. North and west of this there was uncertainty. Men knew only that a great mountain barrier—that of the Rockies—appeared to bar progress from the central plains of the continent to the western ocean. The broadest region of North America had still to be crossed from east to west. The huge territories inland were the province of vast herds of buffalo, deer, and other game that roamed at will across a trackless land almost untouched by the marks of Europeans.

This was the situation during the late 18th century. At that time the fur trade was encouraging hunters and trappers to range across the vast wilderness. One of the centers for the fur trade was Montreal, and to this growing city came Alexander Mackenzie, a 16-year-old boy from Stornoway in the Hebrides off the coast of Scotland.

At the age of 26 Mackenzie found himself in charge of the newly founded Fort Chipewyan on Lake Athabasca in the north of what is today the Canadian province of Alberta. From this lonely outpost on the fringe of known territory Mackenzie set out on two journeys that were to increase vastly man's knowledge of the North American continent. In hopes of finding the Pacific Ocean, he made his first journey in 1789, traveling north to the Great Slave Lake, then along the river now named after him, and eventually reaching what he called the "Hyperborean Sea" (Arctic Ocean). In spite of this remarkable journey through a thousand miles of untamed and unmapped country Mackenzie was disappointed but remained determined to reach the Pacific coast.

On October 10, 1792, he set out from Fort Chipewyan on his second journey, one that was to take him west through country never seen by Europeans. He soon reached the last fur-trade settlement up the Peace River and wintered there to prepare for the journey that lay ahead. He and the other Europeans at the settlement traded with the Indians and occasionally sent back to Fort Chipewyan for additional supplies. By the beginning of May 1793 he was ready and "closed the

Above: John White, one of the first English colonists in North America, painted this view of an Indian village in Virginia in about 1585.

Below: Sieur René de la Salle parleys with Taensa Indians near present-day Natchez while sailing down the Mississippi in 1682.

business of the year for the company by writing my public and private despatches."

With Mackenzie were seven English or French settlers and two Indians, who were to act as hunters and interpreters. At this stage of the journey a single canoe was to carry all of them. "The canoe was put into the water; her dimensions were twenty-five feet long within, exclusive of the curves of stem and stern, twenty-six inches hold, and four feet nine inches beam," Mackenzie later wrote. "At the same time she was so light, that two men could carry her on a good road three or four miles without resting. In this slender vessel, we shipped provisions, goods for presents, arms, ammunition, and baggage, to the weight of three thousand pounds."

After going only a short way up the Peace River the little expedition was forced to land, unload the over-laden canoe, and then recaulk part of it. By the following day they were deep in unknown territory, moving upstream against a current so strong that they were often forced to use long poles instead of paddles.

The country through which Mackenzie and his men were now moving was beautiful, inhabited only by small bands of roaming Indians, and packed with wild life. "This magnificent theatre of nature," Mackenzie wrote, "has all the decorations which the trees and animals of the country can afford it: groves of poplars in every shape vary the scene; and their intervals are enlivened with vast herds of elks and buffaloes; the former choosing the steeps and uplands, and the latter preferring the plains. At this time the buffaloes were attended with their young ones who were frisking about them."

Throughout the month of May, the group continued westward, Mackenzie carefully making notes about where the land might be "opened up" in the future. At one place he described how roads might be cut through the wilderness; at another he said that "this spot would be an excellent situation for a fort or factory, as there is plenty of wood, and every reason to believe that the country abounds in beaver." Everywhere during this first part of the journey Mackenzie was impressed by the amount of game "unmolested by the hunter."

At more than one place the party was forced to un-load the canoe and carry both the boat and supplies past rapids and falls. At other places, however, they were able to tow the canoe through currents that were too strong to allow either paddling or poling. As the days passed there were more and more problems with rapids since the party was steadily approaching the

Rocky Mountains, across which they knew their route must go. At one stage of the journey, Mackenzie wrote, "we had proceeded to where the river was one continued rapid. Here we again took every thing out of the canoe, in order to tow her up with the line, though the rocks were so shelving as greatly to increase the toil and hazard of that operation. . . . The river above us . . . was one white sheet of foaming water."

It now seemed certain that farther advance on the Peace River was impossible, so Mackenzie sent out two reconnoitering parties up the slopes ahead. Both returned that evening with various stories of difficulties ahead. "Unpromising, however, as the account of their expedition appeared," remarked Mackenzie, "it did not sink them into a state of discouragement; and a kettle of wild rice, sweetened with sugar, which had been prepared for their return, with their usual regale of rum, soon renewed that courage which disdained all obstacles that threatened our progress: and they went to rest, with a full determination to surmount them on the morrow."

At dawn the next day the immediate problem was to haul the canoe and their supplies up the steep slope —one of the many uphill stretches they met as they made their way through the foothills of the Rockies. This they accomplished by felling two rows of trees but not separating "them entirely from the stumps, so that they might form a kind of railing on either side." The canoe was then hauled up the slope, with the men belaying the rope round successive stumps. This went on all day, with Mackenzie and his companions cutting a fresh path through the woods in the afternoon.

The same process continued the next day, and the next, and only then were they able to make use of the river again, above the rapids, and continue their journey by canoe.

It was about this time that Mackenzie decided to try to send a message back home, and chose an original way of doing it. "As we had almost expended the contents of a rum keg," he wrote, "and this being a day which allowed of no active employment, I amused myself with the experiment of enclosing a letter in it, and dispatching it down the stream to take its fate. I accordingly introduced a written account of all our hardships, etc. carefully enclosed in bark, into the small barrel by the bung-hole, which being carefully secured, I consigned this epistolary cargo to the mercy of the current." Whether or not this letter was ever "delivered," Mackenzie does not tell us.

Eventually, about the middle of June, the river that

——— 1st journey 1789

——— 2nd journey 1792-3

This map shows the routes of Alexander Mackenzie's two main expeditions from his base at Fort Chipewyan, in the northeast corner of the present province of Alberta.

Mackenzie and his men were following led into a little lake not more than 500 yards or so across and about two miles long. "This I consider as the highest and southern-most source of the Unjigah or Peace River," he wrote. He had, in fact, reached the headwaters of the numerous small streams that join to form what is today called the Finlay River—the upper part of the Peace River. Since setting out nearly five weeks earlier, he had covered more than 500 miles. Now he had reached the crucial part of the journey, the Great Divide, that watershed of the Rockies from which the rivers flow either eastward toward the Great Lakes or westward to the Pacific.

His party paddled along the small lake. Then, wrote Mackenzie, "we landed and unloaded, where we found a beaten path leading over a low ridge of land of eight hundred and seventeen paces in length to another small lake." Along the shore of the lake were Indian canoes, baskets, and fish nets—some of which Mackenzie took, leaving a knife and some beads in exchange. "Here," he said, "two streams tumble down the rocks from the right and lose themselves in the lake which we had left; while two others fall from the opposite heights and glide into the lake which we were approaching . . . and we are now going with the stream."

What Mackenzie had done was to cross the Great Divide, for the westward-flowing river was one of the headwaters of the Fraser. At first it was very narrow and the party went only a short way before camping for the night. Before dark, men sent out to reconnoiter came back with "a fearful detail of rapid currents, fallen trees, and large stones" on the river below. They avoided the first part of these rapids on the far side of the Divide by portaging the canoe, but then came near-disaster soon after they re-entered the river a short way downstream. Carried out of control by the strong current, the canoe struck a rock that shattered her stern. The men were tumbled overboard and had to scramble for their lives, losing most of their ammunition and many of their supplies in the process.

The party was now in a bad way, but they were all still alive; and although their canoe was badly damaged it could be repaired. After some persuasion from Mackenzie the 10 men continued on their way, portaging through country so difficult that at one place it took them 14 hours to blaze a trail and carry the canoe only three miles.

After many more such adventures Mackenzie realized that the quickest way to the coast now lay over-

The Rocky Mountains provided the last great barrier to explorers pushing westward in search of the Pacific Ocean.

land, not along a waterway. The local Indians said that there was a good trail, and Mackenzie estimated that the distance to the sea was about 250 miles in a straight line, and only 300 miles by the track they would be following.

Thinking of their return journey, they put their canoe—a new one that they had by this time built—on a small platform by the river, "shaded by a covering of small trees and branches, to keep her from the sun. We then built an oblong hollow square, ten feet by five, of green logs, wherein we placed every article it was necessary for us to leave here, and covered the whole with large pieces of timber."

They now prepared for their long march to the coast, but they were men who were used to river travel

Only 250 miles short of the Pacific Mackenzie's party almost met disaster in the boulder-strewn rapids of the Frazer River west of the Rocky Mountains.

rather than forest tramping. In addition to guns and ammunition, each man was weighed down by a pack ranging from 90 to 70 pounds in weight. "I had also the tube of my telescope swung across my shoulder," wrote Mackenzie, "which was a troublesome addition to my burthen. It was determined that we should content ourselves with two meals a day, which were regulated without difficulty, as our provisions [largely of pemmican] did not require the ceremony of cooking."

Day after day they marched on, sometimes with a local Indian guide, sometimes without. At one point they had to build a raft to make a river crossing; at another they faced some of the worst weather they had met since they left Fort Chipewyan. Then in the middle of July they reached a river where the local Indians spoke of traveling in two large canoes, many winters before, and meeting white people, who had treated them well. These, Mackenzie decided, were the men of Captain Cook's 1776 voyage—so they must now be near the open sea. On July 19 the little group climbed up a small ridge and Mackenzie saw that the river they had been following (the Bella Coola) appeared to "discharge into a narrow arm of the sea." The following morning there could be no doubt about it. They were on the coast of Queen Charlotte Sound, although here, in a maze of channels, it could hardly be called the "open sea."

For the first time, someone had crossed the full breadth of North America.

Fearing attack by Indians, Mackenzie and his party "took possession of a rock, where there was not space for more than twice our number, and which admitted of our defending ourselves with advantage." Here Mackenzie set up his instruments and the following day checked his position. His group was on the southeast point of what is today known as Elcho Cove, halfway between Ocean Falls and Cascade Inlet, among the maze of channels leading into Queen Charlotte Sound, north of Vancouver Island. Before he left, Mackenzie "mixed up some vermilion in melted grease, and inscribed, in large characters, on the South-East face of the rock on which we had slept last night, this brief memorial—Alexander Mackenzie, from Canada, by land, the twenty-second of July, one thousand seven hundred and ninety-three." This was the famous "Mackenzie Rock."

By comparison with the journey out, the return was fairly easy. They portaged across the Great Divide without too much difficulty, navigated down the Peace River, and toward the end of August found themselves

This portrait of Mackenzie, dividers in hand, stresses his importance as a surveyor as well as explorer.

View of the Entrance of NOOTKA Sound *when the N. point of the Entrance bo*

M.S! Elias

View *when* Mount S! Elias *bore N.W.b.W. 20 leagues*

a

View of Kaye's Island *, bu*

a

Captain Cook's artist sketched the American Pacific coast (above) in 1776. Possibly Cook's men landed near Bella Coola where, 17 years later, Mackenzie Rock (below) marked the first European crossing of this part of North America.

approaching the place they had left four months before. "At length, as we rounded a point, and came in view of the Fort, we threw out our flag, and accompanied it with a general discharge of our fire-arms; while the men were in such spirits, and made such an active use of their paddles, that we arrived before the two men whom we left here in the spring, could recover their senses to answer us."

During the next few decades, Mackenzie was followed westward by others who crossed the prairies and forests of North America, made their own routes over the huge barrier of the Rockies, and in some cases settled on the coast of what is today California.

Among the most important of such men were Captain Meriwether Lewis, who was to become governor of Louisiana, and Captain William Clark. In 1803 the United States bought from France the vast area then called Louisiana, and the following year President Thomas Jefferson decided to send an expedition up the Missouri in an effort to discover its source and then to find the most practicable route across the Rocky Mountains to the Pacific. Although the Spanish had settlements along parts of the West Coast, Jefferson interpreted the Louisiana Purchase to mean that "Upper Louisiana" included regions west to the Rockies and beyond to the Pacific, north of Spanish territory. In joint charge of the expedition that left in 1804 were the president's private secretary, Captain Lewis, and Captain Clark.

On the afternoon of May 14 the group set out from St. Louis. There were some 40 men, and they traveled in a decked vessel that could be either sailed or rowed and that was armed against attack by Indians. The first part of the journey was uneventful—past the mouth of the Kansas River and the future site of Kansas City, past the mouth of the Platte River, through the Dakotas, and on to the villages of the Mandan Indians, near the present town of Bismarck in North Dakota. During this stage of the journey the men were amazed by the abundance of game they saw. One day a member of the expedition said that from a high peak he had seen an enormous herd of buffalo—numbering about 300,000. Early in November, by which time they had traveled some 1600 miles, they decided to camp for the winter. Clark "found a good position where there was plenty of timber, encamped and began to fell trees to build our huts. . . . We now began the building of our cabins, and the Frenchmen who are to return to St. Louis are building a [boat] for the purpose."

The explorers built a fort so that they could defend

themselves if necessary, wintered without trouble, then set off up-river again on April 7, 1805. It seemed that there was never a shortage of game, "particularly the elk and the buffalo, which last is so gentle that the men are obliged to drive them out of the way with sticks and stones."

Next they entered what is today the state of Montana, and on May 26 they caught their first glimpse of the great mountains to the west. "It was here that, after ascending the highest summits of the hills on the north side of the river, Captain Lewis first caught a distant view of the Rock mountains [Rocky Mountains], the object of all our hopes, and the reward of all our ambition. On both sides of the river and at no great distance from it, the mountains followed its course."

Late in July the party came to the Forks of the Missouri and had to decide which river they should now follow—the Jefferson, the Madison, or the Gallatin, as they named the three streams which join here. They correctly chose the Jefferson, and Captain Lewis went on ahead. From this stage onward their luck began to change. So far there had been ample supplies

Lewis (standing) and Clark canoe down the Columbia River at the end of their westward journey across America in 1805. With them are Shoshone Indians who had helped guide the explorers through the Rocky Mountain passes.

of food, with Lewis noting that "two good hunters could conveniently provide a regiment with provisions." But things now began to look different. In addition, it was clear that they would not be able to travel by boat much longer, and that it would be necessary to get horses from the local Indians.

After meeting and bargaining with the Shoshone Indians, who were at first suspicious but eventually became friendly, the party pressed on westward with what horses they could buy. But as they climbed higher and higher, and as the autumn began, cold weather added to their worries. One thing was certain: It was necessary to cross the Great Divide before winter set in. On September 12, Lewis reported a white frost on the ground. The following days the going became difficult; the horses slipped and in some cases fell over precipices. Fresh snow began to appear on the nearby summits, and food became so scarce that the group was forced to kill one of the colts. On Sunday, September 15, they reached the highest point of the trail and camped "near a bank of snow, three feet deep. Some of this we melted and supped on the colt killed yesterday. Our only game today was two pheasants; and the horses on which we calculated as a last resource began to fail us, for two of them were so poor and worn out with fatigue that we were obliged to leave them behind. All around us are high rugged mountains, among which is a lofty range from southeast to northwest, whose tops are without timber, and in some places covered with snow. The night was cloudy and very cold, and three hours before daybreak, Monday 16th, it began to snow and continued all day, so that by evening it was six or eight inches deep. This covered the track so completely, that we were obliged constantly to halt and examine, lest we should lose the route. In many places we had nothing to guide us except the branches of the trees which, being low, have been rubbed by the burdens of the Indian horses. The road was, like that of yesterday, along steep hill sides, obstructed with fallen timber, and a growth of eight different species of pine. [The trees are] so thickly strewed that the snow falls from them as we pass, and keeps us continually wet to the skin, and so cold that we are anxious lest our feet should be frozen, as we have only thin moccasins to defend them."

They ate the rest of the colt they had killed and a little soup together with bear's oil. Lewis later wrote that this was "our only remaining means of subsistence. Our guns are scarcely of any service, for there is no living creature in these mountains, except a few

The Lewis and Clark expedition was chronicled by Sergeant Patrick Gass, a member of the party, from whose journal these pictures are taken. Council Bluffs, a city in Iowa, was named after this conference (right) between the explorers and Indians soon after the expedition started.

Lewis and Clark's men were the first Europeans to encounter the grizzly bear. Here a member of the party, having wounded one, retreats hastily up a tree.

Bitterly cold weather forced the party to build winter quarters near Mandan, North Dakota, where they stayed from November 1804 until the following April.

During the return journey, many of the records and specimens of the three-year expedition were lost when the canoe carrying them was capsized by a floating log.

small pheasants, a small species of grey squirrel, and a blue bird of the vulture kind about the size of a turtle dove or jay, and even these are difficult to shoot." The lack of food was beginning to tell, and Lewis could see that "the men are growing weak and losing their flesh very fast. Several are afflicted with the dysentery, and eruptions of the skin are very common."

The party was now high up in the tangled country of the Montana-Idaho border and there were still no signs that they were yet across the full width of the Great Divide. Then on Friday, September 20, came the sight for which they had so long waited.

"Captain Clark went on through a country as rugged as usual, till on passing a low mountain he came at the distance of four miles to the forks of a large creek. Down this he [went] for two miles, then, turning to the right, continued over a dividing ridge where were the heads of several little streams, and at twelve miles distance descended the last of the [Rocky Mountains] and reached the level country. A beautiful open plain partially supplied with pine now presented itself."

The party was "over the hump," and soon reached a branch of what is now the Clearwater River, near Pierce, Idaho. The Indians here were friendly and assured the party that it was possible to continue westward by water. On September 27 they began to build canoes and were soon moving down the Clearwater. They traveled on to the Snake River and to what Lewis called "the western branch of the Columbia," but which is today called the Yakima. About five weeks later they saw their goal—the open sea. "This cheering view," Lewis wrote, "exhilarated the spirits of all the party, who were still more delighted on hearing the distant roar of the breakers."

The party spent the winter near the mouth of the Columbia, then began the journey home on March 23, 1806. Lewis and Clark separated on the far side of the Rockies, Clark taking a route to the Yellowstone River and then following it down to its junction with the Missouri, where he rejoined the rest of the group. On September 23, 1806, the expedition sailed into St. Louis. They had completed a journey of some 8000 miles that not only opened up much new territory but later strengthened the United States' claim to what are today the states of Oregon and Washington.

By this period of the exploration of North America, the Englishman Samuel Hearne, trying to find a western exit from Hudson Bay, had discovered the Great Slave Lake. In 1805, the Canadian Simon Fraser crossed the Rockies from Lake Athabasca and reached

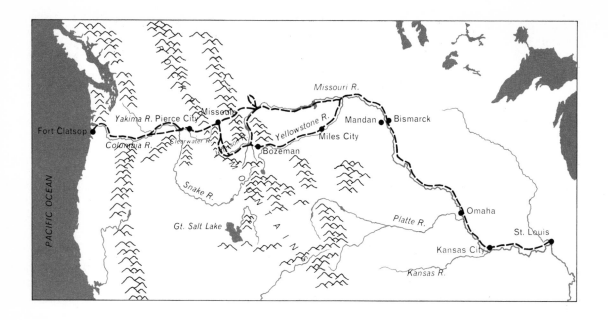

Map of the routes followed by Lewis and Clark in 1804-6. The million or so square miles of land bought from Napoleon more than doubled the size of the American nation. The expedition, organized by President Thomas Jefferson, explored much of the newly acquired land and opened a trail to the Pacific coast.

the junction of the Peace and Parship rivers. Throughout the first half of the 19th century the opening-up of the great spaces of North America continued with increasing speed. In the north, fur traders played an important part, but farther south there were many government surveyors—men such as Lieutenant John Frémont, who went exploring "beyond the call of duty." We shall hear more about such men in the chapter dealing with mountain exploration.

During the latter part of the 19th century the pioneers who followed the explorers slowly but relentlessly pushed back the native Indians and decimated the great herds of buffalo and other wild animals. They brought to the great plains first the covered wagon and then the civilization of the "iron horse," as the first of the railway engines were called. By 1869 the first railway and telegraph system linking the east and west coasts had been completed. And, although much of the West was still sparsely populated, most of the North American continent was mapped in detail, and discovery in the geographical sense had come to an end.

The Exploration of Africa

On the other side of the Atlantic, by the end of the 18th century, men had begun to explore the teeming inland jungles of Africa The coasts of this huge continent had been known since the 15th and 16th centuries, when the adventurous Portuguese sailed around the Cape of Good Hope on their way to India. However, until the latter part of the 18th century few men had tried to press into Africa's mysterious interior as they had into the heart of South America and North America.

The geography of Africa is such that many of the great rivers leading into its interior are interrupted by impassable rapids or high waterfalls near the coasts. So there were few natural "highways" leading into the interior. Another reason lay in the slave trade. For many years Europeans had turned to Africa for slaves; but the traders seldom found it necessary to leave their coastal depots. African middlemen saved them the trouble by going inland, capturing the slaves, and delivering them to the trading stations along the coasts.

Some of the first great explorers of Africa set out in search of knowledge of this vast continent. Others went in search of trade; others to stake territorial claims for their countries; and still others to suppress the slave trade. Suppression of the slave trade and the conversion of the native people to Christianity provided a driving force as strong as any other for the opening-up of this huge land mass.

The exploration of Africa began in earnest with the foundation of the African Association in June 1788. This was achieved largely through the efforts of Sir Joseph Banks, the scientist who had accompanied Cook on his first voyage to the Pacific. The main object of the African Association was the exploration of the continent, and in 1795 its members acquired the services of a 24-year-old Scottish doctor, Mungo Park. He had made a tour of the East Indies and he now offered to search for the source of the Niger, the river that winds its way inland from the west coast. At this time neither its source nor the position of its mouth was known; there was even dispute over which way it flowed. Park had, he says, "a passionate desire to examine into the productions of a country so little known; and to become experimentally acquainted with the modes of life, and character of the natives."

Mungo Park's plan was to travel up the Gambia River as far as he could, then cross overland toward the headwaters of the Niger, which he would then explore.

He left Portsmouth in May 1795, reached Africa, and traveled about 200 miles up the Gambia to a British trading post. Here he stayed during the autumn, learning the native language, then set out on his journey on December 2, accompanied by an interpreter and one native servant. "My baggage was light," he wrote, "consisting chiefly of provisions for two days, a small assortment of beads, amber, and tobacco, for the pur-

In this 17th-century bronze statue a Bini trader from western Nigeria holds a staff of office denoting his right to trade with Europeans. The brass or copper *manilla* in his left hand was used as barter currency and was manufactured in Europe. Trading at the coastal ports of Africa had been carried on for hundreds of years before Europeans began to explore the interior of the continent on a large scale in the 18th century.

Desire to abolish slavery, the search for wealth, missionary zeal, and the spirit of adventure all attracted early explorers to Africa. Some traveled light; others (as here) "showed the flag" and explored in the comfort afforded by large numbers of African servants whose lands they colonized.

chase of a fresh supply, as I proceeded; a few changes of linen, and other necessary apparel, an umbrella, a pocket sextant, a magnetic compass, and a thermometer; together with two fowling pieces, two other pair of pistols and some other small articles."

Although he did not know it at the time, Park was setting out on a journey that was to last 19 months. He was captured by a Moorish king, held for four months before escaping, and reached the Niger near the city of Ségou toward the end of July. From here he traveled about 100 miles downstream, but decided that he must turn back since he was "worn down by sickness, exhausted with hunger and fatigue; half naked, and without any article of value, by which I might procure provisions, clothes or lodging."

The difficulties of his travels are shown by one entry in his diary: "Aug. 5th. I departed from Nyamee; but the country was so deluged that I was frequently in danger of losing the road, and had to wade across the savannahs for miles together, knee deep in water. Even the corn ground, which is the driest land in the country, was so completely flooded, that my horse twice stuck fast in the mud, and was not got out without the greatest difficulty. . . . I did not depart until the 7th; but the water had swelled to such a height, that in many places the road was scarcely passable, and though I waded breast deep across the swamps, I could only reach a small village . . ."

To make matters worse, he was robbed of his horse, weapons, and clothes by three bandits. "After they had gone," he wrote, "I sat for some time, looking around me with amazement and terror, whichever way I turned nothing appeared but danger and difficulty. I saw myself in the midst of a vast wilderness, in the depths of the rainy season; naked and alone; surrounded by savage animals, and men still more savage. I was five hundred miles from the nearest European settlement."

Depressed and utterly worn out, Park pressed on (later recovering his horse and being helped by natives) and finally reached the trading post on the Gambia in June 1797. Back in England, he was able to produce for the African Association a vast amount of fresh information on the area he had visited, even though he had not been successful in finding the source of the Niger. Eight years later he set out again—this time as leader of a government expedition. He followed his previous route, reached the Niger, but was killed on the river. Whether he died by drowning accidentally,

Mungo Park, a 24-year-old Scottish surgeon, led one of the first European expeditions to Africa in 1795, his purpose being to find the source and mouth of the Niger River. His journey began at Gambia on the west coast of Africa. From here he traveled eastward, crossed the Bafing River (below), and reached the Niger at Ségou.

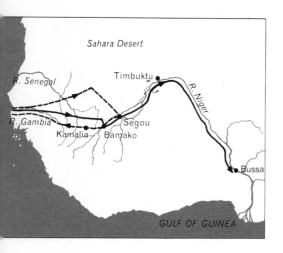

Above: The routes of Park's two expeditions to the Niger. Below: The village of Kamalia where he was seriously ill for a time. Although he followed the Niger for hundreds of miles, Park failed to find its source or mouth. But his account of his adventures is one of the finest in African exploration.

or was murdered by natives is not certain even today.

The mystery of the Niger was solved only in 1830, when the Englishmen Richard Lemon Lander and his brother followed it down to its mouth in the Gulf of Guinea. At the beginning of the 1840s a great 30-year period of exploration began; it was a period that was to define the map of Africa as we know it today. From the north men pushed up the Nile in a continual series of efforts to discover the source of that great river. From the east others worked their way up the Zambezi, through the jungles, and then northward into the higher and more open country of what is today Tanganyika and Uganda.

In 1840 almost the whole of central Africa was still blank on the maps, a massive unknown from whose mysterious depths the waters of the Zambezi, the Congo, and the Nile appeared to flow. Within 30 years explorers had discovered the headwaters of all three rivers, had plotted Lake Victoria, Lake Tanganyika, and Lake Nyasa and had seen for the first time Mount Kenya, Mount Kilimanjaro, and Ptolemy's fabled Mountains of the Moon (the Ruwenzori).

These and similar discoveries in Africa were made by explorers whose interests varied widely. Some, like the brilliant German explorer Heinrich Barth, were scientists. Barth, who ranked with the great missionary-explorer Livingstone, set out in 1850 from Tripoli and explored south across the great Sahara (see chapter 5). Other explorers were sent out by Christian missions. The Rev. Johannes Rebmann in 1845 traveled west from the Church Missionary Society's station near Mombasa and became the first European to see the huge snow-clad slopes of Mount Kilimanjaro rising from the edge of the inland plateau of Africa. Traveling farther north, his companion Dr. Ludwig Krapf, saw the snow of yet another mountain—Mount Kenya's "snow on the equator."

Intrigued by the missionaries' stories of great lakes far inland, two British army officers, captains Richard Burton and John Speke, set out in 1857. They were hoping to solve what was then considered the outstanding geographical riddle of Africa: Where was the source of the Nile?

Together Burton and Speke set out from Zanzibar on the east coast and discovered Lake Tanganyika. But before they could explore the region thoroughly Burton was struck down by fever and was forced to return to Tabora, roughly 250 miles to the east, to recuperate. Speke continued alone, journeying to the north, where, on August 3, 1858, he discovered a vast tract of water—or *nyanza*, meaning lake—which he named Victoria Nyanza after the British queen. Two years later Speke returned to Africa with another British officer, Captain James Grant, and on July 28, 1862, the two men reached a part of Lake Victoria where a great river issued out from it in a long series of falls and rapids. They called these the Ripon Falls and felt sure that here lay the start of the Nile of ancient history. They spent two days at the falls, and Speke records how he watched "the fish flying at the falls, and felt as if I only wanted a wife and family, garden and yacht, rifle and rod, to make me happy here for life, so charming was the place!"

Speke and Grant now set off down the river that issued from Lake Victoria, hoping to prove that it was in fact the Nile. But they had gone only a short distance when hostile tribes barred their way; they were forced away from the river and could return to it only farther downstream at the town of Gondokoro.

Here in the heart of Africa they met a couple who were remarkable even in an age of remarkable explorers—the Englishman Samuel Baker and his Hungarian wife, with their entourage of 90 people, 29 camels, horses, and asses. Baker, a wealthy traveler and sportsman, had followed the Nile upstream from Khartoum. He knew that Speke and Grant were somewhere away to the south, and when, on February 15, he heard that Europeans were approaching he ran out to meet them. "Speke appeared the more worn of the two," he later wrote. "He was excessively lean, but in reality he was in good tough condition; he had walked the whole way from Zanzibar [a distance of about 1500 miles] never having once ridden during that wearying march. Grant was in honourable rags . . . [and] was looking tired and feverish."

Both Speke and Grant felt sure that the river from

The problem of finding the source of the Nile River attracted many explorers to Africa in the mid-19th century. Among the most colorful of these were Sir Samuel Baker (above) and his young Hungarian wife. Baker, a wealthy sportsman, traveled with up to 100 servants and many camels and horses. On one of his journeys (below) from Ismailia in Egypt his "luggage" included a dismantled steamer in which he hoped to travel on the lakes of central Africa.

which they had been forced away by natives was the Nile. But they could not prove it since they had not kept to its course. While Speke and Grant continued on down the Nile toward Khartoum, Baker and his wife continued their journey upstream, encouraged by rumors of yet another great lake to the west of Lake Victoria. The Bakers were now embarking on the most dramatic episode in their long career of exploration.

After two mutinies and an attack of fever and sunstroke, Baker's natives said, on March 13, 1864, that they were now nearing the rumored great lake, which, he felt, must be at least one source of the Nile. Soon after this they came to a deep valley between two hills. On reaching the top, Baker later wrote, "The glory of our prize burst suddenly upon me! There, like a sea of quicksilver, lay far beneath the grand expanse of water —a boundless sea horizon on the south and southwest, glittering in the noon-day sun; and on the west, at fifty or sixty miles' distance, blue mountains rose from the bosom of the lake to a height of about 7000 feet above its level."

Finding a steep zigzag path leading down to the lake —which they named Albert Nyanza—Baker led the way: "After a toilsome descent of about two hours, weak with years of fever, but for the moment strength-

This water color by Baker (above) shows him astride a bullock at the start of a journey to Lake Albert in 1864. The Africans with horned head-dresses were part of an escort provided by a local chieftain.
Below: Baker and his wife are welcomed with a tribal dance on their return to camp after an expedition.

ened by success, we gained the level plain below the cliff. A walk of about a mile, through flat sandy meadows of fine turf interspersed with trees and bush, brought us to the water's edge. The waves were rolling upon a white pebbly beach: I rushed into the lake, and thirsty with heat and fatigue, with a heart full of gratitude, I drank deeply from the Sources of the Nile. . . . No European foot had ever trod upon its sand, nor had the eyes of a white man ever scanned its vast expanse of water. We were the first; and this was the key to the great secret that even Julius Caesar yearned to unravel, but in vain. Here was the great basin of the Nile that received *every drop of water*, even from the passing shower to the roaring mountain torrent that drained from Central Africa towards the North. This was the great reservoir of the Nile!"

Baker was later proved wrong, for the main reservoir of the river is Lake Victoria from which the Nile begins to flow via the Ripon Falls. But the Victoria Nile, as it is sometimes called, then flows into Lake Albert and then out again, where it is known as the Albert Nile, and, farther down, as the White Nile.

While they were exploring the Victoria Nile, Baker and his wife discovered the Murchison Falls, one of the great sights of Africa. After traveling some 18 miles along the river they realized that they were approaching a great waterfall. "Upon rounding the corner, a magnificent sight burst suddenly upon us. On either side of the river were beautifully wooded cliffs rising abruptly to a height of about 300 feet; rocks were jutting out from the intensely green foliage; and rushing through a gap that cleft the rock exactly before us, the river contracted from a grand stream and was pent úp in a narrow gorge of scarcely 50 yards in width. Roaring furiously through the rock-bound pass, it plunged in one leap of about 120 feet perpendicular into a dark abyss below. . . . This was the greatest waterfall of the Nile, and, in honour of the distinguished President of the Royal Geographical Society, I named it Murchison Falls, as the most important object throughout the entire course of the river."

At one point near the falls the river was alive with crocodiles and Baker shot one. As he did so, the boat was caught by the powerful stream and whisked against a thick bank of high reeds. "Hardly had we touched this obstruction when a tremendous commotion took place in the rushes, and in an instant a great bull hippopotamus charged the canoe, and with a severe shock striking the bottom lifted us half out of the water. . . . Crocodile heads of enormous size were

Baker discovered Murchison Falls in 1864. The falls, among the finest in Africa, lie on the Victoria Nile between lakes Albert and Victoria.

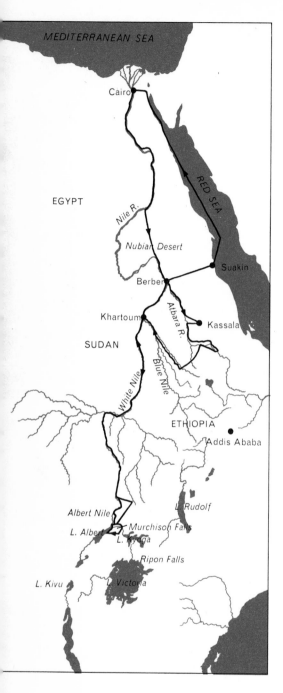

Map of Baker's travels in north and east Africa.

on all sides, appearing and vanishing rapidly as they rose to survey us; at one time we counted eighteen upon the surface. Fine fun it would have been for these monsters had the bull hippo been successful in his attempt to capsize us."

Immediately after this narrow escape, and amid a multitude of crocodiles, Baker ordered that the boat should be kept steady in midstream while he sketched the falls! The adventurous party eventually returned safely to Gondokoro, sailed down the Nile, and then traveled home to England, where Baker's discoveries earned him the coveted Gold Medal of the Royal Geographical Society.

Speke, Burton, Grant, and Baker succeeded in clearing up most of the mystery concerning the source of the Nile. Yet the explorations and careers of all four were overshadowed by a man who set out not to fill in details on maps of the time but solely to bring Christianity to Africa. His name was David Livingstone. Today, a century after his most important work was carried out, he is still seen as the greatest African explorer of all.

Livingstone was born in 1813, the son of humble parents, at Blantyre, Lanarkshire, Scotland; and at the age of 10 he was sent to a local cotton factory, where he worked from six in the morning until eight at night, and then read whatever he could find until midnight. He applied himself in a way that few children have to today. "Were it possible," he wrote in later life, "I should like to begin life over again in the same lowly style, and to pass through the same hardy training."

Livingstone became interested in missionary work, qualified as a doctor, and on November 20, 1840, sailed for Africa to take up work in a settlement started by the Rev. Robert Moffat. Within a few years Livingstone had become the symbol of a new type of explorer —one who treated as human beings the native people among whom he moved. To start with he had not intended to be an explorer, but this role evolved as his travels took him across the great continent in search of new sites for missions.

In 1849 his work took him across the Kalahari Desert, and he gave the first detailed account of that virtually unknown area; he also discovered Lake Ngami. Two years later he struck the great Zambezi River hundreds of miles above the point where it was known, later followed it upstream, and then went westward to the coast, which he reached at Luanda in Angola.

As he traveled, Livingstone became increasingly

African slaves, yoked in pairs, are forcemarched by slave traders to the market. Those who collapsed on the long treks to the trading centers were tied up and left to starve. Among the opponents of slavery was David Livingstone (below), who devoted his life to the cause of African emancipation.

disturbed by the growing slave trade. But what could one man hope to do against such a highly organized activity? If he could find a good trade route from central Africa to the coast, possibly this would encourage merchants to come in search of legitimate goods and drive the slavers from the market. This was his plan, and he stuck fast to it even though he met disappointment after disappointment. In 1855, when he failed to find a route westward to the coast, he turned eastward, navigating the great Zambezi River. It was on this journey that he discovered "The Smoke that Thunders," the great Victoria Falls. "We came in sight for the first time of the columns of vapour, appropriately called 'Smoke', rising at a distance of five or six miles. . . . Five columns now arose [and] they were white below, and higher up became dark, so as to simulate smoke very closely."

Livingstone moved downstream in a light canoe, which his natives directed to a small island on the very lip of the falls. But even from here it was impossible to see what happened to the immense volume of water pouring over. "It seemed," wrote Livingstone, "to lose itself in the earth, the opposite lip of the fissure into which it disappeared being only 80 feet distant. I did not comprehend it until, creeping with awe to the verge,

One of Livingstone's most exciting moments in Africa was his discovery of Victoria Falls, on the Zambezi River, in November 1855. This view of the western fall was painted in 1863 by Thomas Baines, an artist who accompanied Livingstone on several journeys in this region.

I peered down into a large rent which had been made from bank to bank of the broad Zambezi, and saw that a stream of a thousand yards broad leaped down a hundred feet, and then became suddenly compressed into a space of fifteen or twenty yards."

The discovery of the Victoria Falls was a great disappointment to Livingstone. It meant that the Zambezi could not, as he had hoped, provide a water highway to the coast. And farther downstream he found the Quebrabasa Rapids, yet another barrier that trading ships would not be able to navigate.

By May 1856 Livingstone had reached the east coast of Africa. For about two and a half years he had been traveling through the unknown heart of central Africa, recording what he saw and studying the watershed of what is one of the most complicated river systems of the world. He had moved in an almost charmed circle of survival through tribal wars, slave raids, and the dangers of death from disease or wild animals.

He now sailed for England, arrived early in the winter of 1856, went on a series of lecture tours, and settled down to write his first great book, *Missionary Travels and Researches in South Africa*. It was about this time that the missionary society that employed him suggested that Livingstone might devote more of his time to converting the heathen and less to travel. Livingstone did not see the problem in the same way, so he parted company with the society, on the best of terms. When he set sail for Africa again in the spring of 1858, he did so as "Her Majesty's consul at Killimane for the east coast and the independent districts in the interior, and commander of an expedition for exploring eastern and central Africa."

Although this expedition continued for five years, it was only partly successful. There was opposition from local and largely Portuguese slave traders, and there were disagreements among the members of the expedition itself. Again Livingstone returned home, more discouraged than ever by the African slave trade, which he described as "the open sore of the world." But in August 1865 he set out for the third time—as British consul to central Africa—with the double aim of trying to suppress slavery by what he described as "civilising influences" and of untangling the geography of the watershed between lakes Nyasa and Tanganyika. By this time Livingstone had begun to believe that both Speke and Baker might be mistaken about the headwaters of the Nile. He believed that the headwaters might be formed by a river that issued from Lake Tanganyika or by one in the area many miles south of both Lake Victoria and Lake Albert.

On January 28, 1866, Livingstone left Zanzibar with an impressive train of natives, camels, mules, buffaloes, and donkeys. But before the end of the year, by which time he was traveling in the country of the great inland lakes, his party had been reduced to a mere handful. He continued to travel—through 1867, '68, '69, '70, and '71. From time to time he sent reports back to Zanzibar—when he could—but for months and sometimes years he was out of touch with the rest of the world. For weeks he was seriously ill with fever but, as before, he passed unscathed through tribal wars and savage slave raids, sometimes traveling with the slavers themselves. He discovered lakes Bangweulu and Mweru, and spent some time with the ruthless Chief Cazembe, whose executioner nearly always accompanied him.

On more than one occasion Livingstone was, in the eyes of the world, "lost," and more than one unsuccessful effort was made to get in touch with him. Then there came the most famous attempt of all.

It began in a Marseilles hotel in October 1869, when James Gordon Bennett Jr., manager of the *New York Herald*, summoned one of his famous foreign cor-

Many of Livingstone's journeys were full of incident. Once (above) he was lucky to escape with his life when a hippopotamus tipped him into a river full of crocodiles.

The *Ma-Robert*, Livingstone's flat-bottomed paddle steamer (below), was used for several journeys on the Zambezi, where Baines painted this encounter with an elephant.

Although he considered himself primarily a missionary, Livingstone was one of the greatest of central African explorers. He was also one of the few Europeans of his time to befriend the Africans among whom he worked. Here, Susi and his other devoted servants help him escape a soaking in the brackish waters of a jungle swamp during one of his many expeditions.

respondents, Henry Morton Stanley. At the age of only 30 at the time, Stanley had already reported 15 battles and three naval engagements.

"The Suez Canal is going to be opened," Stanley was told. "Go to Egypt and report that little affair. Then go up the Nile and find out what you can about Sir Samuel Baker's expedition. While you're about it, let's have a simple guide to lower Egypt. Nothing fancy. Just plain factual stuff, properly written up. Look in at Jerusalem; and while you're there you can go on to Constantinople. If it's worth while—I leave it to you—take a look at the Caucasus, and then go to India. After that, Livingstone."

The Livingstone assignment, though last on the list, was the job that really mattered.

"Draw a thousand pounds now, and when that is finished, draw another," Stanley was further told. "When that is finished draw another and another. Then another. *But find Livingstone!"*

With those words still in his ears Stanley arrived in Zanzibar in January 1871. He was about to start on a journey that was to bring fame, alter his life, and turn him into a successor of the tired, elderly Englishman whom he hoped to find somewhere in the great vastness before him.

Stanley left Zanzibar on February 5, 1871, with 31 armed natives, 153 porters, three Europeans, two

Livingstone is greeted by the chieftain of a remote jungle village. It was in an attempt to find the "lost" explorer that Henry Morton Stanley (below) set out from Europe in 1870.

saddle horses, and 27 pack animals. For bartering he took great quantities of beads and cloth, as well as 350 pounds of thick brass wire.

From the start, nearly everything went wrong. Stanley knew that he had failed to avoid the rainy season, but he did not understand the consequences. There were mutinies among his bearers and desertions by both armed natives and porters. And, as a final near-disaster, he became involved in a local war, barely escaping with his life.

When he was nine months out from Zanzibar, deep in the interior and his column weakened by mutiny and disease, he heard the first definite news of a European. At Ujiji, on the shores of Lake Tanganyika, seven days' march away, there lived such a white man, he was told. A white man who was old and used medicine to make sick men better. It looked as though he was about to find the human needle in the African haystack.

Just a week later Stanley reached Lake Tanganyika. Ujiji was beyond the reach of the day's march so he camped for the night and the following morning made his way up a ridge overlooking the village. Below lay the lake shimmering in the morning sun, and beside it a tangle of huts in a clearing surrounded by jungle that stretched to the haze of the African horizon.

"Unfurl the flags; load your guns," he ordered.

Nine months after landing in Africa from Zanzibar, Stanley's party reached the village of Ujiji, on the eastern shore of Lake Tanganyika, where Livingstone lived. After climbing a ridge overlooking the village, Stanley ordered a volley of shots to be fired (above) to warn of his approach; then he descended to the village for his celebrated meeting with Livingstone (right).

At the head of the procession stood a gigantic native called Asmani, bearing aloft Old Glory; at the rear, a smaller man with the flag of Zanzibar. Stanley checked along the line. "One, two, three, fire!" he commanded.

Nearly 50 guns volleyed into the air. Below, the villagers heard the announcement of a new caravan arriving, sounds that continued as the men in the column kept up a spasmodic firing. By this time many natives had crowded around the outskirts of the village —Wajiji, Wanyamwezi, Wangwana, Warundi, Waguhha, Wanmanyeuma, and many other tribes.

As Stanley's column crossed the market square, the natives parted, disclosing a tall, elderly white man standing before one of the huts. He wore old gloves, tattered shoes, grey tweed trousers, a red flannel blouse, and a blue cloth cap. Around the cap were tattered remains of the gold band of an officer of Her Majesty's Consular Service. Stanley walked up to the tired-looking old man, removed his helmet, bowed, and spoke:

"Dr. Livingstone, I presume?"

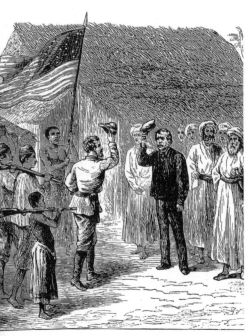

The older man smiled, raised his cap and answered simply, "Yes."

"I thank God, Doctor, that I have been permitted to see you," said the younger man as they shook hands.

"I feel thankful that I am here to welcome you," was the reply.

Weeks later Stanley was still with Livingstone. For the first few days they had talked hour after hour, Livingstone pouring out the tales of five years' adventure and exploration, Stanley explaining what had been going on in the outside world.

It was soon clear that the doctor was neither "lost" nor had he the slightest intention of being taken home. He still had work to do, he maintained. For one thing, he did not believe that Baker had discovered the true source of the Nile; Livingstone felt that this job still remained to be done. One night, when the two men were talking about the unexplored country around the head of Lake Tanganyika, Stanley agreed to travel with Livingstone, at least for a while. A few days later they set off, "bound upon no mercenary errand, after no Golden Fleece, but perhaps to discover a highway for commerce which should bring the ships of the Nile up to Ujiji, Usowa, and far Marungu," as Stanley put it.

Their craft was a hollowed-out tree and into it they packed themselves, two guides, a cook, an Arab boy, and 25 men. For 28 days they paddled first north and then south again, past sandy beaches and forest-covered crags, which dropped down to the water's edge. At places they saw the black figures of the natives gathering ominously in the distance; elsewhere they surrounded their nightly encampments with hedges of thorn. And at the northern end of the lake they found a great river, the Rusizi, flowing into it. Elsewhere, Livingstone argued, there must be an equally large outlet—the source of the Nile itself.

Back at Ujiji, Stanley again tried to persuade Livingstone to return to Britain, but the response was always the same. A slow smile and the words: "I must finish my work before I return." Finally Stanley said that he must leave. On December 27 the doctor set out with him, to accompany him part way back to the coast. The first stage of the journey took them down Lake Tanganyika, each man in his own canoe. Then they landed, struck out across country, and on March 14 reached the parting of the ways. Stanley's route lay eastward to the coast; Livingstone's back toward the west, his work, and the lonely lake.

Stanley promised to send the doctor what supplies he could from Zanzibar, then said, "God bring you

The main routes of Burton, Speke, Livingstone, and Stanley. Stanley's most important journeys were in what is today the Congo Republic— a region then unknown to Europeans.

safe back to us all. Goodbye, Doctor." He turned away and quickly ordered the bearers to march. The track lay slightly uphill and only when he reached its crest did he turn back for a last look at Livingstone, who was standing where Stanley had left him—a small figure around whom the jungle seemed to close in, an old, tired man with his hand raised in a wave of farewell to the American.

When Livingstone's supplies finally arrived, he set off on what was to be his last journey. Traveling around the difficult east side of Lake Tanganyika, he surveyed and mapped the area at the height of the rainy season. He was still searching for the source of the Nile and a water highway to the coast. It was in the Bangweulu swamp that Livingstone became seriously ill with dysentery, but still he pushed on, carried by his faithful natives and mapping the area as he went. But the combination of poor health and overwork was too much. South of the great Bangweulu swamp, at a village in Ilala, Livingstone died at the end of April 1873. His body was embalmed and brought to London to be

Gravely ill and exhausted by a lifetime of hard work, Livingstone returned to his simple home in Ilala in April 1873, and died there a day or two later.

Stanley's large, well-armed party passes between ranks of hostile natives. On several occasions Stanley was involved in skirmishes between warring African tribes.

buried in Westminster Abbey. Stanley, who had hurried back from reporting the Ashanti War, assisted at the funeral.

The following year Stanley set out to solve Livingstone's riddle. He left England with an Anglo-American expedition to investigate the Lualaba, the great river running northward that Livingstone had believed formed the headwaters of the Nile. Over a period of four years Stanley followed the waters of the Lualaba to their sources in the thick forest country west of Lake Tanganyika, in what is today Katanga. He then found that they made a gigantic curve westward, leading him through a great forest region beyond the lakes. They were, in fact, the headwaters of the Congo. With this discovery another riddle involving the source of a great African river had been solved. During his journey down the Congo, Stanley found it necessary to fight off hostile tribes more than once; he lost three European companions and 170 of his native followers. Yet his journey down that 3000-mile-long river was a great feat of exploration.

Stanley's journeys in Africa—he made two more in later years—marked the end of one age of exploration and the beginning of another. When the extent of his discoveries became known, an international association for the opening-up of the new territory was formed. At its head was Leopold III, King of the Belgians, and it was in Leopold's service that Stanley returned to Africa in 1879 to help organize the new enterprise. The result was the founding of the Congo Free State, which, in 1908, became a Belgian colony.

By this time, less than a century after the exploration of Africa had been begun in earnest, the outlines of the continent were known in some detail, as were certain regions of the interior. We have mentioned in this chapter only those explorers who played the most prominent parts; but there were others who helped raise the veil from the Dark Continent. There was the German explorer Georg Schweinfurth, who in 1864 traveled along the coast of the Red Sea as far as Ethiopia and who later helped to survey Upper Egypt. There was Lieutenant Verney Cameron, who in 1874-75 surveyed half of Lake Tanganyika and then crossed tropical Africa on foot from east to west.

Although there was now much "filling in of gaps" to be done on the map of Africa, it was done not so much by explorers as by men who were helping to stake their countries' claims across lands whose main features were understood but whose natural resources were still unexploited.

4 The Polar Regions

Explorers first tried to penetrate the Arctic more than 400 years ago, yet both the North and South poles defied all attempts to reach them until the early years of this century. And today there is still much that we do not know about the geography and geology of the polar regions, particularly the Antarctic. The reasons for this are not hard to find. The areas around the poles are so inhospitable and have exacted so ruthless a penalty for the ignorance or mistakes of explorers that the secrets of both regions could be thoroughly probed only with the help of modern inventions like radio, special motor vehicles, icebreakers, aircraft, and radar.

The polar regions lie between the North Pole and the Arctic Circle, and between the South Pole and the Antarctic Circle—the circles being parallels of latitude running 66°30′ north and south of the equator. Within each region lie nearly eight million square miles of land and sea, and around them are belts of pack ice (large areas of floating ice) that vary in size with the seasons. In the Arctic the temperature ranges from about 70°F. to –65°F.; in the Antarctic it is seldom above freezing and sometimes the temperature plunges to –100°F. and lower.

On the Arctic Circle there is one day each year (about June 21) when the sun does not set, and another day (about December 22) when it does not rise. (On the Antarctic Circle the dates are reversed.) As one travels toward either pole, these periods of continuous light or dark become longer. At the poles themselves, there is a six-month "day" during which the sun rises and falls without ever passing below the horizon, followed by a six-month "night" of almost total darkness.

Apart from the great cold, sparse vegetation, long summer days and winter nights, the two regions have little else in common. The center of the Arctic is a great

Arctic exploration in the early 19th century. The three-masted schooner is locked in the ice and the crew have folded her sails to form a shelter on the top deck. The winter sun is low even at midday; in a week or two it will not appear above the horizon at all, and the explorers will have to make do with the few hours of twilight each day during the long polar winter.

Martin Frobisher, who visited Greenland and Baffin Island in 1576, admired the Eskimos' use of kayaks (above) and dog sledges.

In 1596 the Dutchman Willem Barents sailed to Novaya Zemlya, where his ship was squeezed onto the surface of the pack ice (below). After wintering on the island, his crew sailed 1600 miles in the ship's boats to Kola Peninsula, Barents dying on the way.

frozen ocean surrounded by the land masses of Siberia, Norway, Greenland, and Canada. The Antarctic, by contrast, comprises a huge continental plateau encircled by a belt of stormy seas hundreds of miles wide. Although the icy wastes around the South Pole are desolate and support few species of wild life, the north polar region has a large and varied animal population and the American explorer Vilhjalmur Stefansson called an account of his travels there *The Friendly Arctic*.

It was not its friendliness, however, that attracted man to the Arctic before he turned his attention to the South Pole. As with so many other stories of exploration, man's interest in the Arctic began with his desire to trade with his fellows.

By the 16th century, the maritime nations of Europe were competing for the riches of the East. The Portuguese controlled the sea route around Africa; the Spaniards commanded the only known alternative route, around South America. Might there not be a third route? The English were determined to find one, and were left little choice but to seek a northwest or northeast passage over the top of the world.

To launch this new venture Edward VI of England persuaded the Venetian Sebastian Cabot to leave his service with the Spanish king and to become, as he called it, "Governour of the Mysterie and Companie of the Merchant Adventurers for the Discoverie of Regions, Dominions, Islands and Places Unknowen." These were the Muscovy adventurers, as they came to be known, and in 1553 they sailed from England in three ships, the *Bona Esperanza* of 120 tons, the *Edward Bonaventure* of 160 tons, and the 90-ton *Bona Confidentia*. Commanding the little expedition was Sir Hugh Willoughby, a man chosen "both by reason of his goodly personage (for he was of tall stature) as also for his singular skill in the services of warre." Neither goodly personage nor singular skill, however, proved able to save the expedition from disaster. Willoughby and the crews of the *Bona Esperanza* and the *Bona Confidentia* were wrecked somewhere on the northern shores of Norway or Russia, and perished during the hardships of an arctic winter. Only Richard Chancellor, the chief pilot, and the crew of the third ship were saved. Chancellor pushed on to Arkhangelsk, on the White Sea in northern Russia, but failed to find a northeast passage. He traveled south to Moscow, where he was received by Ivan the Terrible, who ruled Russia, and laid the foundations of a lucrative trade between Russia and Britain.

In 1576 another Englishman, Martin Frobisher, set out in the opposite direction to find a northwest passage to the East, an enterprise that he considered to be "the only thing of the world that was left yet undone, whereby a notable mind might be made famous and fortunate." Commanding a ship of only 20 tons, Frobisher sailed up the southwestern coast of Greenland toward what is now Baffin Island. He reported the first meeting between Englishmen and Eskimos, and was intrigued by their sealskin kayaks and their use of dogs for sledging. As one of his party wrote: "Taking in his hand one of those countrey brydels, he caughte one of our dogges and hampred him handsomely therein as we do our horses, and with a whip in his hande, he taught the dogge to draw in a sledde, as we doe horses in a coatche, setting himself thereon like a guide."

Frobisher returned to England in triumph, convinced by the mongoloid features of the Eskimos that he had reached the threshold of Asia. Any map of the

The top of the world. The map shows the North Pole and the land masses enclosing the Arctic Ocean.

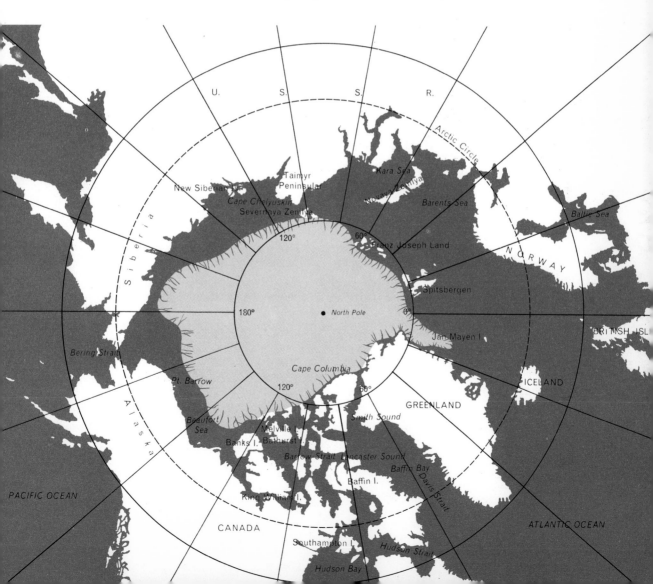

British whalers at work in the Greenland fisheries about 1720. Henry Hudson had reported seeing great numbers of whales in the seas around Spitsbergen in 1607, and by the end of the 17th century bitter rivalry had developed between Dutch and British whaling enterprises.

Arctic shows us how wrong he was. Even so, his voyage encouraged a growing number of seamen to search for a northeast or a northwest passage. In doing so, they laid the foundations of our present knowledge of the arctic islands of Greenland and Spitsbergen, and the complicated, icebound maze of channels and islands on the fringe of the Canadian Far North.

Among these bold explorers was John Davis, who in 1585 sailed up the strait lying between Greenland and Baffin Island, and who reached latitude 72°12′N., little more than 1100 miles from the North Pole. Like many of the explorers who came after him, Davis gave his name to a geographical feature—the huge strait up which he sailed. He was followed by Henry Hudson, who in 1607 discovered Jan Mayen Island and, three years later, the great bay now bearing his name. Hudson reached latitude 80°23′N., only 700 miles short of the Pole, but, more important, he reported that the arctic seas were alive with walruses and whales. This news acted like a magnet upon the seamen of the world and led to the great arctic fishing ventures. The Dutch were especially active in this new industry and brought thousands of men to their base at Spitsbergen for the summer fishing seasons.

There were great fortunes to be won in whaling, and for a time in the 17th and 18th centuries exploration took second place to the development of fisheries off Greenland, Newfoundland, and Spitsbergen. The pressures of competition led to the discovery in these areas of new islands for whaling stations. But it was not until 1773 that a British Admiralty expedition led by Constantine Phipps (and including 14-year-old Midshipman Horatio Nelson) reached farther north than Hudson had been.

Although he was turned back by the ice north of Spitsbergen, Phipps's expedition was a significant one as it was the first with the specific aim of reaching the North Pole. After the end of the Napoleonic Wars in 1815, a growing number of attempts on the Pole were made by the British. About that time, too, explorers began to realize that, instead of trying to force their way through the frozen arctic seas by ship, it might be better to use the Eskimos' technique of sledging.

Ross and Parry

The man who pioneered this method (which was eventually to lead explorers to the Pole itself) was Edward Parry. He was born at Bath, England, in 1790, entered the Royal Navy as a midshipman at the age of 13, and after service against the Danes was sent in 1810

to the Arctic in a ship whose task was to protect the British whale fisheries. This experience fired Parry's ambition to explore the Arctic, and eight years later he was appointed second-in-command of a four-ship expedition led by John Ross. Two of the ships, trying to find a route to the Pole, were stopped by ice north of Spitsbergen. The two others, under Ross, crossed the Atlantic, sailed through Davis Strait and entered Baffin Bay. Then, having rounded the northern shore of Baffin Island, they sailed westward into Lancaster Sound. But here, believing that the exit from the sound was blocked, the expedition turned back. (Not only *is* there a western outlet to the sound but ironically it was in this area, 35 years later, that the last riddle of the Northwest Passage was to be solved.)

Ross was harshly criticized for turning back, but he was not the last explorer to mistake distant clouds for land or ice. When a later expedition, comprising the *Hecla* and the *Griper*, set out in 1819, Parry was given command. His expedition set an example for future explorers in many ways. Parry was not yet 30, and the records of his expedition show much evidence of fresh and controversial ideas. In an attempt to keep scurvy at bay, he not only carried ample supplies of antiscorbutics but insisted that all the men take regular

Seeking a northwest passage in 1818 John Ross encountered these huge icebergs (above) in Baffin Bay. His nephew James Clark Ross reached the North Magnetic Pole 13 years later near an Eskimo camp (below) on Boothia Peninsula.

doses of lime juice. To keep his men fit, Parry organized physical-training sessions, on shore when possible, to the accompaniment of the ships' musicians. Amateur stage plays helped to keep the men's minds occupied aboard ship, and the crew even produced their own newspaper—the *North Georgia Gazette and Winter Chronicle.*

In spite of all his efforts, Parry was beaten back by the ice. But he and his men were the first to sail north of the Magnetic Pole (then at about 71°N., 96°W.)— and to see the compass needle pointing south! In September they also had, Parry wrote, "the satisfaction of crossing the meridian of 110 degrees west from Greenwich . . . by which His Majesty's ships under my orders became entitled to the sum of 5000 pounds." To mark the occasion, he named the nearest land Cape Bounty and, after wintering on Melville Island, the expedition sailed home.

Parry returned to the Arctic in 1821 and again in 1824. Neither expedition made any notable discoveries, but they helped Parry to train his group of officers and men for his final and most famous journey in 1827.

Early the previous year he had proposed to the First Lord Commissioner of the Admiralty that he should "attempt to reach the North Pole, by means of travelling with sledge-boats over the ice, or through any spaces of open water that might occur." The daring plan had been inspired partly, it seems, by the reports of a well-known British whaler, William Scoresby the younger, who had looked out northward toward the

Edward Parry, one of the greatest arctic explorer-navigators, led his first expedition in 1819 when he was only 29 years of age.

Parry's second expedition in 1821 attempted, like his first, to find a northwest passage. His party spent two winters in the Arctic and Parry organized spare-time activities such as cricket (below) for his men while his ships *Fury* and *Hecla* were ice-bound in Foxe Basin.

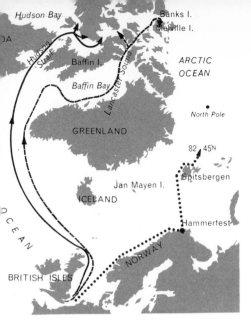

The map shows Parry's expeditions in search of a northwest passage in 1819 and 1821, and his attempt on the North Pole in 1827.

Parry's ships negotiate leads in the ice during his third search for a northwest passage in 1824. Later the *Fury* was wrecked on Somerset Island, west of Lancaster Sound.

Pole and seen "a field that was so free from either fissure or hummock, that I imagine, had it been free from snow, a coach might have been driven many leagues over it in a direct line, without obstruction or danger."

Parry's plan was to sail north of Spitsbergen and then, in the words of his official instructions, to "fix upon some safe harbour or cove, in which the *Hecla* may be placed; and having properly secured her, you are then to proceed with the Boats, whose equipments have, under your own directions, been furnished expressly for the service, directly to the Northward, and use your best endeavours to reach the North Pole. . . ."

These boats had been built to a special design at Woolwich on the River Thames. They had, Parry later wrote, "great flatness of floor, with extreme breadth carried well forward and aft, and possessing the utmost buoyancy, as well as capacity for stowage. Their length was twenty feet, and their extreme breadth seven feet. The timbers were made of tough ash and hickory, one inch by half an inch . . . and a foot apart, with a 'half timber' of smaller size between each two. On the outside of the frame thus formed, was laid a covering of Mackintosh's water-proof canvas, the outer part being coated with tar. Over this was placed a plank of fir, only three-sixteenths of an inch thick; then a sheet of stout felt; and, over all, an oak plank of the same thickness as the fir; the whole of these being firmly and closely secured to the timbers by iron screws applied from without."

Parry's idea was to have amphibious craft—sailing boats that could be quickly adapted for use as sledges across the broad expanses of ice. "On each side of the keel, and projecting considerably below it, was attached a strong 'runner', shod with smooth steel, in the manner of a sledge, upon which the boat entirely rested while upon the ice; and to afford some additional chance of making progress on hard and level fields, we also applied to each boat two wheels, of five feet diameter, and a small one abaft, having a swivel for steering by, like that of a Bath chair; but these, owing to the irregularities of the ice, did not prove of any service, and were subsequently relinquished. A 'span' of hide-rope was attached to the fore part of the runners, and to this were affixed two strong ropes of horse-hair, for dragging the boat; each individual being furnished with a broad leathern shoulder-belt, which could readily be fastened to or detached from the drag-ropes."

Each boat had a 19-foot mast, a sail that could also be used as an awning, and a paddle for every member of the crew of two officers, 10 sailors, and two marines.

When all was ready, the *Hecla* moved down river from London, "received and returned the cheers of the Greenwich pensioners, the children of the Naval Asylum, and of various ships in the river," and on April 4, 1827, sailed northward from the mouth of the Thames.

At Hammerfest, northern Norway, they took on board eight Lapland reindeer to help draw the boats,

Parry's party haul their specially made amphibious boats (above) over the pack ice during their attempt on the North Pole in 1827. The drawing does not exaggerate the difficulties of the terrain, as the photograph (below) of arctic pressure ridges shows. Winds and sea currents make the ice crack and thrust up these jagged ridges.

and in June they anchored off Treurenberg Bay on the north coast of Spitsbergen.

Here they prepared for their journey across the polar ice and, at five in the afternoon of June 21, Parry and his men set off in their two amphibious boats—now named the *Enterprise* and the *Endeavour*. First they paddled to Low Island, off the coast of Spitsbergen, and camped for the night. Next morning they were off again, paddling watch by watch to give the men spells of rest. Their progress was watched with interest by walruses, "here very numerous, lying in herds upon the ice, and plunging into the water to follow us as we passed."

They were forced onto the ice on June 24, and "we now commenced upon very slow and laborious travelling, the pieces of ice being of small extent and very rugged, obliging us to make three journies, and sometimes four, with the boats and baggage, and to launch several times across narrow pools of water."

The expedition was now set on the long trek northward, and as the reindeer were found unsuitable, the men had to haul the boats. From the first, the going was more difficult than they had expected. At times "the glare from the snow produced so painful a sensation in most of our eyes, as to make it necessary to halt . . . to avoid being blinded." At other times, they were so drenched by rain that they had to shelter under the boats. Often, too, thick fog formed so that they could see for only a few paces. Moreover, conditions underfoot were much more difficult than Scoresby had predicted. In places the snow was "so soft as to take us up to our knees at almost every other step, and frequently still deeper; so that we were sometimes five minutes together in moving a single empty boat, with all our united strength."

The main difficulties, however, were the broken surface of the ice—nothing like Scoresby's "carriage track"—and the many "leads" of open water they had to cross. At each of these they had to unload and reload the boats, so that in some places many hours were spent traveling less than a mile.

With the sun above the horizon for all the 24 hours, Parry soon decided to travel by "night" and to sleep by "day." This gave his men greater warmth during their rest, and enabled them to dry out their clothes; moreover it was easier to move at night because the snow was harder.

"When we rose in the evening," he wrote, "we commenced our day by prayers, after which we took off our fur sleeping-dresses, and put on those for travelling;

The arctic regions support a large and varied animal population. These sketches of an arctic fox, a xeme (fork-tailed gull), and a polar bear were made by John Ross.

the former being made of camblet, lined with racoon-skin, and the latter of strong blue box-cloth. We made a point of always putting on the same stockings and boots for travelling in, whether they had dried during the day or not; and I believe it was only in five or six instances, at the most, that they were not either still wet or hard-frozen. . . .

"Being 'rigged' for travelling, we breakfasted upon warm cocoa and biscuit, and after stowing the things in the boats and on the sledges, so as to secure them as much as possible from wet, we set off on our day's journey, and usually travelled from five to five and a half hours, then stopped an hour to dine, and again travelled four, five or even six hours, according to circumstances. After this we halted for the night, as we called it, though it was usually early in the morning, selecting the largest surface of ice we happened to be near, for hauling the boats on, in order to avoid the danger of its breaking up by coming in contact with other masses, and also to prevent drift as much as possible."

The boats were drawn up with their sterns to the wind and the sails and masts arranged to form awnings. Everyone put on dry stockings and fur boots, made any necessary repairs and, after drawing rations for the following day, sat down to supper. "Most of the officers and men then smoked their pipes, which served to dry the boats and awnings very much, and usually raised the temperature of our lodgings 10° or 15° [F.]. After a while they changed into their night attire and lay down to sleep with a degree of comfort which perhaps few persons would imagine possible under such circumstances; our chief inconvenience being that we were somewhat pinched for room and therefore obliged to stow rather closer than was quite agreeable."

Throughout their seven-hour rest, a watch was kept for bears or for any sign that the ice was breaking up, each man doing an hour's turn. At breakfast time, the man on watch boiled cocoa for the company and then roused everyone with a bugle call.

Day by day—or, rather, night by night—the party dragged and paddled its boats farther north. Occasionally they shot and ate a seal to vary their diet. One day they made an hourly record of weather conditions, having arranged that meteorologists in Edinburgh should do the same on this particular day. And, whenever they could, they took readings to fix their position.

In mid-July, Parry began to be disturbed by these readings, for reasons he wisely kept from the men. By the 26th it was obvious that his fears were justified.

The Eskimo house or igloo is made from "bricks" cut from hard snow with a knife and is hemispherical in shape. A block of ice may be wedged in at the top to form a window.

The natural plumpness of this Eskimo child (below), together with several layers of seal-fur clothing, protect him against the arctic cold.

Eskimo dog sledges (above) provide swift and effective transport over the ice fields. The hunter below uses his harpoon to kill seals or walruses when they appear at their air holes in the pack ice.

"We were," he wrote, "but one mile to the north of our place at noon on the 21st, though we had estimated our distance made good at twenty-three miles. Thus it appeared that, for the last five days, we had been struggling against a southerly drift exceeding four miles per day." While the little company had been dragging its boats northward, the ice itself had been drifting away from the Pole, and had canceled out their efforts.

"For the last few days, the eighty-third parallel was the limit to which we had ventured to extend our hopes; but even this expectation had become considerably weakened since the setting in of the last northerly wind, which continued to drive us to the southward, during the necessary hours of rest, nearly as much as we could gain by eleven or twelve hours of daily labour."

Parry decided that they should now have one day's complete rest before the 150-mile march back to their ship. They stopped at 82°45′N., 435 miles from the Pole, and closer than anyone was to get for another 50 years. On his return, Parry was knighted. Although only 37, he had made his last arctic journey, and took up the first of several important posts at the Admiralty.

Parry's expedition showed that, given favorable conditions, it might be possible to reach the Pole on foot or by sledge over the ice. Yet, even now, the hope of finding a northwest passage to the East had the stronger grip on the imaginations of explorers. And it was the fate of the historic Franklin expedition to the northwest in 1845 that was to trigger off the long period of intensive arctic exploration leading to the conquest of the Pole itself.

The Franklin Tragedy

Sir John Franklin was 58 when he was given command of the 1845 expedition, and had lately returned from seven years' duty as governor of Tasmania. He was no stranger to polar regions, having explored the Canadian Arctic with Sir George Back in 1819 and 1825. The 1845 expedition, which was sponsored by the Admiralty, consisted of two ships—the *Erebus* (under Franklin) and the *Terror* (commanded by Francis Crozier)—with a combined crew of about 130 carefully chosen officers and men. Each ship had a 20-horsepower auxiliary engine, and they were the first arctic vessels to be fitted with propellers.

The *Erebus* and *Terror* left London on May 19, 1845, under instructions to pass westward through Lancaster Sound and then make southwest for Bering Strait. They reached Greenland without trouble and put in at Disko, halfway up the western coast. Then they continued northward through Baffin Bay, and on July 26 were making progress through the pack ice at 74°48′N., where they were spotted by a whaler captain. And that was all—not a single member of the expedition was ever seen alive again.

The ships had enough food and other supplies for three years, so there was little anxiety when nothing was heard from them for the rest of 1845. When two more years passed without news, however, the alarm was raised and the long search began—a search that lasted for over 10 years and involved no fewer than 40 expeditions. A verse from a sailors' song popular at the time runs:

> *In Baffin's Bay where the whalefish blow*
> *The fate of Franklin no man may know*
> *The fate of Franklin no tongue can tell*
> *Lord Franklin long with his sailors do dwell.*

The first relief expedition was launched from England in 1848. Sir James Ross, a veteran of polar exploration, led two ships that were to try to follow Franklin's route. Captain H. Kellett commanded two more ships, which were to make for the Bering Strait

Sir John Franklin commanded four expeditions to the Arctic. The camping scene above was drawn on his overland journey westward from Hudson Bay to the Great Slave Lake in the Canadian Far North in 1819-21.

The map shows the route believed to have been followed by the ships *Erebus* and *Terror* during Franklin's tragic last voyage in 1845-48.

and then press on to relieve Franklin if he were found completing his journey to Asia. The third group, commanded by an old friend of Franklin, Dr. John Richardson, made an overland journey through the wastes of arctic America, to discover if the lost explorers had tried to escape overland somewhere between Lancaster Sound and the Bering Strait.

Not one of these relief expeditions found a trace of Franklin (though we know now that Ross's party got within 200 miles of where the *Erebus* and *Terror* had become locked in the ice). Then a series of further efforts were launched—commanded by Richard Collinson and Robert McClure in 1850; by Dr. John Rae in 1851; by Sir Edward Belcher, Edward Inglefield, and Captain Leopold McClintock in 1852. These and many other explorers led parties up through the maze of channels in which the ships had vanished; over the wastes of northern Canada and Alaska; or up and around the Bering Strait. None of these expeditions found any trace of the *Erebus* or *Terror*, though in 1850 Captain Erasmus Ommanney had discovered a cairn at the entrance to Wellington Channel, traces of a camping party, and then the graves of three men from the missing ships who had apparently died nearly five years before. Another four years were to pass before further details of the tragedy were revealed.

Then, in 1854, Rae, exploring northward for the Hudson Bay Company, was told by Eskimos that a few years previously they had seen about 40 white men dragging a boat across the ice near King William

Reconstruction of an incident during Franklin's last voyage: The crew of the *Erebus* haul their boats onto a floe after searching for a passage between massive icebergs in the area of Lancaster Sound in 1846.

Portrait of Sir John Franklin

Franklin's last official note, dated 28 May, 1847, from a position north of King William Island. In the margin is the announcement of his death the following month.

Island and, later in the year, they had discovered the bodies. Rae's report persuaded the government to renew the search in this area, while in 1857 Lady Franklin sent out a private expedition under the command of McClintock. The discoveries they made, together with the reports of the earlier expeditions, enabled the story of the Franklin Expedition to be pieced together at last.

By the autumn of 1846 the *Erebus* and the *Terror* had forced their way through the western exit from Lancaster Sound and had turned southwest into the waters north of King William Island. Here Franklin was almost within sight of country he knew—country from which a passage could be made to the Bering Strait. And here, almost within reach of their goal, the *Erebus* and *Terror* became locked in the ice. The men spent the winter of 1846 on the ships. The following June Franklin died. All efforts to free the ships failed, and another winter was spent in the same grim, silent surroundings. Then, on April 22, 1848, the 105 sur-

The four pictures on the right are of incidents during an expedition led by the American Dr. Elisha Kane in 1853–55. Commanding a 17-man party aboard the brig *Advance*, Kane sailed north from Baffin Bay into Smith Sound, explored the Greenland coast near Etah, and finally returned south in two small boats after having to abandon his ship.

Kane's party preparing a meal

Advance ice-locked in Smith Sound

Crossing a crevasse in Greenland

Trapping a walrus on the pack ice

vivors abandoned the ships and began a desperate march southward, led by Crozier, who took command when Franklin died. Not one member of the expedition survived, and the relics discovered later told their own story of starvation and death. The epilogue was written 30 years later when, in 1878-80, an expedition commanded by Lieutenant Frederick Schwatka of the United States Army discovered the skeletons of the crews.

Ironically, the search for Franklin brought about the first crossing of the Northwest Passage. Collinson and McClure's relief expedition of 1850 decided to approach the Canadian Arctic from the west. McClure, commanding the *Investigator*, passed through Bering Strait and sailed eastward until he was stopped by the ice at the entrance of Prince of Wales Strait. The following summer he pressed on, was stopped again by the winter ice and sheltered in an anchorage, which he named the Bay of God's Mercy. Here he and his men were forced to spend two winters—during which McClure providentially made a sledge journey to the east across the ice and left a record of his journey in a cairn. The men were able to live on the abundant supplies of musk ox that they killed, but in the spring of 1853 McClure decided to abandon his ship, still locked in the ice north of Banks Island, and trek southward as Franklin had done.

The party had hardly set out when a lone figure appeared and approached them with the words: "I'm Lieutenant Pim of the *Resolute*."

The *Resolute* was one of five ships under Belcher that in 1852 formed the last official Franklin relief expedition. The ships had sailed from the east, and then split into two groups. One group had explored Melville Island after their ship, the *Resolute*, had become locked in the ice in Barrow Strait. They had found McClure's message in the cairn, had determined to find the *Investigator*, and had sent Lieutenant Pim on a reconnaissance.

McClure's party, with Pim, now sledged eastward to Barrow Strait. They found that the *Resolute* had been abandoned, but another of Belcher's ships, the *North Star*, was free of the ice a little farther to the east and could take them aboard. McClure returned home in 1854, having completed the Northwest Passage by ship, foot, and then another ship. He was knighted, and the government voted the officers and men of his expedition a £10,000 reward for their work.

So the Northwest Passage had at last been found. McClure's route was the first of several discovered; but

Robert McClure's ship *Investigator* (above) locked in the ice north of Banks Island in 1850–52. McClure, searching for Franklin's party, led the first group to make a northwest passage. Abandoning ship, he marched eastward (see map below), and was picked up by the *North Star*, another Franklin search ship, near Barrow Strait.

the dangers of the ice and the problems of navigation prevented the Canadian Arctic from ever providing a trade route to the Indies.

What, then, of the North*east* Passage? This was finally discovered by Baron Nils Nordenskjöld, a Swedish scientist, who sailed from Norway in the *Vega* in 1878. Passing the southern tip of Novaya Zemlya, he entered the Kara Sea and on August 19 rounded Cape Chelyuskin, the most northerly point of the Asian mainland. Then he called at the New Siberian Islands, turned southeast, and became locked in the ice of the Chukchi Sea to the north of Bering Strait. Here he wintered aboard ship, then passed through the strait in July 1879. Although Nordenskjöld's route was of little use for trading with the Indies, his expedition yielded important scientific results.

The interest in arctic exploration inspired by the search for Franklin continued vigorously even after the mystery had been solved. Moreover, once the Northwest and the Northeast passages had been discovered and their uselessness as trade routes had been confirmed, explorers turned with renewed vigor to the remaining problem—reaching the Pole itself.

The Adventure of the "Polaris"

One such man was Charles Francis Hall, a middle-aged American, who lived for two years (1860-62) among the Eskimos of King William Island, hoping to discover more about the fate of Franklin and his men. Later in the same decade he spent five consecutive

Baron Nordenskjöld's ship *Vega* fires a salute (above) as she rounds Cape Chelyuskin, northernmost point of mainland Asia, in August 1878. Having sailed eastward from Norway, the *Vega* completed the first northeast passage (see map below) when she passed through Bering Strait in July 1879 after being ice-locked in the Chukchi Sea.

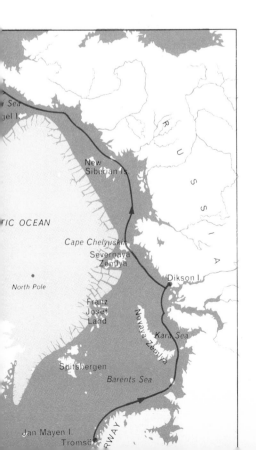

winters in the Arctic and became possessed by a desire to reach the Pole. An entry in his diary about this time reads: "North, *north*, farther and farther NORTH I long to get. . . . I never will be satisfied in voyaging and traveling in the Arctic regions until I reach that spot of this great and glorious orb of God's creation where there is no North, no East, no West."

In 1871 Hall left the United States in a converted naval tug renamed the *Polaris*, and steamed through Smith Sound into the arctic seas north of Greenland before being forced back. He planned to winter on the Greenland coast beneath the shelter of a huge iceberg called Providence Berg, and then push northward with the help of Eskimos. But on a sledging trip he became ill, and on his return to the *Polaris* died of a stroke.

During late October, when the ship drew free from the ice, its commander, Captain Buddington, decided to return to the United States. It was now that 19 members of the expedition began one of the most remarkable and terrifying of all arctic adventures.

The *Polaris* was almost out of Smith Sound when a gale lashed the pack ice and sent a great splinter of ice through the ship's hull. Fearing she might sink, the captain ordered stores of food, fuel, and clothes to be unloaded onto the neighboring floes. Then, in the words of the report later compiled by the United States Navy, "the wind, still strong, now drove the vessel from the floe, and, the anchors dragging at the strain, she swung round to the forward hawser. The latter slipped, and the vessel was carried rapidly away from

141

the ice. The night was black and stormy, and in a few moments the floe and its precious freight could no longer be seen through the drifting snow."

Aboard ship, the crew watched, unable to help, as the floe broke into pieces, each carrying different groups of men and provisions. They saw one of the Eskimos rush to pick up a bundle—his three-month-old baby—from the edge of the ice. Then, in the gathering gloom, they heard the voice of the steward calling out faintly through the darkness: "Goodbye, *Polaris*!"

The ship was blown northward along the coast. Its crew landed stores near Port Foulke, spent the winter there with an Eskimo community, built two boats, and in the summer began to row southward. Soon they were picked up by a whaler, and from its crew heard the fantastic story of their comrades on the ice floe.

It was October 15 when the marooned party had drifted away from the *Polaris*, and the long arctic night was beginning. Luckily, all the members of the group had been able to join one another—Captain Tyson, nine other Americans, and nine Eskimos.

The *Polaris* was little more than a speck on the horizon as the castaways turned to examine the ice floe, about 150 yards square, which was to be their home for many months. With them were two whale boats and two kayaks, a small tent, and provisions consisting of 14 cans of pemmican, 12 bags of bread, 132 cans of meats and soups, one can of dried apples, 14 hams, and a small bag of chocolate.

It was obvious that they would have to depend on the Eskimos for survival. These hardy men now built three snow huts, hunted for food, and helped the Americans to make an Eskimo-type lamp, using a pemmican can, a wick made from canvas, and seal blubber as oil.

The arctic twilight (which lasted for only three hours at first and decreased each day) made hunting difficult, but the party managed to kill seals, an occasional bear, and several birds. These and the other food were rationed with the help of a pair of scales made from a broken barometer and a ruler, and using "weights made of gun shot wrapped in chamois skin." Day by day the party became weaker and weaker as the floe drifted southward through the arctic night.

Then, toward the end of March, the floe began to break up, and on April 1 the whole party had to crowd into the one tiny boat that had not been destroyed or lost. They drifted south, landed on another floe—and then, late in the month, sighted a passing ship! It failed to see them, and it was only on the morning of April 30

The American Charles Hall died of a stroke during his first attempt on the North Pole in 1871. He was buried (above) at his base on the north coast of Greenland.

Lieutenant Tyson and 18 others from Hall's ship *Polaris* were marooned for over six months on an ice floe and drifted south for 1300 miles before being picked up (below) off the Labrador coast.

that a second ship was seen. "Hans shoved off in his kayak, of his own accord, to intercept her, if possible; the morning was foggy, but the steamer's head soon turned toward them and in a few moments she was alongside of the floe. The three cheers given by the shipwrecked people were returned by a hundred men on deck and aloft." The ship was the Newfoundland sealer *Tigress*, and she soon had the whole party aboard. All had survived, and they learned that they were now off the Labrador coast, having drifted some 1300 miles since the previous October.

In the 1870s the character of arctic exploration changed as scientists began to take an active interest in the climate, wild life, vegetation, and geology of the polar regions. This interest was crystallized at a German scientific conference in 1875, when Lieutenant Karl Weyprecht (who had helped discover Franz Josef Land, east of Spitsbergen) proposed an International Polar Year in which scientific observations were to be made at many stations in both the Arctic and the Antarctic. At a conference in Berne, Switzerland, in 1880, it was decided that observations should be made from August 1882 until September 1883 from 12 stations around the Arctic Circle. Norwegians at Alten Fiord, Swedes in Spitsbergen, Dutch and Russians in Siberia, Americans and British in the arctic regions of North America, as well as Germans, Danes, and Austrians—all collaborated in studies of the weather, the magnetic attraction of the Pole, and the northern lights.

The work of scientists gave a tremendous fillip to polar exploration, and by the turn of the century many of the remaining gaps on the arctic map had been filled in. Among the explorers of this period, perhaps the greatest was Fritdjof Nansen, a Norwegian scholar, who in 1882 had first traveled north to collect zoological specimens in Spitsbergen and Greenland.

The Drift of the "Fram"

In 1888 Nansen (then 27 years old) and five companions crossed the Greenland icecap from coast to coast on skis—a daring expedition that showed what could be achieved by a small party of brave, tough men who were all expert skiers. The crossing of Greenland, however, was only the first of many amazing adventures undertaken by Nansen. He had studied the fate of the *Jeannette*, which, with an American party under Lieutenant George Washington De Long, had become lodged in the ice north of Siberia in 1879, and had drifted with the ice until it had crushed her. Nansen

Nansen the explorer (left) and Nansen the statesman. Already supreme as a scientist-explorer of the Arctic, Fritdjof Nansen was in 1922 awarded the Nobel Peace Prize for his work for the League of Nations on behalf of refugees and prisoners of war.

Nansen made this sketch of "moon rings" and "mock moons" during the polar night in November 1893. At this time his ship *Fram* was drifting with the pack ice north of the New Siberian Islands.

This cartoon appeared in the Christmas Eve 1893 edition of *Framsjaa*, the expedition's paper. It pokes fun at the "patent footgear" worn by Nansen's second-in-command Otto Sverdrup, captain of the *Fram* and a noted explorer.

reasoned that if he built a ship that would rise under the pressure of the ice, it would be able to drift, unharmed, with the pack ice into areas beyond the reach of normal ships. The *Jeannette* had passed through the Bering Strait, but relics from the ship had been washed ashore onto the Greenland coast on the other side of America. Nansen therefore deduced that a northwesterly drift in the pack ice ran right across the polar basin, and possibly even across the Pole itself. The outcome of Nansen's reasoning was the *Fram*, a third as broad as she was long, with sides up to two feet thick, and a screw that could be hoisted upward if threatened by the ice.

In the summer of 1893, Nansen turned the bow of the *Fram* north from Cape Chelyuskin in northern Siberia. Soon, he hoped, he would be locked in the ice and drifting across the top of the world. The first test came when the ice closed in during October. "As we were sitting idly chatting, a deafening noise began and the whole ship shook," Nansen wrote in his book

Farthest North. "This was the first ice pressure. Everyone rushed on deck to look. The *Fram* behaved beautifully. On pushed the ice, but down under us it had to go, and we were slowly lifted up."

During the winter of 1893 and the summer and winter of 1894, the *Fram* drifted with the ice. At the end of this period, the ship was at 83°N. (less than 500 miles from the Pole). It was at this point that Nansen, having abandoned hope that his ship would ever be carried to the Pole, decided to embark on a daring adventure. He and one companion planned to leave the ship, sledge to the Pole, and then make their way back to civilization.

On March 14, 1895, Nansen set off with one companion, Frederik Johansen, and with three sledges, each drawn by nine dogs. Otto Sverdrup was left in charge of the *Fram*, to sit out the long months ahead in hopes that the ship would eventually be carried into open, navigable water. The two-man expedition that now set out was faced with a race against time. Nansen knew that before he could reach the Pole his supplies would run low and that he and Johansen would have to live on animals they could kill along the way.

After nearly a month of traveling over the ice a discouraged Nansen realized that the drifting ice was carrying him not toward the Pole but *away* from it, so on April 8 he and Johansen abandoned the idea of attempting to reach the Pole, and decided to make their way to Franz Josef Land. The two men were at this time closer to the North Pole than anyone had been before—at latitude 86°13′36″N., a distance of 224 miles from the top of the world.

Not until mid-August did they reach Franz Josef Land, east of Spitsbergen, and realized that they would have to spend the winter there. They built a hut that was to be their home throughout the winter of 1895, living on what they could shoot, and getting light and heat from walrus blubber. With the coming of the sun they set off south once more—but without their dogs, which they had been forced to kill during the winter.

It was on June 17, 1896, that Nansen heard a sound other than the wind over the ice. In the distance he

Nansen and Frederik Johansen leave the *Fram* for their attempt to sledge to the Pole. The windmill on board ship helped to generate electricity.

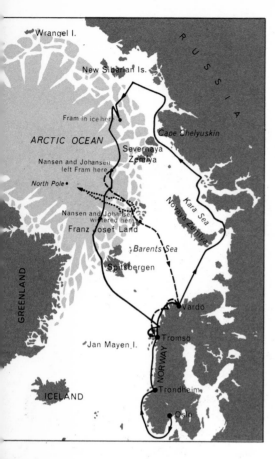

————— Fram 1893-96

— — — Nansen and Johansen 1895-96

········· Cagni 1900

The map shows the *Fram*'s voyage,
its drift in the ice, and Nansen's and
Johansen's route by sledge. Also
included is the route of the party
from Franz Josef Land led by the
Italian Lieutenant Umberto Cagni,
which in 1900 exceeded Nansen's
farthest north by 22 miles, little
more than 200 miles from the Pole.

could hear dogs barking. Nansen wondered if they
could possibly be those of his men from the *Fram*, or
whether they might be with a party from a British expedition, led by Frederick Jackson, which had been
making preparations when the *Fram* had set out about
three years before.

Nansen went up onto the highest ice hummock he
could see and shouted. Then, in the distance, he saw a
figure coming toward him. "We approached one
another quickly, I waved my hat; he did the same,"
wrote Nansen later. "I heard him speak to the dog and
I listened. It was English, and as I drew nearer I
thought I recognised Mr. Jackson whom I remembered
once to have seen."

It was indeed Jackson. "A more remarkable meeting
than ours was never heard of," the Englishman wrote
later. "Nansen did not know that I was in Franz Josef
Land, as I did not leave England until a year after he
had started, and I had not the slightest idea he was
within hundreds of miles of me."

Before the end of August, Nansen and Johansen
were back in Norway. Only one worry remained, and
it was dispelled a week later when Nansen received a
telegram announcing that the *Fram* was safe. After
being locked in the ice for 35 months she had broken
free and sailed back to Tromsö in Norway.

The voyage of the *Fram* added much to what men
knew about the Arctic, and it brought nearer the day
when the Pole itself would be reached, for the whole
tempo of polar exploration was now quickening. Sir
Martin Conway, the English mountaineer, made the
first crossing of Spitsbergen in 1896-97. The Duke of
the Abruzzi, an Italian mountaineer, led a large expedition to the north of Franz Josef Land at the turn
of the century. And, already in the field, was the American explorer Robert E. Peary.

Peary Reaches the Pole

This tough, restless man with his broad figure, huge
walrus moustache, and determination to be the first
man at the Pole, would have been the last to deny that
his successes rested on a foundation built by the generations of arctic explorers who had gone before him. All
the same, Peary made his own important and dis-
tinctive contribution to arctic exploration.

He had been in South America, attached to naval
forces surveying a route for the proposed Nicaraguan
canal, when he had read Nordenskjöld's book on
Greenland. Shortly afterward, in 1886, he made a brief
summer visit to the enormous island, and soon found

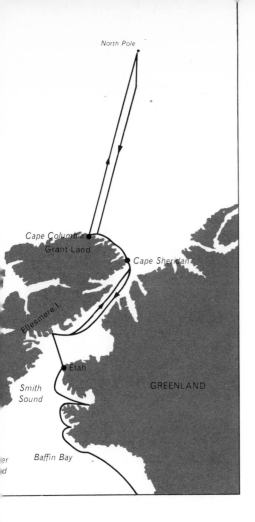

North Pole

Cape Columbia
Grant Land
Cape Sheridan

Ellesmere I.

Etah

Smith
Sound

GREENLAND

Baffin Bay

Above: Robert E. Peary's route to
the North Pole in 1908–09, via
Smith Sound and Cape Columbia.
Cagni had also suggested this route
after he failed to reach the Pole from
Franz Josef Land eight years before.

Below: Peary and his wife, Marie

himself under the spell of the great arctic wastes. "It is a strange and powerful thing," he was later to write. "More than once I have come back from the great frozen spaces, battered and worn and baffled, sometimes maimed, telling myself that I had made my last journey thither, eager for the society of my kind, the comforts of civilization and the peace and serenity of home. But somehow, it was never many months before the old restless feeling came over me. Civilization began to lose its zest for me. I began to long for the great white desolation, the battles with the ice and the gales, the long, long Arctic night, the long, long Arctic day, the handful of odd but faithful Eskimos who had been my friends for years, the silence and vastness of the great, white, lonely North. And back I went accordingly, time after time, until, at last, my dream of years came true."

At the start Peary had the kind of bad luck that would have discouraged most men. His first serious expedition to Greenland was made in 1891, and even while his ship, the *Kite*, was nosing through the offshore ice, Peary had an accident and broke two bones in one of his legs. He was advised to return to the United States and rejoin the party when they were ready for their journey northward. Peary refused. He recuperated in Greenland, and was ready the following spring to strike northward with a single companion onto the great plateau that covers the center of the island. He sledged north for 500 miles, arrived at Independence Bay on July 4, 1892, and proved beyond doubt that Greenland was a separate island and not part of a great Arctic continent. Two years later he crossed the island again. Then in 1898 he set out on the first of his three attempts to reach the North Pole.

Peary had decided early in his arctic career that the only way for Europeans to conquer the great white spaces was for them to adopt the Eskimos' way of life. Like them, arctic explorers must live in igloos; like them they must live off the "land" by fishing and hunting. In order to make the best time on the long, lonely trek to the Pole, they would have to plan the expedition scientifically, with advance parties preparing the way for those who followed. All these ideas were tested during the years 1898-1902, when Peary and his men explored and surveyed hundreds of miles of the north coast of Greenland. What held him back during this period was the pack ice, which prevented his ship from entering the Arctic Ocean. He was unable, therefore, to set up a base camp nearer than 700 miles from the Pole; as a result, even his longest sledge journey left

Peary designed his ship the *Roosevelt* and used it for his attempts on the Pole in 1905 and 1908–09. Specially strengthened for crashing its way through pack ice, the ship differed from previous arctic vessels in relying primarily on steam engines for power, its sails being used only in the event of engine failure.

him 350 miles short of his goal. A new method of approach would have to be used.

Convinced that a special vessel would be needed to force its way through the ice, Peary returned to the United States and planned his next expedition. First he designed the *Roosevelt*, and then he raised the money that enabled it to be built and manned for his next journey. The ship differed in two important ways from any other that had been built for the Arctic. First, its wooden hull was constructed so that it would be able to crash its way through the ice; second, and more important, it relied primarily on 1000-horsepower steam engines. Previous explorers had used engines (usually quite small ones) only as a support for sail. With the *Roosevelt* the order of priority was reversed; steam would be used to push the vessel northward through the ice, and sail would be used only as an auxiliary.

In 1905 Peary sailed in the *Roosevelt*, and eventually set off from Grant Land (west of the northern tip of Greenland) with his sledging party across the frozen Arctic Ocean. When he reached latitude 84°38′N., a wide lead opened in the ice before him and a week passed before he could cross it. Then, when this obstacle had been overcome, a great storm arose, and at 87°06′N. his party was forced to turn back. Yet, by this time, they had reached farther north than any human had ever been before.

When he returned to the United States, Peary was 50 years old. He knew that he would probably have only one more chance to accomplish what had now become for him the goal of all human hope and endeavor. In July 1908 he left New York, once again in the *Roosevelt*, determined to force himself to the utmost in his efforts to reach the Pole. That autumn Peary assembled 49 Eskimos and 246 dogs at Etah on the northwest coast of Greenland, and on the afternoon of August 18 the *Roosevelt* steamed northward up Smith Sound between Greenland and Ellesmere Island.

They had gone only a little way when the ship struck a great berg; and, as Peary relates, while most vessels would have been seriously damaged, the *Roosevelt* merely "shook herself like a dog coming out of the water" and continued on her way. From Etah to Cape Sheridan, which was to be their base camp, was a voyage of 350 miles, not in open sea but through solid ice—"ice of all shapes and sizes, mountainous ice, flat ice, ragged and tortured ice, ice that, for every foot of height revealed above the surface of the water, hides seven feet below—a theatre of action which for

Where normal ships like this one would have become ice-locked, the *Roosevelt* could crash its way without damage through the pack ice in Smith Sound.

diabolic and Titanic struggle makes Dante's frozen circle of the Inferno seem like a skating pond."

There were 13 days of desperate tussle with the ice before the *Roosevelt* at last rounded Cape Rawson at the northern end of Smith Sound, and Peary and his men, who had not taken off their clothes since they left Etah, saw before them the sloping headland of Cape Sheridan, looking "more beautiful than the gates to paradise to our vigil-wearied eyes."

Throughout the autumn and the winter months, the crew of the *Roosevelt* sledged supplies and equipment across 90 miles of land to Cape Columbia (only 413 miles south of the Pole) that Peary had decided should be his starting point for the great trek. It was desperately difficult work, even with the 13-foot sledges of oak with bent ash runners that Peary had designed and which he found better than the nine-foot Eskimo sledges. Eventually, toward the end of February, all was ready for the dash to the Pole.

Peary's great venture was a "dash" in the sense that no time was to be wasted on the long trail from Cape Columbia. But the astonishing speed at which the party traveled depended on Peary's careful planning of the entire operation. Such factors as how many men and dogs could be supported by a given amount of food; exactly how the food and equipment were to be stowed on the sledges—these and many other matters were calculated to the last detail.

The plan, on which the success of the expedition rested, was that a number of supporting parties would open the trail and lay down stocks of provisions, each one nearer the Pole than the last. Then Peary, in charge of the "assault party," would make the final dash from an advance base set up as near to the Pole as possible.

The standard daily rations consisted of a pound of pemmican, a pound of ship's biscuits, four ounces of condensed milk, and half an ounce of tea, while the dogs were given a pound of pemmican daily. The supplies were loaded on the sledges as follows: "On the bottom was a layer of dog pemmican in red tins, covering the entire length and width of the sledge," wrote Peary. "On this were two tins of biscuits, and crew pemmican in blue tins; then the tins of alcohol and condensed milk, a small skin rug for the men to sleep on at night in the igloo, snowshoes and spare footgear, a pickax and a saw-knife for cutting snow."

On February 22, 1909, Peary left the *Roosevelt* for Cape Columbia. Here the North Pole parties concentrated—seven Americans, one Newfoundlander, 19 Eskimos, 140 dogs, and 28 sledges. From here, on

February 28, the advance party, led by the Newfoundlander, Captain Robert Bartlett, set off north across the ice to open the trail.

The long winter was ending—it was light now by 10 A.M.—and next morning, March 1, the main parties prepared to leave. Some of the Eskimos were ill, and an unexpected wind was whistling around the camp, but otherwise everything was going according to plan.

"One by one the divisions drew out from the main army of sledges and dog teams, took up Bartlett's trail over the ice and disappeared to the northward in the wind haze," wrote Peary. "This departure of the procession was a noiseless one, for the freezing east wind carried all sounds away. It was also invisible after the first few moments—men and dogs being swallowed up almost immediately in the wind haze and the drifting snow. . . . An hour after I left camp my division had crossed the glacial fringe, and the last man, sledge and dog of the Northern party—comprising altogether twenty-four men, nineteen sledges, and one hundred and thirty-three dogs—were at last on the ice of the Arctic Ocean, about latitude 83°."

Between them and the Pole lay 413 miles of white untracked wilderness.

Their first setback came on the second day. Ahead lay a dark cloud on the horizon—an obvious indication that a lead of open water split the ice across which they were advancing. Shortly afterward Peary, who was bringing up the rear to ensure that there were no stragglers, had his fears confirmed by the dark dots of

Peary's assault party sledge across the white wilderness during their 413-mile dash from Cape Columbia to the Pole.

the parties ahead of him drawn up on the edge of the water. They camped for the night, only to be awakened before dawn by the grinding of the ice, a sign that the lead was closing up. Using convenient ice floes as stepping stones they crossed immediately. On the far side, they found no sign of Bartlett's trail, for there had been a lateral movement of the ice that had caused the lead. The trail was eventually picked up a mile and a half away.

On March 4 Peary caught up with Bartlett, whom he found camping on the edge of another great stretch of water. It was some days before they were able to cross. The leads formed one of their main problems, and soon the members of the expedition were to see the wisdom of Peary's plan that they should sleep with musk ox skins below them and caribou skins over them, rather than in sleeping bags. The latter, he argued, would be too difficult to get out of quickly in an emergency.

On March 28 Peary was suddenly awakened by shouting outside his snow igloo. "Leaping to my feet," he wrote, "and looking through the peephole of our igloo, I was startled to see a broad lead of black water between our two igloos and Bartlett's, the nearer edge of water being close to our entrance; and on the opposite side of the lead stood one of Bartlett's men yelling and gesticulating with all the abandon of an excited and thoroughly frightened Eskimo." The ice had split near the igloo, and only a foot from the fastening of one of the dog teams, which was saved by the distance of only 12 inches from being dragged into the icy water. Luckily the floe that had broken away, and on which Bartlett's party was camped, soon brushed against the main ice and the two groups were reunited.

On March 30 Bartlett turned back with the first of the supporting parties, leaving five sledges and 40 dogs with Peary, who was now 133 miles south of the Pole. He had with him Matthew Henson, his Negro personal assistant, who had been with Peary for more than 20 years; and the four Eskimos, Ootah, Ooqueah, Egingwah, and Seegloo. "All these men had a blind confidence that I would somehow get them back to land," he later wrote. "But I recognized fully that all the impetus of the party centered in me. Whatever pace I set, the others would make good; but if I played out, they would stop like a car with a punctured tire."

His plan was to make five marches of at least 25 miles each, timing them so that he ended the fifth at noon, and would thus be able to observe the latitude. All was now ready for the final spurt, and shortly after midnight on the morning of April 2 they set off. "Up

First to the North Pole! Peary and four of his five companions pose for a triumphant photograph on April 6, 1909. Behind them, atop a hastily built igloo, flutters an American flag made by Marie Peary.

to this time," Peary wrote, "I had intentionally kept in the rear, to straighten out any little hitch or to encourage a man with a broken sledge, and to see that everything was in good marching order. Now I took my proper place in the lead. Though I held myself in check, I felt the keenest exhilaration, and even exultation, as I climbed over the pressure ridge and breasted the keen air sweeping over the mighty ice, pure and straight from the Pole itself."

They sledged on for 10 hours that first day, watching the moon as it circled the skies opposite the sun, "a disk of silver opposite a disk of gold." The moon was full; they knew spring tides might stir the ice, causing new leads to form and block their way north. Next day they again traveled for 10 hours, and near the end of it

Peary confirms his position at the Pole by taking readings from the Sun. "East, west, and north had disappeared," he wrote. "Only one direction remained and that was south."

they only just missed disaster. They had come to a lead about 100 yards wide, covered with ice so thin that they had to distribute their weight as evenly as they could, with the last two men coming over on all fours. Peary watched the ice bending with the weight of the sledges and the men—and then, as one of the sledges reached the north bank, one of its runners cut clean through the ice. But they managed to haul the sledge onto the bank and were on their way again.

On the third day they found a lead going north but it was covered by ice firm enough to sledge on. For two hours they traveled over it, "the dogs galloping along and reeling off the miles" in a way that delighted Peary's heart.

There was a fourth day's sledging. Then a fifth—and at the end of it, about 10 o'clock on April 6, the five men set up camp while Peary took his first observation. It showed that they had reached 89°57′—about three miles from the Pole! Peary turned in and slept for a few hours. The first thing he did on waking was to write in his diary: "The Pole at last. The prize of three centuries. My dream and goal for twenty years. Mine at last! I cannot bring myself to realize it. It seems all so simple and commonplace."

Then Peary loaded a light sledge with his instruments, a tin of pemmican, and one or two skins. Drawn by a double team of dogs, the little party sledged on for what they estimated to be 10 miles. Then, as the sky cleared, Peary took his reading. It proved beyond doubt that he and his party had crossed the North Pole.

This final stage was a curious journey. For the first part of it, the party had been going due north; then, while continuing in the same direction, they had been going due south. "East, west, and north had disappeared for us," wrote Peary. "Only one direction remained and that was south. Every breeze which could possibly blow upon us, no matter from what point of the horizon, it must be a south wind. Where we were, one day and one night constituted a year, a hundred such days and nights constituted a century. Had we stood in that spot during the six months of the Arctic winter night, we should have seen every star of the northern hemisphere circling the sky at the same distance from the horizon, with Polaris (the North Star) practically in the zenith."

Peary's great triumph ended one phase of arctic exploration just as another was about to begin. Salomon Andrée, the Swedish scientist, had been the first man to go by air into the arctic regions when, in 1897, he set out with two companions on a balloon trip north-

In 1897 a Swede, Salomon Andrée, and two others made the first arctic flight. Departing from Spitsbergen, they were never seen alive again.

Aircraft transformed polar exploration in the 1920s and 1930s. The Soviet Union made many flights in the Arctic (below) and in 1937 four Russian scientists were flown to the North Pole for a nine-month research project.

eastward from Spitsbergen. None of them was seen alive again. Just 17 years later a Russian, Nagursky, became the first man to fly a heavier-than-air craft in the Arctic when, in 1914, he made a short flight over the Barents Sea.

The coming of flight, for both commercial and military purposes, completely changed the character of arctic exploration. For the "Great Circle routes"—the shortest routes—between many of the world's most important centers lay across the Arctic Ocean, and in the years after the First World War, men from many countries began to discover that it would be practicable to fly such routes. In 1924 the Oxford University Expedition to Spitsbergen under Professor George Binney carried out many experimental flights; in 1925 Roald Amundsen, the Norwegian explorer, tried to reach the Pole in two flying boats; and in the following year the American, Commander (later Admiral) Richard Byrd, became the first man to fly over the North Pole. From this time onward aircraft became as regular an aid to arctic exploration as radio had already become. And men were no longer so much concerned with geographical exploration as with the investigation of the Arctic's geology, meteorology, and glaciology.

One mystery remained—and still does: a detailed knowledge of the great Arctic Ocean beneath the ice. The most dramatic step toward investigating it was taken in 1958 by the United States nuclear-powered submarine *Nautilus* under Commander William R. Anderson.

The *Nautilus* had already had some experience with arctic ice when she left the Hawaiian Islands in July, bound for the Bering Strait. To the north of Point Franklin the submarine entered the Barrow Sea Valley and began her historic journey under the ice. Eleven hundred miles ahead lay the North Pole, and 800 miles beyond that the far edge of the ice pack and the open sea near Spitsbergen.

The *Nautilus* was able to cruise submerged at a steady 20 knots for much of the time, with Anderson watching the fathometer intently: "I saw incredibly steep cliffs—undersea ranges—rise thousands of feet above the ocean floor," he wrote later. "Several times I ordered speed slackened, then resumed, as a promontory leveled off or descended as rapidly as it had risen. The shape of these undersea mountains appeared phenomenally rugged, and as grotesque as the craters of the Moon." The *Nautilus* sped silently onward, all eyes on the mass of flashing and clicking instruments in the control room. In case of emergency the ship's torpedo tubes were kept ready to blast a hole in the ceiling of ice above.

Then, on August 3, after 62 hours under the ice, the submarine reached the North Pole and soon after radioed its exciting three-word message to the world— NAUTILUS 90 NORTH. After a celebration, Anderson and his crew continued south to Iceland and the Atlantic Ocean. This voyage typifies the roles that science and technology are playing in 20th-century exploration of the polar regions.

Little is known about the Arctic Ocean beneath its permanent ice cap. A big step toward investigating it came in July 1958 when a voyage of 1900 miles under the ice and across the North Pole (see map above) was made by the United States nuclear-powered submarine *Nautilus* (below) under Commander William R. Anderson. The voyage was quite uneventful and *Nautilus* was often able to speed at 20 knots.

EXPLORING THE ANTARCTIC

Antarctic exploration began relatively late—about 300 years after Europeans began to venture into the northern polar regions. It was not until between 1818 and 1820 that man caught his first, brief glimpse of the Antarctic continent beyond the pack ice, while the first landing, by a Norwegian, Captain Carsten Borchgrevink, on the mainland did not take place until 1895.

When Magellan passed the tip of the South American mainland in 1520, he and most other explorers of the time believed that Tierra del Fuego (the large island off the southern end of South America) was part of a vast southern continent called *Terra Incognita* (Unknown Land). For more than two and a half centuries the discovery of new lands—New Guinea, the New Hebrides, and New Zealand—kept alive the myth of a huge southern continent that stretched up into the temperate regions. Then, in 1768, came Captain James Cook's first voyage, during which he began to destroy

Map of the Antarctic continent. Whereas the Arctic is a frozen ocean hemmed in by land masses, Antarctica is a plateau surrounded by huge expanses of stormy seas. Each region has an area of nearly eight million square miles.

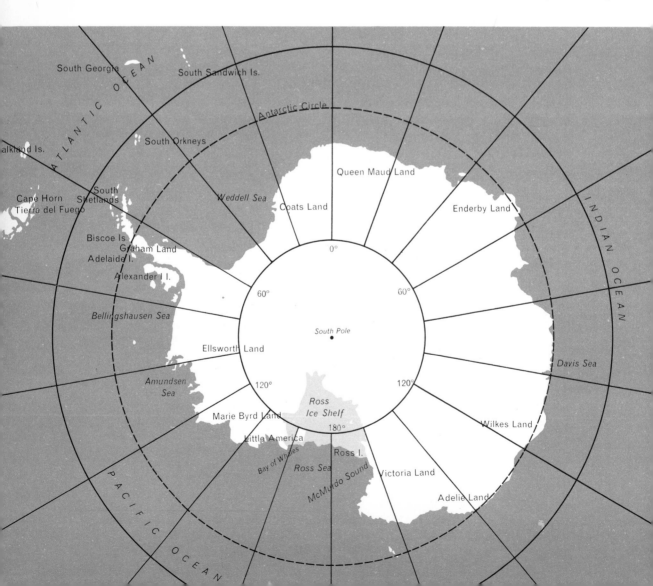

the myth, as we have seen, by circumnavigating New Zealand. On his second voyage, between 1772 and 1775, he crossed the Antarctic Circle, sailed completely around Antarctica, and so proved once and for all that any land lying south of his route had no link with Asia, South America, or Australasia. In the course of his voyages Cook discovered the South Sandwich Islands and annexed South Georgia for Britain—an act that was to have an important effect on the future of the Antarctic.

South Georgia, which lies about 1200 miles east of Cape Horn, is a rocky island that since the end of the 18th century has grown steadily more important as a sealing and whaling base. Within three years of Cook's voyage Samuel Enderby, an adventurous London merchant, was sending his vessels to South Georgia. And during the next few decades British and American whalers sailed in growing numbers into this area.

The South Shetlands, South Orkneys, and other small groups of islands lying on the fringe of the polar land mass were seen by whaler captains and plotted on the maps. The Russians, under Captain Fabian von Bellingshausen, circumnavigated Antarctica in 1819-21 as Cook had done, and in the process discovered Peter Island and Alexander I Island. About the same time the British and the Americans first reported the peninsula called Graham Land on British maps, but Palmer Peninsula on American maps. And in 1831 John Biscoe, one of Enderby's master mariners, sailed around the south polar region, discovered the Biscoe Islands and nearby Adelaide Island off Graham Land and, on the other side of Antarctica, the great promontory of Enderby Land. When we say that the early explorers "discovered" these islands and other land areas, it usually means that they merely took note of their existence. In most cases, the pack ice prevented them from landing, or from even getting very close to the shore. Biscoe, for instance, was unable to get within 20 miles of Enderby Land.

Ross Reaches the Continent

Only in the 1840s was the existence of the Antarctic continent finally confirmed. The man responsible was James Clark Ross, nephew of Sir John Ross, with whom Parry had sought the Northwest Passage in 1818. James Ross, who was born in 1800 and entered the Royal Navy at the age of 12, had accompanied his uncle on two arctic voyages including the 1818 expedition. In 1831 he plotted the position of the North Magnetic Pole and in 1839, by this time a captain, he was

In the 1840s James Clark Ross became one of the first explorers to penetrate the antarctic pack ice and sail along the mainland coast.

Ross and other antarctic explorers of the 19th century put in at Christmas Harbor on Kerguelen, a lonely island 1200 miles north of Antarctica on the southern fringe of the Indian Ocean.

put in command of the British Antarctic Expedition sponsored by the Admiralty.

Ross's vessel was H.M.S. *Erebus*, while as escort she had H.M.S. *Terror* under Commander Francis Crozier. Both vessels (later to be lost in Franklin's tragic expedition) were "bombs"—bombarding vessels with specially strengthened hulls capable of plowing through the pack ice. They left England in the autumn of 1839, and on November 12, 1840, sailed south from Hobart, Tasmania. "Joy and satisfaction beamed in every face," wrote Ross later. He had on board provisions for three years, good officers and crew, and felt that he had "nothing to desire but the guidance and blessing of Almighty God throughout the arduous duties we were about to commence, and without which all human skill and courage must prove utterly unavailing."

They sailed at first through gales and heavy seas and then, when the storms abated, began to see whales and giant icebergs. The latter, unlike the arctic bergs, "presented very little variety of form, but were generally of large size and of very solid appearance, bounded by perpendicular cliffs on all sides. Their tabular summits varied from one hundred and twenty to one hundred and eighty feet in height, and several of them were more than two miles in circumference." They passed sperm whales, humpback whales, and many others "so tame that our ships sailing close past did not seem to disturb them."

Early in January 1841 Ross and his men had their first glimpse of the pack ice, extending as far as the eye could see, and after skirting it for four days, Ross decided that the time had come to tackle the first problem of his voyage.

"The signal was made to the *Terror*, and we bore away before the wind, selecting the most favourable point to break through the outer edge of the pack, which, as usual, was formed of much heavier ice than the rest, and which we accomplished without sustaining any serious injury, although necessarily receiving some very heavy blows.

"After about an hour's hard thumping, we forced our way into some small holes of water, connected by narrow lanes, for which we had purposely steered; and, closely followed by the *Terror*, we found the ice much lighter and more scattered than it appeared to be when viewed from the distance. It consisted chiefly of small floes of ice, of last winter's formation, with a quantity of hummocky ice of much older date, formed by great pressure into very heavy masses; but it was by no means

Although a dangerous hazard to sledging expeditions, leads like this one provided ship-based explorers with useful channels through the pack ice before the days of icebreakers.

Beset by huge blocks of pack ice, *Erebus* and *Terror* ride out a gale during Ross's second voyage to Antarctica in 1842.

of so formidable a character as we had been led to expect. . . ."

For five days the *Erebus* and *Terror* pressed southward through the pack. The crew saw seals basking on the ice and many penguins. The penguins "followed our ships, answering the call of the sailors, who imitated their cry; and although they could not scramble over the ice so fast as our ships sailed past it, they made up for it when they got into the water, and we soon had quite a flock of them in our wake, playing about our vessel like so many porpoises." On the evening of January 9 a strong wind from the northward sprang up, and by 5 o'clock next morning they found that they "had accomplished the object of our exertions, and found ourselves again in a clear sea."

Ross and his companions now believed that little might lie between them and the South Pole. Soon, however, they were to have doubts, for there appeared on the horizon a strong "land-blink"—a reflection in the sky that suggested land. And at 2 A.M. the officer of the watch reported land dead ahead. Ross and his companions were now sailing straight for the Antarctic continent, which few explorers had glimpsed before, and then only from a great distance.

Soon it could be seen that the land—or rather the ice—stretched far to the east and west. The two ships continued south under full sail throughout the morning and afternoon. "It was a beautifully clear evening," Ross later recorded, "and we had a most enchanting view of the two magnificent ranges of

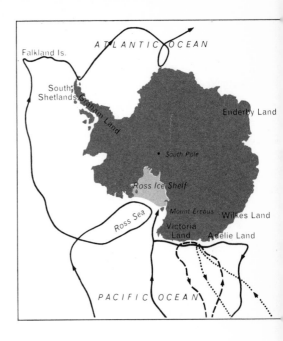

——— J. C. Ross ――― d'Urville ·········· Wilkes

This map shows the routes of antarctic explorations by Ross and by the Frenchman Jean Dumont d'Urville and the American Charles Wilkes, both of whom beat Ross to the continent.

mountains whose lofty peaks, perfectly covered with eternal snow, rose to elevations ranging from seven to ten thousand feet above the level of the ocean. The glaciers that filled their intervening valleys, and which descended from near the mountain summits projected in many places several miles into the sea, and terminated in lofty perpendicular cliffs. In a few places the rocks broke through their icy covering, by which alone we could be assured that land formed the nucleus of this, to appearance, enormous iceberg."

Ross now realized that his way to the Pole might be barred, but he had discovered land farther south than any man before him, and the following day he landed to stake Britain's claim to what he named Possession Island. "We saw not the smallest appearance of vegetation, but inconceivable myriads of penguins completely and densely covered the whole surface of the island, along the ledges of the precipices, and even to the summits of the hills, attacking us vigorously as we waded through their ranks, and pecking at us with their sharp beaks, disputing possession. . . ."

The coast in this area (now called Victoria Land) ran south, and the two little ships now sailed along it, their crews plotting the islands, capes, and mountain peaks that appeared in astonishing array.

Then, on January 27, they approached land, which had been in sight since the preceding day and which they had named High Island. "It proved to be a mountain 13,200 feet of elevation above the level of the sea, emitting flame and smoke in great profusion; at first

Mount Erebus (above), which Ross discovered in 1841 and named after one of his ships, is an active volcano over 13,000 feet high lying on Ross Island. The photograph of the volcano (right) was taken in 1957 by a member of the Commonwealth Transantarctic Expedition which had a base nearby on McMurdo Sound.

the smoke appeared like snow drift, but as we drew nearer, its true character became manifest."

This was Mount Erebus, as they named it, an active volcano, which the crews of the *Erebus* and *Terror* were soon to see belching out great smoke clouds above a bright red flame filling the mouth of the summit crater. A little to the east lay another volcano, which they named Mount Terror.

Ross now sailed nearer to the astonishing spectacle. As he did so, an even more remarkable sight came into view. "As we approached the land under all studding-sails, we perceived a low white line extending from the western extreme point as far as the eye could discern to the eastward," he wrote. "It presented an extraordinary appearance, gradually increasing in height, as we got nearer to it, and proving at length to be a perpendicular cliff of ice, between one hundred and fifty and two hundred feet above the level of the sea, perfectly flat and level at the top, and without any fissures or promontories on its even seaward face."

This was the huge Ross Ice Barrier, or Ice Shelf, as it was later called, and the *Erebus* and the *Terror* now followed it to the east for five days. They covered 250 miles but the great white wall continued, seemingly endless, into the distance. "You could no more find a way through than you could through the cliffs of Dover," Ross later commented. It was obvious that he would be unable to sail farther south, at least by this route, so he turned back northward through the pack ice once again and returned to Hobart.

Erebus and *Terror* (below left) cruise along the great floating ice shelf named after Ross. Below right is a recent photograph of the ice shelf, which towers about 150 feet above the water, is over 400 miles long, and juts nearly 500 miles into the Ross Sea from the mainland glaciers that feed it.

At the time Ross had been preparing for his first voyage to the Antarctic, the French and the Americans were also preparing expeditions. Both, in fact, beat Ross to the continent, which annoyed him. The French expedition was led by Jules Dumont d'Urville and got to within four degrees of the South Magnetic Pole. Its members had hoped to be able to sail over it until they realized that it was inland. D'Urville named this area Adélie Land, in honor of his wife. The American expedition, led by Captain Charles Wilkes of the United States Navy, reached the same position along the coast nine days after the French had left. Wilkes proved that the mountainous coastline was part of a continental land mass and not a group of islands linked by ice.

Ross made two more voyages. The first was during the following winter when the *Erebus* and the *Terror* spent 40 days breaking through 800 miles of pack ice before they reached the Ross Barrier; the second in 1842-43 took the ships to the Antarctic continent once again, but bad weather limited the work that could be done.

After the return of the two ships to England, there came a definite break in the story of antarctic discovery. The main cause was the search for the Franklin expedition that concentrated attention on the northern polar region. Moreover there was little to suggest that Antarctica might be of commercial value except to whalers and sealers. It offered no trade routes, as the Arctic had seemed to do; nor was there any reason

Members of Wilkes's American expedition in 1839 relax on the coast of the huge region of Antarctica named after their leader.

D'Urville reached a neighboring region of Antarctica a few weeks before Wilkes and called it Adélie Land after his wife. Above, with the winter pack ice closing in, d'Urville's crew manage to haul one of his ships toward open water.

to think it might contain valuable mineral resources. When explorers returned once more to Antarctica, after a gap of nearly 40 years, most of them were seeking scientific knowledge as much as adventure.

By the 1880s expeditions were once again charting the coastlines of what was now realized to be a vast continent. In 1893-94 the Norwegians added many new names to the map. In 1897 the Belgian Lieutenant Adrien de Gerlache led a purely scientific expedition; trapped in the ice in 1898, they were the first men to winter within the Antarctic Circle. In the early years of the present century the Germans, the Swedes, and the French all sent expeditions south. It was during this period, moreover, that an expedition to Antarctica was led by Captain Robert Falcon Scott, the Englishman who 12 years later was to be the central character in one of the great dramas of exploration.

First Attempt on the Pole

Scott was aged 32 when at the turn of the century the Royal Society and the Royal Geographical Society raised more than £90,000 for a full-scale government expedition to Antarctica. A naval officer with little knowledge of polar exploration, he was put in command of what was in effect a naval expedition (30 of its members were officers or men of the British navy). In the summer of 1901 the party sailed south in the *Discovery,* a wooden ship specially prepared for breaking through the ice.

Scott's brief was to discover, as accurately as he could, the extent, position, and nature of the Antarctic continent and to make a magnetic survey. He was reinforced by a physicist, a biologist, and a geologist, and the expedition, although organized by the British Admiralty, had aims that were largely scientific. The idea worked well and within three years Scott and his companions had added enormously to man's knowledge of the south.

It seemed—correctly as we know today—that a way up and across the Ross Ice Shelf might provide one of the best routes into the interior, and it was to the Ross Sea coast that the *Discovery* sailed first. Because it is from this part of the Antarctic that most explorations of the continent have started, it is as well to understand its peculiar and dramatic topography. Here the arms of the continent enclose an immense bay, more than 400 miles across and extending 500 miles outward from the shore, bounded on the west by the slopes of Mount Erebus and completely filled by the white mass of the Ross Ice Shelf. Down into this V-

Roald Amundsen

Robert Falcon Scott

Ernest Shackleton

Rivals in the race to the South Pole these three are perhaps the greatest names in antarctic exploration.

shaped, ice-covered bay, comparable in size to the British Isles or France, run glaciers from the great inland plateau—one of which, Scott hoped, would lead toward the Pole itself.

Early in 1902 the *Discovery* broke its way through the pack ice. New land to the west of the Ross Ice Shelf was discovered and a balloon ascent was made from atop the Shelf itself. Then the party sailed to McMurdo Bay at the western end of the Shelf, wintered there, and discovered that Mount Erebus lay on an island (now called Ross Island) and was separated from the mainland by what was renamed McMurdo Sound.

From his base in McMurdo Sound, Scott set off on one of the most important antarctic journeys ever made. With him went Ernest Shackleton and Dr. E. A. Wilson, a scientist and the artist of the expedition. They had 19 dogs, and with them they hoped to sledge partway to the Pole, if not reach it. In fact, they went as far as 82°17's.—much farther south than men had gone before. But at this point lack of supplies forced the small party to turn back. As they traveled into the interior, they realized that their track was leading them onto the great plateau that forms the mass of the Antarctic continent. This approach from the Ross Shelf remains one of the only three land routes by which men have been able to attain the South Pole, and its discovery was due solely to the Scott expedition of 1901-02.

The expedition was to have another, if unexpected, result. It convinced Scott that it was cruel to use dogs for sledging. He had used them on this journey south and, by the time his party returned to base, all the dogs had died—mainly through illness. "Conquest is more nobly and splendidly won without them," Scott concluded—a conviction that, possibly, was to cost him his life 10 years later.

The *Discovery* spent a second winter in the ice, and the following September (1904) Scott returned home, having found the key that would unlock one door to the Pole.

The pace of antarctic exploration increased during the first 10 years of the 20th century. Dr. Jean Charcot, a Frenchman, opened up new country adjoining Graham Land in 1903-05 and 1908-10. A Scotsman, Dr. William Bruce, discovered Coats Land, named after the man who had backed his expedition. And in 1908 Shackleton, who had accompanied Scott and Wilson on their journey to 82°17's., led a small expedition.

Shackleton's aim was clearer than that of many pre-

This view northward from McMurdo Sound was painted by Dr. Edward Wilson, the zoologist-physician who accompanied Scott on both his antarctic expeditions.

An iceberg dwarfs Scott's ship *Terra Nova*, at anchor in the pack ice near the McMurdo Sound base in December 1910. The photographs of Scott's expedition in these pages were by Herbert Ponting, among the greatest photographers of Antarctica.

This view of the *Terra Nova*'s deck includes some of the 33 dogs that Scott used for hauling supply sledges to Beardmore Glacier.

vious polar explorers. "I do not intend to sacrifice the scientific utility of the expedition to a mere record-breaking journey," he told the Royal Geographical Society, "but say frankly, all the same, that one of my great efforts will be to reach the Southern Geographical Pole."

Shackleton believed that ponies would do better than dogs on the Ice Shelf. With four of them, four sledges, three companions, and provisions for 91 days he set out from Ross Island on October 29, 1908. Within a month they had passed Scott's farthest point south. By the time they got to the foot of a great glacier rising up toward the heart of the plateau—named by them the Beardmore Glacier in honor of one of the expedition's backers—all the ponies had died. Shackleton and his companions were now faced with the task of manhandling the sledges up the snow and ice—a back-breaking task that continued for 17 days.

On December 27 they reached the top of the high plateau, only 250 miles from the South Pole, which lay somewhere ahead in the white wilderness. They marched on, hauling their sledges for one more day—then another and another. Finally, on January 9, 1909, they realized that they would have to turn back if they were to have even a sporting chance of survival. They had reached 88°23's.—only about 100 miles from the Pole. Now they were faced with the long march back—on scanty rations, and weakened by dysentery. All four survived the nightmare journey back to McMurdo Sound—but only just.

Shackleton's great achievement confirmed that the Pole was now attainable by a determined, well-equipped expedition, and at the beginning of 1910 Scott was already preparing for his historic journey.

The Race to the Pole

The British Antarctic Expedition of 1910 sailed in the *Terra Nova* in midsummer. On board was a large team of scientists—a physicist, a geologist, biologists, zoologists, and a chemist, all of whom were to play their parts in Scott's ambitious plans. He was to set up his base on the shores of McMurdo Sound and then cruise eastward along the edge of the Ross Ice Shelf and land a second party to investigate the almost unknown King Edward VII Land. If possible, supply dumps would be put ashore at one or two intermediate points along the edge of the Ice Shelf, thus providing a link between the two parties, which would be separated by some 400 miles of icy wastes. The *Terra Nova* would then return to the western base and land more supplies.

During the winter, preparations would be made for an attack on the Pole.

Motor transport, ponies, and dogs were all to be used to get this southern party to the foot of the Beardmore Glacier. Beyond that, Scott estimated, they would probably be on their own—"it is only possible, certainly not probable, that any means of transport can be taken [up the glacier]," he had said before leaving Britain. But he believed dumps could be laid for a lot of the way along the route. Three four-man teams, pulling their own supplies, would climb the glacier, and one of them would make the final attack on the Pole.

In New Zealand, where the *Terra Nova* called on her way south, Scott received disturbing news. Roald Amundsen, the Norwegian explorer who had been planning an expedition to the North Pole and had been forestalled by Peary, had now switched his attention to the South Pole, and was preparing to sail to Antarctica in Nansen's old ship, the *Fram*. He sent Scott the following brief telegram: BEG LEAVE TO INFORM YOU PROCEEDING ANTARCTICA—AMUNDSEN.

By January 1911, Scott had set up his base on McMurdo Sound, and throughout the following months he and his men established a series of depots across the Ross Ice Shelf to the foot of the Beardmore Glacier. At the end of October the main southern party set off for the Pole—the plan being that ponies and dogs should help to get three four-man teams to the foot of the glacier, that here the dogs should be sent back and the ponies shot, and that the three teams should then haul their sledges for the 100-mile journey up to the plateau. Then, one team would try for the Pole. "So here," wrote Scott on October 31 as they set out, "end the entries in this diary with the first chapter of our History. The future is in the lap of the gods; I can think of nothing left undone to deserve success."

It took them 40 days to cross the Ice Shelf—from Corner Camp, which they left on November 1, past One Ton Depot, Mid Barrier Depot, and South Barrier Depot, to Lower Glacier Depot, which they reached on December 10. There was trouble with the motor sledges, and there were many blizzards that made the going worse than expected. "The snow which had fallen in the day remained soft and flocculent on the surface," Scott wrote on November 11. "Added to this we entered an area of soft crust between a few scattered hard sastrugi [ridges of wind-blown snow]. In pits between these places the snow lay in sandy heaps. A worse set of conditions for the ponies could scarcely be imagined."

On June 6, 1911, Scott (center, above) celebrated his 43rd, and last, birthday at McMurdo Sound base. As a relief from many months of hard work in the bitterly cold antarctic winter, members of the expedition (below) attend Ponting's lantern lecture on Japanese culture.

On December 10 the three parties set off up the glacier. Here Shackleton had found blue ice, which made for easy going; Scott and his men, however, had to make their way through soft snow. Sometimes they were able to use their skis, but elsewhere they and their sledges sank deeply into the snow, adding to the labor and difficulties of the work. By December 18 they were 4000 feet above the Shelf.

On December 21 they reached 8000 feet, and stopped at what they named Upper Glacier Depot. They were now almost at the summit of the plateau, and one of the four-man teams unloaded its supplies and the following day started on the journey back to the base. "We ought to get through," Scott noted in his diary.

The two remaining teams now struck due south across the plateau, and two nights later, December 24, treated themselves to a four-course Christmas Eve supper. "The first, pemmican, full whack, with slices of horse meat flavoured with onion and curry powder and thickened with biscuit; then an arrowroot, cocoa and biscuit hoosh, sweetened; then a plum pudding; then cocoa with raisins, and finally a dessert of caramels and ginger."

By January 3, 1912 the two teams had reached 87°32′s., less than 150 miles from the Pole, and Scott decided to reorganize his party. He also made a surprising decision. While Captain Edward Evans was due

Captain Lawrence Oates, who was to reach the Pole with Scott, inspects the party's team of Siberian ponies (above). Scott declined to use either ponies or dogs in his final assault on the Pole. Instead, the heavy sledge was hauled by members of the assault party (below)—an exhausting task that may have cost them their lives on the journey back.

to turn back here as planned, only two of his team were to go with him. Henry "Birdie" Bowers, Evans's other man, was to join Scott's four-man team and press on to the Pole with him. "The decision to take a fifth man was a surprise," Evans wrote later. "It gave more pulling power but it meant less food, and our organization—tents, rations, equipment—was built on a four-man basis. It took half an hour longer to cook for an extra man. Moreover, Bowers had left his skis at Third Degree Depot, and until they reached that point on the return journey he had to plod through the snow whilst the others were running on skis."

On January 4 Scott pushed on with his four companions—Dr. E. A. Wilson, chief of the scientific party (and a member of his previous expedition), Bowers, Lawrence Oates, who had been in charge of the ponies and the dogs, and Petty Officer E. Evans. "A last note from a hopeful position," Scott had written in his diary the previous evening. "I think it's going to be all right. We have a fine party going forward and arrangements are all going well."

By January 10 they were within 85 miles of the Pole but the going was worse than they had expected. The following night Scott noted that they had made 11 miles during the day and were now only 74 miles from the Pole. "Can we keep this up for seven days?" he added. "It takes it out of us like anything." In spite of the conditions, they covered 11 miles the next day and the same distance the next. By the night of the 15th they were only 27 miles from the Pole and Scott noted in his diary, "We *ought* to do it now." The following morning they started off in high spirits, covering seven and a half miles in the morning and knowing that if their pace held they would be at the Pole the following day.

That afternoon Bowers saw ahead what he at first thought was a cairn but then felt must be an unusual snow formation. "Half an hour later he detected a black speck ahead," Scott wrote. "Soon we knew that this could not be a natural snow feature. We marched on, found that it was a black flag tied to a sledge bearer; near by the remains of a camp; sledge tracks and ski tracks going and coming and the clear trace of dogs' paws—many dogs. This told us the whole story. The Norwegians had forestalled us and are first at the Pole. It is a terrible disappointment, and I am very sorry for my loyal companions."

The following day Scott reached the Pole, "but under very different circumstances from those expected." The psychological effect of Amundsen's suc-

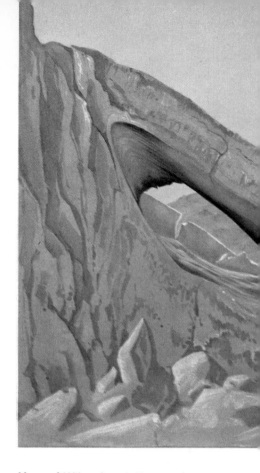

Many of Wilson's paintings and sketches caught vividly the drama and hostility of the polar scene. Above is his impression of a freak ice formation on the coast of Ross Island.

In the sketch below a member of a sledging party prepares to spend a night away from base. In the foreground his sledge is half buried by the gale-swept snow.

cess must have been immense, and is reflected in the entries Scott made in his diary on that day, January 17, 1912: "Great God! this is an awful place and terrible enough for us to have laboured to it without the reward of priority."

Amundsen had in fact reached the Pole a month earlier. He and his men had sailed south in Nansen's *Fram*, and set up base on the Bay of Whales, several hundred miles east of McMurdo Sound. Compared with Scott's expedition, which planned to carry out a lengthy program of scientific research and investigation, Amundsen's was a small affair whose efforts were concentrated on the one aim of reaching the Pole. He and his men had set out less than two weeks before Scott in three sledges drawn by a total of 52 dogs, 18 of which were killed when the party had reached the plateau.

The Norwegians faced conditions almost as bad as those of Scott's party, but their dog teams made their problems considerably less, and after no major difficulties, at three in the afternoon of December 14, the three sledge drivers simultaneously cried out "Halt." "They had carefully examined their sledge meters, and they all showed the full distance—our Pole by reckoning," wrote Amundsen. "The goal was reached, the journey ended. I cannot say—though I know it would sound much more effective—that the object of my life was attained. That would be romancing rather too barefacedly. I had better be honest and admit straight out that I have never known any man to be placed in such a diametrically opposite position to the goal of his desires as I was at that moment. The regions around the North Pole—well, yes, the North Pole itself—had attracted me from childhood, and here I was at the South Pole. Can anything more topsy-turvy be imagined?"

The five weather-beaten men planted the Norwegian flag, and then set about putting up their tent. "When we had got the tent up," Amundsen wrote, "Hanssen set about slaughtering Helge, and it was hard for him to have to part from his best friend. Helge had been an uncommonly useful and good-natured dog; without making any fuss he had pulled from morning to night, and had been a shining example to the team. But during the last week he had quite fallen away, and on our arrival at the Pole there was only a shadow of the old Helge left. He was only a drag on the others and did absolutely no work. One blow on the skull and Helge had ceased to live." The carcass was then portioned out among the other dogs and "within a couple of hours

there was nothing left of him but his teeth and the tuft at the end of his tail."

After sledging around the area the Norwegians estimated the exact position of the Pole, and the tent was put up again.

One of the three sledges had been unloaded and set upright in the snow. The party now reorganized their supplies and the next day set out on the return journey. It was as easy as Scott's was to be difficult, with ample food for both men and dogs.

On January 18 Scott and his companions had found Amundsen's tent. They built a cairn, raised the Union Jack, and then, with the help of a string pulled by Bowers, photographed themselves in a group. Then they set out—for "800 miles of solid dragging."

At first all went well. They picked up their earlier tracks, but in places these were already half covered by drifting snow. There were periods of bad weather and on January 23 they found that Evans was suffering from frostbite. The following day there came the first ominous note in Scott's diary—"things beginning to look a little serious."

That day there was a howling blizzard and Scott

Frostbite, exhaustion, and bitter disappointment at being beaten by Amundsen mark the faces of Scott's party in this photograph taken soon after they had discovered the Norwegians' tent at the Pole.

Thirty-five days before Scott, Amundsen's party (above) pose for a historic photograph at the South Pole on December 14, 1911. Favorable weather, and their leader's audacity and exceptional skill, won the great prize for the Norwegians.

The map below shows the routes followed by Amundsen, Scott, and Shackleton in their polar journeys.

····· Shackleton 1909 ▬▬ Amundsen 1911 ▬ ▬ ▬ Scott 1912

South Pole •

Queen Maud Range

Axel Heiberg Glacier

Beardmore Glacier

Queen Alexandria Range

Ross Ice Shelf

Bay of Whales

Ross I.

McMurdo Sound

added: "Is the weather breaking up? If so, God help us, with the tremendous journey and scant food." On January 28—"we are getting more hungry." In spite of this they were covering 20 miles a day.

By the second week in February, Evans's condition was bad, Wilson had a strained leg, and Scott had injured his shoulder during a fall. It was only on February 11 that their first serious setback occurred and "gave a horrible feeling of insecurity." They became involved in a maze of crevasses and broke through to easier ground only after about 12 hours of strenuous marching. They had similar trouble the next day; and on the night of the 12th had "one meal only remaining in the food bag." It was essential to reach the Mid Glacier Depot the following day. They reached it, but had only three and a half days' food in hand.

On February 14 Scott noted that they were becoming ever slower with their camping arrangements and that none of them was going strongly. On February 17 Evans collapsed and died, one day away from Lower Glacier Depot and its supplies of horsemeat.

For the next few days, with the food from the depot, things looked better. On February 24 they reached the South Barrier Depot and, with only 70 miles to the next depot, estimated that on their short rations they had food enough for 10 days.

But the position was more critical than these figures suggested. All four men were by now suffering from the effects of short rations and heavy sledging, and Wilson was having bad attacks of snow blindness. Their fate was now in the hands of the weather.

They reached the Mid Barrier Depot on March 1, but here they suffered three blows: There was less oil than they had expected; Oates announced that his feet were frostbitten; and, during the night, the weather began to worsen.

From now on the balance began to swing against the weak but still determined party. It became more and more difficult even to pull on their boots each morning. Oates, with frostbitten hands and feet, was unable to help with the sledge hauling. Food—what little there was of it—was warm rather than hot due to the shortage of fuel, and more than once they were confined to their tent by lashing wind and snow.

Oates pleaded to be left behind in his sleeping-bag, but the others insisted that he carry on as long as possible. Then, a few days later, at the height of a blizzard, Oates got up and said: "I am going outside and may be some time." He was never seen again.

On March 19 Scott reported in his diary that they

Scott, Wilson, and "Birdie" Bowers spent the last few days of their lives huddled in a small tent. The sketch (above) of three men in just such a tent was made by Wilson himself on his first journey to Antarctica in 1901-04.

were only 15 miles from One Ton Depot, and that they should be there in three days. But they now had only two days' food and barely a day's fuel, and all three men were suffering from severe frostbite.

On March 21 they were only 11 miles from safety—but a raging blizzard prevented further movement and kept them in their tents. On Friday, March 29, Scott made what was to be the last entry in his diary: "Since the 21st we have had a continuous gale from w.s.w. and s.w. We had fuel to make two cups of tea apiece and bare food for two days on the 20th. Every day we have been ready to start for our depot *11 miles away,* but outside the door of the tent it remains a scene of whirling drift. I do not think we can hope for any better things now. We shall stick it out to the end, but we are getting weaker, of course, and the end cannot be far. It seems a pity but I do not think I can write more—R. Scott." As a postscript, he added: "For God's sake look after our people."

The bodies of Scott, Wilson, and Bowers were found eight months later by a party that had set out from McMurdo Sound as soon as conditions allowed. Their tent had been pitched so well that it had withstood the buffetings of an unusually hard winter. Inside it were found Scott's diary, the photographs taken on the trek to the Pole, and the letters that he had written when he knew that they could not survive.

The fate of Scott and his four companions remains one of the classics of human drama. But it has tended, unjustly, to obscure the astonishing feat of Amundsen who, beaten by Peary in the Arctic, promptly sailed for the South Pole and conquered it at his first attempt. In assessing the problems of route and weather, Amundsen showed superior judgment to Scott; this, and his unsentimental attitude toward the use of dogs, enabled him to complete his task with a brilliance and economy of effort unexcelled in polar exploration.

With Scott's death, the "heroic" era of antarctic exploration ended. In 1914 the veteran Shackleton commanded a trans-antarctic expedition that sailed in the *Endurance* in an attempt—that failed—to cross the continent by land from the Weddell Sea on the Atlantic side to the Ross Sea on the Pacific side. After the ship had been crushed in the ice Shackleton made an epic small-boat journey of about 600 miles through gale-swept seas to bring help to his companions. But by this time the First World War had begun, and within a few years the techniques of radio and the art of flight had been so developed that the new polar exploration was very unlike the old.

The last entry in Scott's diary (left) is an astonishing example of courage in the face of certain and lonely death.

For nine months in 1915, Shackleton's ship *Endurance* (above and below) was ice-locked in the Weddell Sea and ground to matchwood. Marooned for several months on ice floes, the 27-man party at last drifted into open water, launched their boats, and reached a bleak island from which they were rescued in August 1916, after one of the most terrifying ordeals in antarctic exploration.

Modern Exploration of the Antarctic

During the years between the two World Wars, a number of expeditions went to Antarctica, traveling overland onto the central plateau, mapping further areas of the coast and gathering much valuable scientific information. But already the airplane was transforming the technique of exploration.

The Australian Sir Hubert Wilkins, who had been second-in-command of a British Imperial Antarctic Expedition in 1920-21 and the naturalist of the *Quest* expedition under Shackleton in 1921-22, made many flights with four Lockheed Vega aircraft in 1928 and 1929. In 1933 others under Wilkins's management were made by the American Lincoln Ellsworth.

But it was Commander Richard E. Byrd who revolutionized antarctic exploration by the use of aircraft during the 1920s and 1930s. Byrd served in the navy during the First World War. In 1925 he commanded the Naval Flying Unit of the MacMillan Arctic Expedition, and the following year (as we have seen) he flew with Floyd Bennett from Spitsbergen to the North Pole and back.

In 1929 Byrd made the first of many expeditions to the Antarctic, which by this time was estimated to have a coastline of about 13,000 miles, only some 4000 of which had been either discovered or explored. This was, as Byrd described it, "a continent greater than the combined areas of Mexico and the United States, more than half of whose coasts had never been seen, and whose desolate interior had felt only the hurrying feet of the parties under, or directed by, Shackleton, Mawson, Scott, and Amundsen, tracing relatively a few narrow paths in its infinite immensities."

Byrd chose as his base an area at the eastern end of the Ross Ice Shelf behind the Bay of Whales. Here, near the spot from which Amundsen had started on his successful journey 18 years earlier, Byrd founded Little America, as it later became known. And from this impressive base, with its huts and its radio towers, explorations were made for up to 250 miles into the interior, and led to the discovery of new mountains, new ranges, and the territory later called Marie Byrd Land. Many flights were made, during which vast territories, which had taken many days to sledge across, were photographed in a few minutes. Then, on November 29, Byrd set out for the Pole.

His plane, the *Floyd Bennett*, was a three-engined Ford metal monoplane with a total horsepower of just under 1000 and a top speed of 122 miles an hour. Its skis left the ground at 3:29 P.M. on November 29;

after a half-minute rush across the snow, four men were airborne for the first flight to the South Pole—Richard Byrd, Bernt Balchen (who was in charge of the expedition's aviation unit), Harold June, the radio operator, and Ashley McKinley, the photographer.

Byrd planned to follow the trail already marked by the expedition's geological party from the Ross Ice Shelf to the edge of the mainland—roughly the line that had been taken by Amundsen. Then—the most difficult stage of the flight—the plane had to be coaxed up some 8000 or 9000 feet as it followed the trail of the earlier explorers onto the high plateau. There were two alternative routes: one, by the Axel Heiberg Glacier which had been taken by Amundsen; the other, by the Liv Glacier, a little to the west. The possibility of getting the small, heavily laden plane "over the hump" depended on the weather conditions they would meet at the head of these glaciers.

Within a few hours the *Floyd Bennett* was above the geological party, "a cluster of little beetles about two dark-topped tents," and Byrd dropped overboard for them a parachute load of recent air photographs to help them in their work—a striking example of how times had changed. "A wing, pistons, and flashing propellers had taken the place of runners, dogs, and legs," he wrote. "Amundsen was delighted to make 25 miles per day. We had to make 90 miles an hour to accomplish our mission. We had the advantages of swiftness and comfort, but we had as well an enlarged fallibility. A flaw in a piece of steel, a bit of dirt in the fuel lines or carburetor jets, a few hours of strong head winds, fog or storm—these things, remotely beyond our control, could destroy our carefully laid plans and nullify our most determined efforts."

There was also "the hump." They chose the Liv Glacier and were soon flying up it. When their altimeters showed 9600 feet, they found it increasingly difficult to gain altitude. "We were still climbing, but at a rapidly diminishing speed." It was soon clear that it would be touch and go when it came to breasting the little col where the glacier gave onto the plateau.

Then came the first decision—a 250-pound bag of food was jettisoned to lighten the load. The *Floyd Bennett* rose sharply. But a few minutes later her nose was still only level with the head of the pass, which she was now approaching. Another bag of food went over —250 pounds, enough to feed four men for a month. This did the trick and they were "over the hump" with 500 feet to spare. The Pole now lay dead ahead over the horizon, less than 300 miles away.

In 1926 the American Commander Richard Byrd flew over the North Pole and, three years later, over the South Pole—in each case the first man to do so.

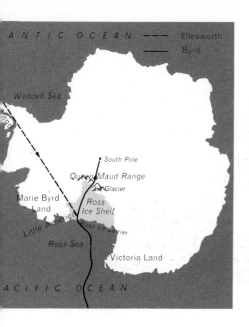

The map shows the route of Byrd's flight to the South Pole, and of Lincoln Ellsworth's flight from Dundee Island (off Graham Land) to the Bay of Whales in 1935.

The Liv Glacier (left) provided the greatest test for Byrd's plane, the *Floyd Bennett* (above) on its flight to the South Pole. Byrd was forced to jettison 500 pounds of food supplies before he could coax the little monoplane over the top of the 10,000-foot glacier.

They flew on across the huge white wilderness, their only worry the possibility of bad weather that at one point appeared to be looming over the horizon. Then, at 1:14 A.M., their calculations showed that they were over the Pole.

Byrd dropped the American flag; then, in honor of the great contest 18 years previously, the British and Norwegian flags. "There was nothing now to mark that scene; only a white desolation and solitude disturbed by the sound of our engines," he wrote. "The Pole lay in the center of a limitless plain. That, in brief, is all there is to tell about the South Pole. One gets there, and that is all there is for the telling. It is the effort to get there that counts."

Byrd's flight, a total distance of 1700 miles, was merely the high spot of a long series of probes made by him and his companions into and across the still unknown continent. In 1933 Byrd returned to the Antarctic, one purpose of his expedition being to set up a base deep in the interior to gather meteorological data during the long winter. Byrd himself manned this station alone for five long months, radioing weather data to the main base. His expeditions added vastly to man's knowledge of the Antarctic; they also underlined the value of modern aircraft in surveying the great white south and in bringing supplies to parties which would otherwise be isolated.

It was the successful results of Byrd's two expeditions that induced the United States to form the U.S. Antarctic Service under his command in 1939.

This American project was planned to last for a minimum of five years but was interrupted by the outbreak of the Second World War. By this time, however, Byrd was already deep in a vigorous scientific program that was being carried out from two separate bases, one on Stonington Island and the other on a new Little America—Little America III—again sited in the Bay of Whales.

It was the experience gained here by Byrd and his companions that led to the greatly enlarged scale of postwar antarctic exploration, typified by Operation Highjump, a United States Naval expedition which Byrd commanded in 1946-47. This expedition was the largest that had ever come to the Antarctic, and in planning and execution it set the pattern for many that followed it. With 4700 men, 13 ships—including an aircraft carrier and a submarine—and 23 aircraft, Operation Highjump brought to the south all the technological improvements that had been developed during the war—radar and mechanical transport of the

The helicopter above symbolizes the great variety of communication and research tools that are transforming antarctic exploration today. Though much of its surface has been explored, the continent still offers great opportunities to researchers in geology, glaciology, and meteorology.

latest kinds, long-range weather reports, and a huge stock of scientific equipment. When the Bay of Whales froze, for instance—an event that would have disrupted earlier expeditions—a 10,000-horsepower ice-breaker was sent in to smash millions of tons of ice in a few days.

During the years that followed, many other expeditions made spectacular use of new equipment. On the Norwegian-British-Swedish expedition of 1954, for instance, one member of the team traveled 300 miles inland on equipment drawn by a "weasel"—a mechanical vehicle specially adapted to moving over snow—and did so at the rate of 100 miles a day. Aircraft surveyed 100,000 square miles in a few days, while a vast stretch of coast was surveyed by ship-borne radar in a couple of days. Radio kept the expedition in constant touch with whaling fleets to the north, so that if there had been a shortage of supplies it would have been possible to "ring up for more." And by using radiotelephones the Swedes were able to talk directly to their families at home.

By the early 1950s most of the physical difficulties of exploring Antarctica had been overcome, and the gaps in its geography were being rapidly filled in by aerial photographic surveys.

The largest expedition yet sent to the Antarctic was Operation Highjump mounted by the United States in 1946-47, which brought 4700 men, 13 ships, and 23 aircraft to the Ross Sea and other areas. The work was concerned mainly with photographic reconnaissance and weather research—as with this meteorological balloon used to determine wind speed and direction at high altitudes.

In April 1950, Dr. L. V. Berkner of the United States suggested that the prospects of making useful scientific investigations were now so good that another International Polar Year should be held. The first had been in 1882-83, and the second in 1932-33. The plan was encouraged by the International Council of Scientific Unions and by 1952 a far bolder scheme had been proposed. This was to hold an International Geophysical Year to begin in July 1957 and extend for a period of 18 months. During this time, observations would be made on a world-wide basis. It was out of this scheme that there came two events that put the seal on antarctic exploration—the setting up by the Americans of a base at the South Pole itself, and the first crossing of the continent by the Commonwealth Transantarctic Expedition under Dr. Vivian Fuchs.

Seventeen nations took part in the International Geophysical Year and set up stations on the coast of Antarctica and in the interior. The biggest of the operations that planned, built, and worked these stations was Operation Deepfreeze, run by the United States Navy, which sent 1800 men to the south in icebreakers, tankers, landplanes, and helicopters.

With Rear Admiral George Dufek in charge of the naval force and Admiral Byrd in charge of the United States antarctic program, bases were set up once again at Little America and on McMurdo Sound beneath Mount Erebus, as well as on the Weddell Sea on the far side of the continent. Then, by airlifting building materials and equipment from McMurdo Sound, they established a 16-man base at the South Pole itself.

On McMurdo Sound, 35 major buildings were put up. The washrooms for these buildings were larger than had been Scott's solitary hut on the same site. Hundred-kilowatt generators helped to supply power, fuel was pumped ashore through rubber pipelines five miles long, and special equipment was used to construct aircraft runways. Helicopters were used for dropping and supplying survey parties, while on one occasion an aircraft, with its bird's-eye view of the terrain, was able to drop trail flags for about 100 miles, enabling a ground party to avoid the worst crevasses.

The Russians also set up a number of stations that they established with the aid of airlifts and snow tractors in remote regions of the high central plateau. In 1960 at their Vostok station they measured the lowest temperature ever recorded on the plateau—it was 159° below the freezing point of fresh water!

The advance party of the Commonwealth Transantarctic Expedition, aboard the *Theron*, arrived at

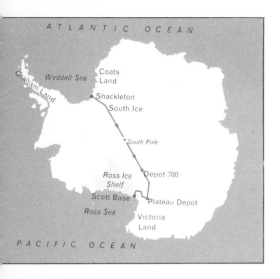

One of the highlights of the International Geophysical Year in 1957-58 was the crossing of the continent by the Commonwealth Transantarctic Expedition, whose route is shown above.

Dr. Vivian Fuchs's party camp on their journey to the South Pole. This, the larger of the two Commonwealth teams, carried out a large scientific program en route.

Shackleton, their new base on the Weddell Sea, late in 1955. As ice threatened to lock her in, the *Theron* left the base as soon as the men and supplies were unloaded. Bad weather swept away many of the stores and the eight members of the party spent nearly all of their first winter under canvas, using a 21-foot packing case as a messroom! In spite of their ordeal they set up a scientific station, known as South Ice, 300 miles inland.

The main party, which arrived in Antarctica in January 1957, was divided into two teams, which were to set out from opposite sides of the continent. Vivian Fuchs, the English leader of the expedition, was to establish his base at Shackleton, while Sir Edmund Hillary (the New Zealander who in 1953 had climbed Mount Everest) would set up Scott Base 2158 miles away on McMurdo Sound. The plan was for the two teams to meet at the American base at the Pole and then for Fuchs's team to continue to Scott Base.

While Hillary was establishing his base during early 1957, a sledge party set off from McMurdo Sound, reached the inland plateau, and built Plateau Depot, which was then stocked by airlift. Later in the year Hillary set out with weasels and sno-cats (tracked vehicles), passed Plateau Depot, and by December 15 had reached Depot 700 (also stocked by airlift), which was only 500 miles from the Pole. From here he continued his journey with four companions and reached the South Pole on January 4, 1958. He was then flown back to McMurdo Sound. Their trek had been

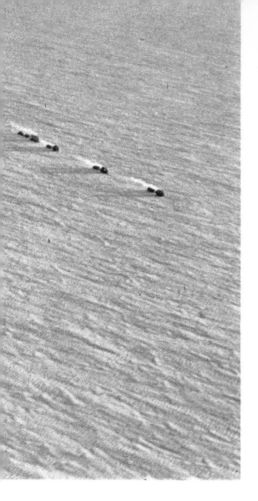

Fuchs's fleet of sno-cats (above) leaves Shackleton Base, on the Weddell Sea, at the start of its long trek to the Pole.

Below: Meeting at the Pole. Sir Edmund Hillary, who had flown from Scott Base, is flanked by Fuchs (right) and Rear Admiral George Dufek, commander of the United States naval force in the Antarctic.

completed swiftly and with remarkably few incidents —in stark contrast with Scott's terrible journey in this region of Antarctica 46 years before.

Meanwhile on November 24, Fuchs and his team had set out from South Ice with four sno-cats, three weasels, and a tractor. They carried much scientific apparatus, special aluminum equipment for bridging crevasses, and were constantly in touch by radio with their base and the Pole station. Nonetheless, the going was difficult and dangerous and their progress was slowed by the need to make scientific observations. They completed the first part of their journey—over 900 miles—in just under two months, arriving at the Pole on January 19. Here they were met by Hillary, Admiral Dufek, and several newspapermen who had flown up for the day from Scott Base.

The longest and most difficult part of the journey still lay before Fuchs and his men. The distance from the Pole to Scott Base was more than 1200 miles, the first 500 of which—to Depot 700—were through cruelly inhospitable territory. They arrived at the depot without any serious accidents, however, and were joined by Hillary, whose knowledge of the route to McMurdo Sound helped them to make good time. Fuchs and his small fleet of vehicles drove into Scott Base on March 2. He had calculated that the journey from South Ice would take 100 days; he was slightly ahead of schedule—it had taken 99. The many seismic soundings made by Fuchs (about every 30 miles) showed that the thickness of the ice along his route varied from about 2000 to 6000 feet.

The vast amount of scientific knowledge acquired in the Antarctic during the International Geophysical Year was not won without danger or hardship. But it was danger and hardship different from that which men faced only half a century earlier. In spite of the many modern expeditions to Antarctica, much still remains to be done in the way of surveying and mapping the great hump of ice and the land hidden beneath it. It would be unwise to claim that explorers of the 20th century have "conquered" this vast region. Clearly they have not, but perhaps the way has been paved for doing so one day. In 1959 the governments that took part in the International Geophysical Year drew up a unique treaty, one that defines Antarctica as a special domain for scientific research. In part it reads: "It is in the interest of all mankind that Antarctica shall continue forever to be used exclusively for peaceful purposes and shall not become the scene or object of international discord."

5 Sand and Sun

As we have seen, the jungle and forest regions of the world attracted men for a variety of reasons—mainly the desire to colonize and exploit commercially the new-found territories, and to convert their peoples to Christianity. The deserts have attracted explorers for quite different reasons. Men first crossed these huge, empty wastes for the same reason that they voyaged across uncharted seas—to discover what lay beyond. Desert and ocean travel, in fact, have much in common. The desert caravans that from time immemorial have traversed most of these oceans of sand can be likened to convoys of ships. The oases in the parched wastes are rather like islands at which vessels can take on fresh supplies—mainly water in the case of desert travelers.

The great deserts of the world lie in two belts, one north and one south of the equator. The northern and more important belt contains the great Sahara and the Libyan and Nubian deserts of North Africa, then continues eastward across the peninsula of Arabia, through Persia and Turkistan, and onward to the Gobi and the other huge deserts of central Asia. On the eastern side of the Pacific the belt continues as the deserts of Nevada and Arizona. The southern belt—less impressive since there is less land at this latitude—includes the Kalahari Desert of South Africa, the deserts of central Australia, and the smaller ones of South America.

Some of the deserts, like the Sahara, are low-lying or are even in depressions below sea level. Others, such as the deserts of central Asia, lie at an altitude of many thousands of feet. Some are rocky and mountainous in character; others are relatively flat, consisting merely of vast, uninterrupted plains of sand. All have certain things in common, however. First is

A caravan of traders arrives at a small oasis for water and a few hours of rest. Hundreds of years ago, men like these became the first desert explorers when they crossed the central Asian and Sahara deserts in search of new markets for trade. Many of their original routes are still the main highways across these vast and inhospitable regions.

the lack of rainfall, which makes travelers dependent either on the water they can carry or on the oases. Second, the absence of moisture on the ground and the low humidity of the air help to produce extreme variations in temperature. By day the desert can be searingly hot, with a ground temperature as high as 150° F.; but at night the sand rapidly loses its heat and temperatures may drop to below freezing point.

The Central Asian Deserts

One of the largest and most inaccessible desert areas stretches eastward for more than 2000 miles from the Hindu Kush and the Pamirs, the high knots of mountains that rise just beyond the northernmost point of India. At its western end, the desert is only between 300 and 400 miles across, bounded on the north by the Tien Shan mountains and on the south by the edge of the great Tibetan plateau. Much of this area, known today as Sinkiang, consists of the huge Takla Makan Desert; while on the northeastern side of the Tien Shan the sandy wastes are continued by the Dzungaria Desert. Roughly 1000 miles to the east of the Pamirs the Tien Shan peters out and the desert land broadens until it meets the Altai Mountains farther north. Much of the country from here to Peking—the northern area in Mongolia and the southern in China—is filled by the Gobi Desert, the last great obstacle guarding the lowlands of China and the Pacific coast.

It was in a camel caravan much like the one above—from a medieval Persian manuscript—that Anthony Jenkinson attempted to reach fabled "Cathay" (China) in 1558.

Below: Map of routes followed by Francis Younghusband, Sven Hedin, and Sir Aurel Stein in central Asia.

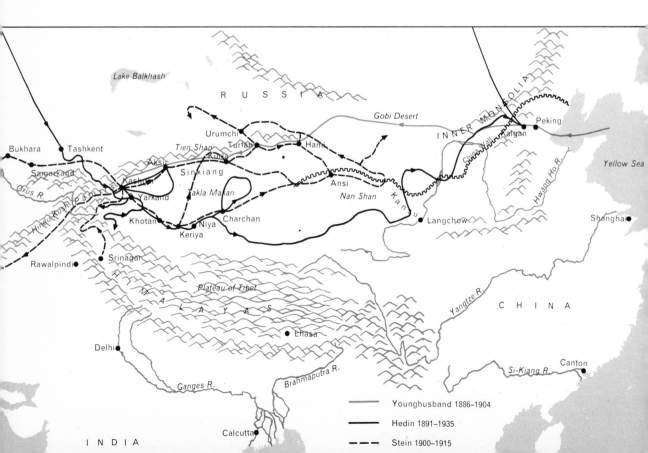

———— Younghusband 1886–1904

———— Hedin 1891–1935

– – – – Stein 1900–1915

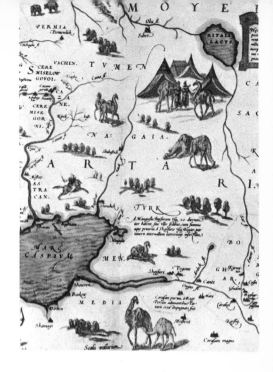

Not all of this immense area is parched and unrelieved desert. There are occasional rivers, lakes, and large tracts of rough steppe land on which nomads scrape a meager living. Over the centuries changes in the geography of central Asia have caused rivers to alter course or dry up and have even altered the position of lakes such as Lop Nor in Sinkiang. In the dry desert atmosphere valuable relics of the ancient past have been preserved; as a result the whole of this area has attracted adventurous archaeologist-explorers.

Marco Polo was one of the first Europeans to cross these wastes to China and bring back detailed accounts of what he saw. About 300 years later a remarkable attempt to reach "Cathay" was made by an English trader, Anthony Jenkinson, who set out from Moscow with his two companions, Richard and Robert Johnson, on April 23, 1558. They sailed down the Moskva and the Volga rivers to Astrakhan. Here they took ship across the northern corner of the Caspian, landed on its eastern shore, and in September set out eastward in a huge caravan of 1000 camels.

Five days out in the desert the caravan was stopped by Tartar horsemen who demanded a levy for their master. Most of the company paid, but Jenkinson insisted on being taken to the "Prince" who "lived in the fields without Castle or towne . . . in a little rounde house made of reedes covered without with felt, and within with Carpets." Jenkinson was treated well, and together with his companions allowed to go on his way. "So having leave I departed and overtooke our Caravan, and proceeded on our journey, and travailed 20 days in the wilderness from the sea side without seeing towne or habitation, carrying provision of victuals with us for the same time, and driven by necessitie to eate one of my camels and a horse. . . ."

At Bukhara, Jenkinson's way was barred by what is now called the Alayskiy Khrebet range, but he and his companions returned home with stories of how from Bukhara merchants went in 30 days to "Cashar" —Kashgar—and how another 30 weeks' journey across great deserts would bring them to Cathay, "which they praise to be civil and unspeakably rich."

The first Europeans since Marco Polo to investigate this area in any detail were Jesuit fathers, who from the 17th to the early 19th centuries traveled either westward from Peking, where they had established missions, or eastward from India, over the Himalayas and across the deserts to China. One of the first was Matteo Ricci, who arrived at the Chinese court in Peking in 1598. He and his companions were allowed to survey the

Part of the map of Russia made by Anthony Jenkinson in 1562 after his return to England.

Matteo Ricci (below, left) was one of the first of many Jesuit fathers who explored and established missions in China and India in the 17th to 19th centuries.

country, and within a century they and their successors had produced the first European maps of China.

One of the most remarkable journeys across the central Asian deserts was made in 1886 by Francis Younghusband, then a young British army officer. He had been sent first to India, and later to Peking where he heard that a Colonel M. S. Bell was planning to visit the city and then travel overland to India, by a desert route that had never been taken by a European. Younghusband was granted leave to join Bell, and then arranged with the colonel that they would travel by different routes across the great Gobi Desert. If possible they would meet on the far side and continue their journey together but, as it happened, they failed to make contact and traveled on by separate routes.

Younghusband set out on a camel from Peking on April 4, together with two companions. One was to act as interpreter, and the other as interpreter, cook, servant, and groom. "Nowhere in Peking," wrote Younghusband later, "had we been able to obtain information about the road across the desert. I had never been in a desert, and here were a thousand miles or so of one to be crossed. Nor had we any information of the state of the country on the other side."

In two weeks they reached the edge of the Gobi at the town of Kwei-hwa-cheng, and here Younghusband and his two companions met their first problem. Hami, their goal on the far side of the desert, lay some 70 or 80 days' march westward, and the people of the town were loath to provide camels or guides to so small a party making such a long journey. Eventually the matter was settled and Younghusband obtained five camels and a guide to take him across the desert.

Knowing little about the route from Peking to Hami, Younghusband (above, left, with his two companions) hired a guide for his journey across the Gobi Desert (right) in 1886.

But first they had to consult the Chinese calendar to discover an auspicious day for starting the journey. "The guide," Younghusband noted, "was very particular about this, as he said it would never do to start in a casual way on a journey like this."

Finally, on the morning of April 26, the little caravan set out from the north gate of the town. There were eight camels in all, one ridden by Younghusband, four others carrying his baggage and over half a ton of stores. The other three carried water, brick tea (for use as money), and the men's baggage.

Within two weeks they were well into the Gobi Desert. The country rapidly became more barren, streams disappeared, and water could be obtained only from the rough wells or water holes dug by former caravans. "No grass could be seen, and in its place the country was covered with dry and stunted plants, burnt brown by the sun by day and nipped by the frost by night. Not a sound could be heard and scarcely a living thing seen as we plodded along slowly, yet steadily, over those seemingly interminable plains," wrote Younghusband later.

Each day the little group began their journey at three in the afternoon to escape the worst of the heat and traveled until midnight. In the evening "the stars would appear one by one, and through the long dark hours we would go silently on, often finding our way by the aid of the stars alone, and marking each as it sank below the horizon, indicating how far the night was advanced."

The ground and the atmosphere were as dry as a bone so that their belongings became charged with static electricity, and "in opening a sheep-skin coat or a blanket a loud cracking noise would be given out, accompanied by a sheet of fire." Toward the end of June they reached the worst part of their journey, the crossing of the eastern end of the desert of Dzungaria. "Nothing we have passed hitherto can compare with it—a succession of gravel ranges without any sign of life, animal or vegetable, and not a drop of water. We were gradually descending to a very low level, the sun was getting higher and higher, and the wind hotter and hotter, until I shrank from it as from the blast of a furnace."

At last, after a march of 28 hours in which they covered about 70 miles, they reached an oasis. The most easterly section of the Tien Shan now lay before them—country that varied, sometimes within a few miles, from stretches of pure desert to areas of rough vegetation and occasional streams.

Sven Hedin, the Swedish explorer, covered thousands of miles in little-known areas of central Asia between the 1890s and 1930s. Four of his many hundreds of sketches and paintings appear on these pages.

A village market near Khotan

Onset of a storm in northern Tibet

On July 24, after crossing the Tien Shan at a height of 8000 feet, Younghusband and his companions rode into the town of Hami. "My desert journey was now over," he wrote, "and I had accomplished the 1255 miles from Kwei-hwa-cheng in just seventy days; in the last week of which I had travelled 224 miles, including the crossing of the Tien Shan mountains."

Younghusband still had far to go, however. First he rode 900 miles westward through the Takla Makan Desert and on to the city of Yarkand. Then, continuing west into the Pamirs, he became the first European to cross the Muztagh Pass. Now he made his way south, skirted the Karakorams, crossed the Indus River and continued south to Srinagar. A few weeks later he rejoined his regiment at Rawalpindi in what is now northern Pakistan.

The crossing of central Asia from Peking to Kashgar was one of the greatest exploratory ventures of its time, and was the first of many that Younghusband made at the end of the last century, mostly in the complex mountain tangle of the Pamirs. The great desert areas of Sinkiang, Turkistan, and Mongolia are so vast, however, that even after Younghusband's journeys they continued to challenge the courage and ability of explorers for many years.

Two such men whose paths in central Asia were to cross for nearly 50 years were Sven Hedin and Sir Aurel Stein. Hedin, a Swede born in 1865, and one of the most brilliant explorers of his time, had been fired by an ambition to venture into unknown territories since early boyhood. His first chance came in 1885 when he was asked to work as a tutor for six months in Baku, on the Caspian Sea. This gave Hedin his first sight of the Caucasus and of the peoples of the East. It also gave him the chance to learn the Tartar and Persian languages. So he was well equipped when, with his wages sewn into a belt, he set off for an adventurous journey on horseback through the heart of Persia.

About four years later, in 1890, Hedin became interpreter at the Swedish Embassy in Constantinople. The following year he visited Bukhara and Kashgar,

Temple Buddha in Inner Mongolia

Mongolian beggar

and crossed the Tien Shan. When he returned home to Sweden he had served his apprenticeship in Asian travel and was, as he wrote, "burning with desire once more to take the road of wild adventure."

Hedin's first major expedition began at the end of 1893. It was to last three and a half years, during which time he traveled a distance greater than that from Pole to Pole. Quite early in the expedition Hedin nearly died. He had set out from Merket (northeast of Yarkand) on April 10, 1894, with four companions and eight camels. His immediate target was the Khotan River, about 175 miles farther east in the center of the Takla Makan Desert—a journey Hedin hoped would take about a month. The camels were heavily laden with food, 455 liters of water, three rifles, six revolvers, two heavy ammunition boxes, scientific equipment, books, three cameras, and about 1000 photographic plates.

On April 22 they reached the last-known water on their route and the following day struck eastward across the desert. "There was nothing now but fine yellow sand," Hedin wrote. "As far as the eye could reach only high dunes, quite bare of vegetation, were visible. Strange that I should not be amazed at this sight, and that it did not make me halt."

On the 24th he found that their water tanks had been only partly filled at the last supply point. Even though the water had to be severely rationed, Hedin refused to turn back.

A few days later they decided to dig for water and recklessly drank most of what remained in their tanks. Then came the horrifying discovery that there was no water to be found beneath the sand. "Our entire [remaining] supply was less than a tenth of what a camel would need to drink its fill," Hedin wrote.

Two of the camels had to be abandoned, and then on April 28, to add to their misery, a sand storm broke over the caravan. "Even at noon the darkness was more pronounced than at dusk. It was like marching at night. The air was filled with opaque clouds of drift-sand. Only the nearest camel was dimly visible, like a shadow in this otherwise impervious mist.

A sand storm enveloped Hedin and his party in the depths of the Takla Makan desert in April 1894. Four days after this, two of Hedin's companions died of thirst only a few miles short of the Khotan River.

Shouts could not be heard [above the wind]. Only the deafening roar of the storm filled our ears."

After the wind had died down they killed one of their chickens and drank its blood, then a sheep. But one by one men and camels were unable to go on. Eventually only Hedin and two others had the strength to crawl to the top of a sand dune, from which they could see on the horizon an "absolutely even, dark green line." They were in sight of the poplars on the Khotan River.

Hedin's escape from the sands of the Takla Makan was the prelude to three years of adventure during which he crisscrossed Asia on journeys to Tibet, across the Gobi, and into the Pamirs. He discovered cities that had been lost and covered by the desert sands for 2000 years, surveyed hundreds of square miles, and helped to trace the course of many unmapped rivers and hill ranges.

Hedin returned in triumph to Stockholm in May 1897 and geographers throughout Europe paid tribute to his work. Yet his travels were to continue for another 40 years. In the summer of 1899 he set out once more for central Asia, then again in 1906 and in 1908. At the age of 62 he organized and led a large Sino-Swedish expedition to Inner Mongolia, western Kansu, and Sinkiang. Then in 1933, when he was 68, he put his immense knowledge at the service of the Chinese government and made a three-year survey of the ancient silk-trade route across the heart of central Asia.

Sir Aurel Stein was a very different kind of man—shy, unassuming, and a distinguished scholar. Born in Budapest in 1862, he went to England to complete his studies, and became much influenced by the orientalist and soldier Sir Henry Rawlinson, and by Sir Henry Yule, then the greatest living expert on the travels of

Sir Aurel Stein devoted much of his life to exploring ancient communities buried beneath the desert sands of central Asia. The relics on this page he found in the Sinkiang region. Top: Painted panel from a ruined dwelling near Khotan. Bottom: Clay monster found in a cemetery near Turfan in the Tien Shan.

Marco Polo. Stein was intrigued not only by stories of the great deserts of central Asia, but also by the knowledge that their sands covered the relics of great civilizations that had risen and fallen many centuries before.

In 1888 Stein took a job at the Punjab University in Lahore. He worked for 12 years, first there and later in Calcutta, spending his vacations in archaeological exploration along the frontiers of India. Then in the spring of 1900 he set out on the first of his many great expeditions.

On this journey Stein traveled over the Pamirs to Kashgar, on to the town of Khotan, and then along the southern fringe of the Takla Makan Desert where Hedin had so nearly perished. In these areas Indian, Chinese, and Hellenistic cultures had mixed for nearly 1000 years, and he found hundreds of ancient tablets and Buddhist manuscripts. Throughout the Takla Makan Desert, Stein confirmed, there had once been thriving towns and villages, watered by rivers that had dried up over the centuries. He visited many of the abandoned sites and brought back or photographed a large number of manuscripts and paintings.

Stein's greatest discovery came in 1907. He had set out the year before from Chitral, crossed the Hindu Kush, forded the Oxus—dipping his hand in it "as a pious salute to a great river, touched at last after many years' waiting"—and reached Khotan. Continuing eastward for hundreds of miles, he found important ruins as far as 100 miles from drinkable water—an indication of how the geography of the region had changed during the passing centuries. Still farther east, he found himself, as he later put it, "rewarded by a big and fascinating task after my own heart." This was the discovery of the westernmost portion of the Great Wall of China, which nearly 2000 years earlier had protected the lands of the Chinese from the raids of the Huns.

Many archaeologists knew that the wall had existed and that it might be possible to trace its ancient course. But little was known about it until the day Stein saw, in the desert distance before him, the unmistakable ruins of a watchtower. "It rose in a solid mass of brickwork, about fifteen feet square, to a height of some twenty-three feet," he wrote.

After clearing away sand that had drifted around the tower, he and his men found the remains of a regular wall made of reed bundles set on a mixture of clay and gravel. There was still no clue to the age of the wall, but then came a lucky find. Within the reed

This 5th-century wall painting was found in the Caves of a Thousand Buddhas, a storehouse of ancient Chinese culture that was Stein's most celebrated discovery.

Stein's excavations at Niya, east of Khotan, revealed this room in an ancient ruined dwelling.

bundles the explorers found a bunch of coarse fabric, several pieces of silk, and a piece of wood bearing five Chinese characters. The letters meant "the clothes bag of one called Lu Ting-shih." Later research proved that these materials came from the Han period, about 2000 years ago.

Stein and his little party followed the wall for 200 miles to the east, gathering valuable relics from the ruined fortifications. Then they came to the "Caves of the Thousand Buddhas." Here, to the southeast of the town of Tun-huang, were a large number of sacred Buddhist grottoes. It seemed to Stein that they might yield material of great archaeological interest; just how great he did not suspect as he rode out of Tun-huang and caught his first sight of the cliffs in which the grottoes lay. "A multitude of dark cavities, mostly small, was seen here," he later wrote, "honeycombing the sombre rock faces in irregular tiers from the foot

A Buddhist prayer, the *Diamond Sutra,* was another discovery of Stein's in the Caves of a Thousand Buddhas. Made in A.D. 868, it is the world's oldest-known printed book.

of the cliff, where the stream almost washed them, to the top of the precipice. Here and there flights of steps connecting the grottoes showed on the cliff face."

All these grottoes had been shrines, and they still had their guardians. Earlier, someone had discovered a vast collection of manuscripts in a number of the grottoes. A few had been inspected but had been put back with the rest, which had then been sealed up in a small chapel in one of the caves. Stein was determined to see this priceless collection. After much persuasion the guardians escorted him to the store of hidden manuscripts and he was allowed to inspect them. It was obvious that they were of great age. Among the manuscripts were paintings on fine silk and on linen as well as long scrolls of parchment. Here was a vast library of the ancient world from which a picture of the Chinese past could be built up.

When Stein and his caravan left Tun-huang they carried with them 24 cases packed with manuscript treasures and five more filled with paintings and other art relics. Four months later he returned—and was allowed to take away another 200 bundles. In all, there were more than 9000 Chinese manuscripts—many of them now in the British Museum, London.

Stein's success was only the first of many. During the next 25 years he made several more journeys—some lasting for two or three years—through the central Asian deserts, each producing a rich harvest of archaeological treasures.

Also found in the cave was a paper scroll (below) with drawings of arms and hands in mystic poses.

The Arabian Deserts

Until a few years ago there were still large tracts of Arabia that were unknown to European explorers. At the heart of this huge peninsula lies a great area of true desert. Although caravans have crossed its northern portions since ancient times, the southern half—sparsely peopled by nomadic tribes—was not crossed by western explorers until this century.

Bounded on the north by the mountains of Syria and the plains of Iraq, Arabia stretches southeastward for some 1800 miles; it is about 700 miles across at its northern extremity and widens to over 1200 miles toward the south. Behind Arabia's Red Sea coast rises a narrow mountain range reaching to a height of 7000 feet in the south. To the east of the mountains the land slopes down from the central tableland to the shores of the Persian Gulf. In the extreme southeast mountains rise again to nearly 10,000 feet in the peaks of Oman. The great desert area in the center of the subcontinent is called the Nejd. To the southeast is Rubal Khali—the great "Empty Quarter."

--- ---	Niebuhr 1761–3
··········	Burckhardt 1812–15
———	Burton 1853–77
·—·—·	Doughty 1875–78
– – –	Philby 1917–36
··········	Thomas 1928–31
———	Thesiger 1934–50

This map of the Arabian subcontinent shows the routes of its principal European explorers.

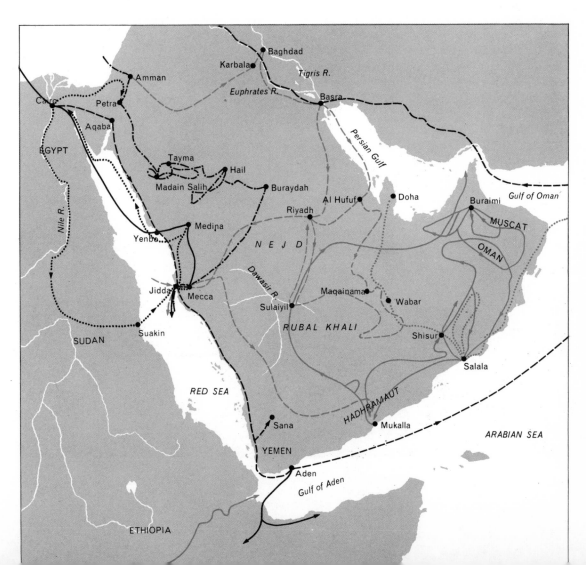

Two factors combined to discourage western travelers from exploring and surveying this huge peninsula. One was the terrain itself and the hazards of its sand seas. The second was the fact that the ancient city of Mecca was the center of Islam, and both the city and its surrounding regions were barred to "infidels."

It was in the middle of the 18th century that the first party of European explorers made a serious attempt to probe the secrets of Arabia. The journey was sponsored by King Frederick V of Denmark, and its purpose was to explore the Yemen (in southwest Arabia) and to discover, if possible, something about the rest of the subcontinent. Of the party of five men who set out, only one—Carsten Niebuhr, a soldier and surveyor—survived; the rest died of various diseases in the course of the journey. The travelers were well received at the port of Jidda, and continued down the Red Sea coast to the Yemen. From here they traveled about 100 miles inland to Sana, a town 7000 feet up in the mountains, where they were received in state by the *imam*, or local ruler. "The Imam sat upon the throne between cushions, with his legs crossed in the eastern fashion, his gown was of a bright green colour, and had large sleeves," Niebuhr observed. "On each side of his breast was a rich filleting of gold lace, and on his head he wore a great white turban. We were first led up to the Imam, and were allowed to kiss both the back and the palm of his hand, as well as the hem of his robe. It is an extraordinary favour when the

Carsten Niebuhr was the only one of a party of five Danish explorers to survive a journey to Arabia in 1761. Above: Niebuhr receives an audience with the imam of Sana, in the Yemen.

Below: Niebuhr's sketch of soldiers exercising in a palace yard.

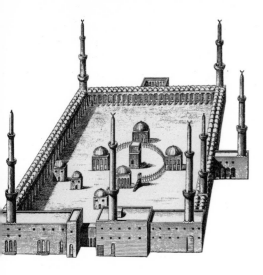

Niebuhr's journal included this drawing (above) of the great mosque at Mecca. The small building in the center houses the Black Stone, most sacred emblem of Islam.

The Swiss explorer John Burckhardt traveled widely in the deserts fringing northern Arabia during the early 1800s and was the first European to visit the ancient city of Petra (below) in modern Jordan.

Mahometan princes permit any person to kiss the palm of the hand."

Niebuhr sailed to India and returned to Europe by landing at Oman and traveling up the Persian Gulf. When he arrived in Denmark, he brought with him not only his own notes, but those of his companions who had died; and the journal he wrote later provided the Western world with its first detailed description of southwestern Arabia.

Another 50 years were to pass before Western knowledge of Arabia was much increased. The explorer responsible was a Swiss, John Burckhardt, born in Lausanne in 1784. In 1806 Burckhardt was employed by the African Association to explore Africa. He learned Arabic and in 1809 left for Malta on the first stage of several remarkable journeys. In Malta he changed into oriental dress, sailed for Aleppo (in Syria), and spent two years wandering across the northern deserts. During this period he became the first European to see Petra (in modern Jordan)—the "rose-red city—'half as old as Time'!"—a great stronghold of ancient times but by Burckhardt's day a city of rock ruins. During these years, and like others who followed him into this desert country, he gradually assumed the character of a Bedouin Arab.

In the 1850s, Arabian exploration was dominated by the colorful exploits of Richard Burton—orientalist, adventurer, and, as he styled himself, "the last swordsman of Europe." Like many other travelers in Arabia, Burton was greatly affected by the romance and

Richard Burton (above) was more a romantic adventurer than explorer. Today he is best remembered for his translation of the *Thousand and One Nights*, from which this picture (below) of Scheherazade is taken.

"mystique" of the desert and its peoples. Apart from his translation of *The Thousand and One Nights* it is mainly for the journey described in his *Pilgrimage to Al-Medinah and Meccah* that Burton is remembered today.

His original idea was to make a crossing of the Empty Quarter from east to west. By the time he set out for Arabia he could already pass as a member of half a dozen Eastern cultures, and decided that he would first make the pilgrimage to Medina and Mecca. Disguised as an Arab, Burton traveled to Egypt and Suez, and then took ship to Yenbo, the Red Sea port from which the caravans set out for Medina.

At seven in the evening on July 18, 1853, he and his small party, including 12 camels walking in single file and tied head to tail, passed through the gate of Yenbo on the track to Medina. The complete caravan consisted of about 600 animals and was protected from marauding Bedouins by Turkish troops. On more than one occasion, however, shots were exchanged between the escort and raiding horsemen who hovered on the outskirts of the group. At night, the party unsaddled the camels, stacked their belongings in a circle, and slept on top of them—all, that is, except Burton himself. Offended by the snoring of his companions, he slept apart from the main group, with a drawn sword beside him and a cocked pistol under the saddlebag he used as a pillow.

Two days out from Yenbo, they entered "a country fantastic in its desolation—a mass of huge hills, barren plains, and desert vales. . . . The road wound among mountains, rocks and hills of granite, and over broken ground flanked by huge blocks and boulders piled up as if man's art had aided Nature to disfigure herself. Vast clefts seamed like scars the hideous face of the earth; here they widened into dark caves, there they were choked with glistening drift sand. Not a bird or a beast was to be seen or heard; their presence would have argued the presence of water; and, though my companions opined that Badawin [Bedouin-Arab nomads] were lurking among the rocks, I decided that these Badawin were the creatures of their fears. Above, a sky like polished blue steel, with a tremendous blaze of yellow light, glared upon us without the thinnest veil of mist cloud. Below, the brass-coloured circle scorched the face and dazzled the eyes, mocking them the while with offers of water that was but air. The distant prospect was more attractive than the near view, because it borrowed a bright azure tinge from the intervening atmosphere; but the jagged peaks and the perpendicular streaks of shadow down the flanks of the mountainous background showed that yet in store for us was no change for the better."

Burton and his party reached Medina and Mecca without much difficulty. At Mecca he performed all the rites and ceremonies of a devout Moslem, becoming a *hadji* for having completed his pilgrimage to the holy city.

Burton's account of his journey to Mecca increased interest in Arabia, and in the last 40 years of the 19th century many travelers added to Western man's knowledge of the desert and its peoples.

The greatest of these was Charles Montagu Doughty, who in 1875 settled in Damascus (Syria) to learn Arabic. He joined the annual pilgrim caravan to Mecca the next year, then left it to travel with a tribe of Bedouins in order to widen his knowledge of the desert and its peoples. For over two years he wandered across northern Arabia, visiting Madain Salih and Taymā, then traveling inland to Hail and Buraydah, and finally back to the coast at Jidda from which he returned to England in 1878. This was his only Arabian journey, yet Doughty is still considered one of the greatest explorers of the huge peninsula. His poverty obliged him to live much the same kind of life as an ordinary Arab and his book *Arabia Deserta* is still regarded as one of the finest descriptions of Arabia and its people.

Arabia Deserta, like Burton's book, had a profound effect on travel-minded Europeans at the time, and

This Islamic ceremony of Stoning the Great Devil (above) was sketched by Burton at Muna in the Nejd.

Burton traveled as a pilgrim. At Medina (below) and Mecca in 1853-54 he performed all the rites and ceremonies of a devout Moslem.

it also inspired a growing number of archaeologists and explorers. Typical of many were David Hogarth and T. E. Lawrence, who helped to excavate the ruins of Carchemish (today the town of Jerablus on the Euphrates) and were active in Arabia during World War I. One of their colleagues at the Arab Bureau in Cairo was Gertrude Bell, an Englishwoman who journeyed from Jerusalem to Konya (Turkey) in 1905, explored the ancient ruined city of Ukheidir near Karbala (Iraq) four years later, and made several attempts to penetrate central Arabia shortly before the outbreak of war.

During World War I, much of northern Arabia (especially those areas now comprising Jordan and Iraq) became familiar to British soldiers fighting against the Turkish army. As a result, these areas were surveyed and mapped for the first time. Farther south, Lawrence, who encouraged the local tribes to revolt against Turkish rule, was exploring, fighting—and gathering material for his book *The Seven Pillars of Wisdom*. As a result of the war, there came to Arabia two outstanding explorers, H. St. John Philby and Bertram Thomas, both of whom crossed the vast Empty Quarter.

An officer in the Indian Civil Service, Philby was sent to Basra (Iraq) in 1915 and then to Baghdad, about 300 miles to the north. Two years later, in 1917, he traveled on a diplomatic mission to Riyadh, about 700 miles southward. Soon after he arrived here he crossed the peninsula to Jidda on the west coast, riding off into the desert on a journey that was to take him across hundreds of miles never before visited by Europeans.

The outbreak of World War I had brought anarchy to an already lawless land. In addition to tribal wars there was much brigandage and at night, wrote Philby, "we had to adopt the then usual precaution of announcing the identity and credentials of our party to the four winds of heaven. This nightly advertisement was always accompanied by a cordial invitation to anyone who might be prowling about in search of trouble to partake of our dinner."

Most of the country was completely unmapped but Philby kept a compass record of his route, checked his latitude by the sun, and took readings of the altitude of the land. His detailed notes enabled a map to be made of a huge segment of unknown central Arabia.

One of Philby's great ambitions was to cross the great Empty Quarter that fills so much of the southern part of the Arabian peninsula. But by the time he set out in 1932 the first crossing of this

Charles Doughty (above) spent only two years in Arabia in the 1870s, but his book *Arabia Deserta* marked him as perhaps the wisest and most objective European observer of this land and its peoples.

T. E. Lawrence (below), a scholar turned soldier, explored and fought in many parts of Arabia during World War I. His flair for guerilla warfare played an important part in ending Turkish domination in this part of the Middle East.

immense region had already been made by Bertram Thomas.

By December 1930, when Thomas began his journey from Salala on the southeast coast, he could speak many of the local dialects and, although a Christian, he had worked as vizier (councilor) to the sultan of Muscat. A celebrated figure throughout southern Arabia, he wore Bedouin dress and, like those who accompanied him, neither smoked nor drank alcohol. As the British authorities did not encourage exploration of the interior, Thomas had been forced to keep his plans secret. Even most Arabs thought it impossible to cross the Empty Quarter from the Arabian Sea to the Persian Gulf.

The caravan made its way over the Qara Mountains, reached Shisur about 100 miles inland, then continued northward. "The open state of war existing between the tribe I travelled with and their powerful neighbours made this stage of my journey very dangerous," Thomas wrote later. "Many had been (and will be) the bloody conflicts upon this road along the southern borderlands, for waterless no-man's-lands as they are, yet they are the fairway between water-holes which are used only and inevitably by raiders on murder and plunder bent. Any party we met would be a potential enemy."

Across sands that sang in the wind, Thomas rode for nearly two months, checking his position and taking notes of all he saw. During the first week in February, the party arrived safely at Doha on the Persian Gulf.

Thomas's journey of over 600 miles had been made from south to north. Philby's was made from northeast to southwest beginning at Al Hufuf, inland from the Persian Gulf. From here his caravan traveled 220 miles southwest to the oasis of Maqainama, whose position had never been accurately fixed before, even though the oasis was well known to Arabs. He then made direct for Wabar (about 250 miles south of Al Hufuf), which the Arabs said had once been a great city and had been destroyed by "fire from heaven." Philby did not know exactly what to expect when he arrived at Wabar, but he thought that there might be some ruins. He was greatly surprised when "I looked down not on the ruins of a city, but into the open mouth of what I took to be a volcano with twin craters side by side, surrounded by low walls of what looked like outpoured slag and lava." Philby continued farther south, then turned westward through more than 300 miles of waterless desert to the oasis on the dried-up Dawasir

Bertram Thomas poses with his armed Arab escort during his journey across the Empty Quarter in 1930. He followed a route used only by "raiders on murder and plunder bent. Any party we met would be a potential enemy," he wrote.

Wilfred Thesiger's party pauses at the top of a sand hill in the Empty Quarter. Thesiger explored this vast and desolate region of southern Arabia in 1946-47.

River. On reaching it he became the first European to cross the most difficult part of the Empty Quarter.

Philby's explorations of Arabia continued throughout the 1930s and well into the postwar years. However, after World War II there appeared on the scene a new and important explorer of Arabia, Wilfred Thesiger, who had traveled extensively in Ethiopia while a member of the Sudan Political Service during the years before the war. Thesiger made his first great journey in Arabia in 1945-46 when he traveled for hundreds of miles in the Hadhramaut through country that had been visited neither by Thomas nor Philby. His second journey started in October 1946 and took him from Salala north across the Empty Quarter to settlements near the coast of the present Trucial States, then back by a route farther to the west—some 2000 miles in all. Soon after Thesiger and his party had left Salala some of the Arabs in his party decided to turn back. He continued with only four companions. "We divided the food and water, taking as our share 40 pounds of flour, a pint of liquid butter, some sugar, tea and coffee, and four skins of water," he later wrote. "We now lived on bread baked in the embers of the fire and lightly smeared with butter, which we divided into five portions each evening, casting lots for them as is the custom among these Bhadu [tribesmen]. We fed but once a day at sunset. Our water was only sufficient for a daily allowance of two pints each, which we drank mixed with some sour milk given to us here by the Rashid. This improved the taste of the water, which each day became more brackish."

They went on, first north and then east, often traveling by moonlight "through the first half of the night, our camels stepping out into the cold across the crackling salt flats beneath the dimly seen, unreal sand dunes, encouraged at times by the full throated roar of Arab war songs." On they continued across the dunes, at one place seeing "a red, mountainous range of sand, very lovely in the light of dawn as it rose in jagged peaks and spurs 500 to 700 feet above the ice-coloured [dunes]." At another place, "while descending a sheer-sided dune our camels were frightened by a loud, ever-growing, vibrant hum, evidently caused by a layer of sand slipping down the face of the dune."

Thesiger's journeys ended the pioneering phase of European exploration in Arabia. Today, less than 20 years later, petroleum engineers have established bases in many parts of the subcontinent, and even the Empty Quarter seems a little less empty.

Greek terra-cotta camel of about 250 B.C. The Greeks were among the earliest Europeans to explore the fringes of the Sahara, founding colonies at Cyrene and other coastal areas of Libya in 700-600 B.C.

The map below shows European exploration of the Sahara from the beginning of the 19th century on.

The Sahara Desert

The Sahara is the largest desert in the world. It consists of the gigantic rectangular area in northern Africa between the Atlantic Ocean and the Red Sea, bounded on the north by the Atlas Mountains and the Mediterranean coastal strip, and extending as far south as the Niger River and Lake Chad. If we include its "satellites," the Libyan, Nubian, and Western deserts, the Sahara measures 3000 miles from east to west and is rarely less than 1000 miles from north to south.

The first peoples to make tentative explorations into the Sahara were the ancient Egyptians, who penetrated the Libyan and Nubian deserts. In the last three or four hundred years B.C. the Phoenicians, based at Carthage (near modern Tunis), explored the northern fringe of the desert, and also its western edge from their colonies along the coast of what is now Rio de Oro.

By the middle of the eighth century most of the northern half of Africa was under Islamic domination and was to be vigorously defended against Christian "infidels" for 800 years. The Moors and Arabs took over the practice of slavery started by the earlier Mediterranean civilizations. To transport the slaves from the interior to markets on the north and east coasts of Africa the Arabs developed caravan routes across the Sahara and Nubian deserts. Many of these trade routes remain the principal "highways" across the deserts today.

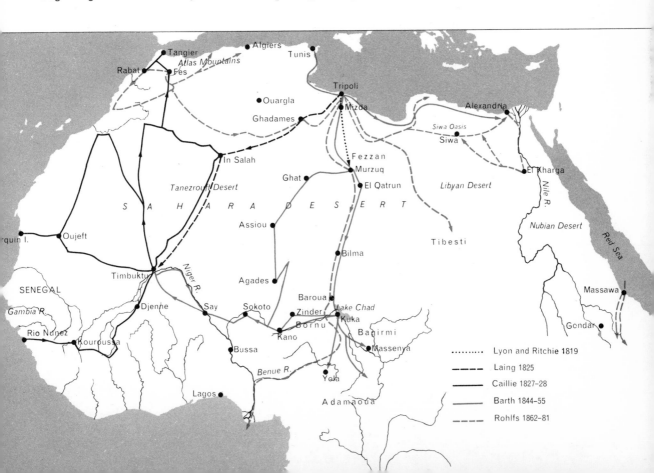

··········	Lyon and Ritchie 1819
- - - - -	Laing 1825
———	Caillie 1827-28
———	Barth 1844-55
– – – –	Rohlfs 1862-81

One of the first recorded European explorations into the interior of the Sahara took place in 1819, when Joseph Ritchie and G. F. Lyon traveled south from Tripoli to the Fezzan and visited the town of Murzuq, which lies on the trans-Saharan caravan route between the Mediterranean and Lake Chad. Six years later Captain Alexander Gordon Laing, who had made several journeys into the interior from Sierra Leone on the west coast, was instructed to make a journey from Tripoli on the Mediterranean coast to Timbuktu—a distance of more than 1200 miles. His object was to establish trade links with Timbuktu. He left London in February, and by July 14, 1825, had not only prepared for his one-man expedition but had married the daughter of the British consul at Tripoli. Two days later he departed for the south, leaving behind the bride he was never to see again.

By October he had passed through Ghadames, and two months later arrived at In Salah, an important staging post on the caravan routes between Algiers and the southern Sahara. The Tuareg—fierce tribesmen of the central Sahara—were astounded to find a lone infidel in their midst, and Laing was saved from assassination only by the lucky intervention of an influential Arab nobleman.

Laing failed to learn from this experience, and pressed on south alone. By February 1826 he was well into the Tanezrouft Desert, about 600 miles north of Timbuktu. His journey was to take another seven months, however, for he became involved in several skirmishes with Tuareg raiders and was seriously wounded. He reached Timbuktu in September, only to find that he was not allowed to enter the city. Discouraged, he left Timbuktu on September 24, heading north and hoping to find a way into Morocco on the

In 1825-26 Captain Alexander Gordon Laing (above) crossed the Sahara from Tripoli to Timbuktu, where he hoped to establish British trade. His journey ended in tragedy, Laing being murdered by his Arab guide soon after leaving Timbuktu.

Six years before Laing, Joseph Ritchie and G. F. Lyon explored the Fezzan and visited the town of Murzuq (below) in central Libya.

The French explorer René Caillié (above), a convert to Islam, evaded the usual hostility toward Europeans by his knowledge of local dialects and by dressing as an Egyptian. In 1828, he completed a journey of nearly 1200 miles to Morocco from Timbuktu—one of the first Europeans to return alive from the city.

Timbuktu (below) was founded by Tuareg traders in the 11th century, and by the 16th century had become a great center of Islamic culture in western Africa.

northwest coast. He did not get far, however, for on the night of the 26th he was strangled to death by his Arab guide.

Laing's courage cannot be denied; but this apart, his journey was a lesson in how *not* to explore the Sahara. Neither he nor the British authorities seem to have had any idea that his reception at In Salah and Timbuktu would be anything but cordial.

Another lone traveler was the Frenchman René Caillié. To prepare for his Saharan travels, Caillié spent several years in Senegal (on the Atlantic coast), living with the natives, becoming a convert to Islam, and studying the language, local dialects, and customs of the Arabs. In 1827 he joined a caravan traveling inland from what is now the Republic of Guinea, posing as an Egyptian Arab returning to his homeland. He arrived in Timbuktu in 1828 and stayed there for two weeks. Then, having explored the middle reaches of the Niger River, he joined another caravan going north. He crossed the Sahara and, after a journey of nearly 1200 miles, reached the city of Fès in Morocco. From here he went to Tangier and took ship to France—one of the first Europeans to return alive from Timbuktu.

The greatest explorer of the Sahara was the German Heinrich Barth. In 1845 his first important journey took him from Tangier in Morocco across the entire breadth of North Africa to Egypt.

Five years later Barth and Adolf Overweg, a German astronomer, were invited by the British government to join an Englishman, James Richardson, in an expedition to establish trade with local rulers in western and central Sudan—an area that today includes the Niger and Chad provinces and much of eastern Nigeria. The party left Tripoli in March 1850

in a small caravan. Their route took them south to Murzuq, then southwest along an arm of the central uplands to the city of Ghat, which they reached at the beginning of July. By this time they were well into the country of the ferocious Tuareg. Next they turned south making for Agadès, a city once as important as Tunis. In the desert between Assiou and Agadès, Barth's caravan was constantly harried by the Tuareg, who demanded money or the lives of the "infidels"— or both. At one stage, three Tuareg joined the caravan, offering "friendship." Two nights later they were replaced by three others who stole several camels under cover of darkness. The explorers' plight was made

Heinrich Barth and his two European companions parley with a band of Tuareg in the Sahara in 1850. The German explorer was later obliged to surrender much of his money and equipment to the warlike tribesmen.

even more difficult by the unpredictable behavior of the caravan's escort and camel drivers. One moment they swore allegiance to Barth; the next they were making obvious preparations to help the Tuareg. Even Barth's personal servant, Mohammed—whose "insupportable insolence" is a recurring theme in Barth's journal—seemed to be engaged in some sinister plot. The fact that Barth and his European companions had pistols and rifles was all that saved them from certain death. After a journey of more than 1000 miles the party arrived in Agadès in October. By January 1851, the travelers had no money left and Barth and Overweg separated from Richardson. The plan was that both groups would have to manage as well as they could until supplies arrived from home. As it happened, Richardson died before he could link up again with his companions.

Barth and Overweg (who wanted the expedition to travel more quickly) separated near Zinder, and Barth pushed on slowly southwestward to Kano, which he reached in February. This city, which he called "the great emporium of central Africa," had long excited Barth's imagination. But he was unable to move about the city, or even very far from his stifling lodgings, until he had permission from the governor. Permission would be granted, Barth knew, if suitable gifts were presented. But before he could see the governor he had first to pay his respects—with more gifts—to the lord of the treasury and then be interviewed by an official close to the governor. After the lord of the treasury "had examined and approved of the presents . . . [and] manifested his satisfaction with them by appropriating to himself a very handsome large gilt cup, which with great risk I had carried safely through the desert, he accompanied us on horseback to the palace," Barth wrote. After his interview Barth had to wait for two hours before gaining an audience with the governor.

"The governor's hall was very handsome . . . and was the more imposing as the rafters supporting the very elevated ceiling were concealed, two lofty arches of clay, very neatly polished and ornamented, appearing to support the whole. At the bottom of the apartment were two spacious and highly decorated niches, in one of which the governor was reposing on a *gado*, spread with a carpet."

After the introductions were made, Barth's mediator gave an account of his travels, with special emphasis on the thefts of the Tuareg. The governor replied that, luckily, Barth still had ample presents for him. "Nor was he far wrong, for the black *kaba* (a sort of burnous,

For five years Barth (above) journeyed along the southern fringes of the Sahara between Lake Chad and Timbuktu and his writings added greatly to European knowledge of these regions.

Barth called Kano (below) "the great emporium of central Africa." The city has been a key trading center for more than 900 years.

The German Gerhard Rohlfs explored widely in the central and eastern Sahara during the 1860s and 1870s. He visited this temple (above) at El Kharga during a journey from the Nile to Siwa Oasis in 1874.

Colonel Paul Flatters, a French officer, interviews Tuareg leaders. French pacification of western and central Sahara led to many bloody skirmishes with Arab tribes. In 1881 Flatters and about 90 soldiers were killed by the Tuareg near the town of Ouargla.

with silk and gold lace) which I gave him was a very handsome garment. . . . Besides, he got a red cap, a white shawl with a red border, a piece of white muslin, rose oil, one pound of cloves, a razor, scissors, an English claspknife, and a large mirror."

Barth obtained permission to stay in Kano and remained in the city for about five weeks. On March 8, 1851, he set off eastward in the direction of Bornu (in the northeast corner of modern Nigeria), where he was reunited with Overweg. Barth was to remain in Africa for nearly four more years, traveling thousands of miles in the Bornu, Adamaoua, and Bagirmi regions near Lake Chad in the east and in the areas around Sokoto and Timbuktu in the west. His great reputation rests not only upon the extent of his travels but also upon the extraordinary care with which he described the geography of each region he visited and the life and customs of the people he met.

The pace of Saharan exploration now began to quicken. During the next 20 years other Germans, notably Gerhard Rohlfs, made important journeys. Rohlfs was an adventurer who joined the French Foreign Legion in 1855, and soon acquired a remarkable knowledge of the languages and customs of Islam. On one of his first expeditions into the Sahara he was attacked and left for dead by his guides. It was quite by chance that two nomads found him and brought him back to Algeria. During a period of 10 years from 1864, Rohlfs explored the city of Ghadames (in modern Libya) and the surrounding desert areas; the Fezzan and Tibesti farther south; the Niger River and its largest tributary, the Benue; and the Siwa Oasis in the Libyan Desert.

It was the French who first conquered the vast stretches of the central and western Sahara and eventually subdued the warlike Tuareg. But their conquest was not without considerable bloodshed. In 1881 Colonel Paul Flatters, together with 10 other Europeans and about 80 Arab soldiers were massacred by the Tuareg near Ouargla (about 350 miles southeast of Algiers) while surveying a route for a trans-Saharan railway that was never built. It was not until World War I that the French finally succeeded in pacifying the Tuareg and freeing travelers on the ancient caravan routes from extortion and death.

Today the Sahara is more peaceful. Its modern explorers—surveyors and engineers—have discovered and are beginning to develop the vast reserves of petroleum and (surprisingly) fresh water that lie beneath this enormous ocean of sand.

The Australian Deserts

Australia has sometimes been called the oldest continent on earth. While it is one of the most recent to be explored and colonized, the vast central region of this land has an exhausted, time-worn appearance. Here are vast tracts of sand, baked mud, and loose stones, veined by parched river beds and drained of color by the brilliant sunlight.

Compared with most other deserts of the world, Australia's Gibson and Simpson deserts seem specially unfriendly to man. Extending across hundreds of miles, they are relatively featureless, for even the mountains in the central Macdonnell Ranges are only three or four thousand feet high; they support little vegetation except patches of stunted eucalyptus trees and thorny spinifex bushes, and there are few spots in the worst areas of the deserts where the explorer can rely on water supplies. In spite of their hostile nature, the deserts of Australia provide the last refuge of one of the most primitive peoples on earth—the aborigines. These people can survive in the desert only because of their remarkable skill as hunters and their seemingly magical ability to find water where, even to the most experienced European "bushmen," there seems to be none.

Sturt 1829–44
Leichhardt 1844–45
Burke and Wills 1860–61
Stuart 1861–62
J and A Forrest 1869–79
Warburton 1873
Giles 1875–76

The map below shows the routes of the most important explorers of the Australian deserts.

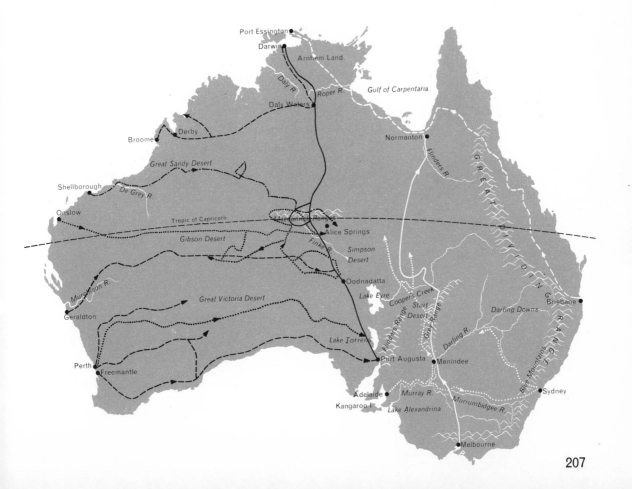

207

The exploration of the interior did not begin until seven years after the British had established their convict settlement at Sydney in 1788. One reason for the push inland was that much of the land along this area of the coast was unsuitable for farming, contrary to the reports of Captain Cook. Another reason was the need for Britain to strengthen her control over the continent in case other European powers became interested in colonizing Australia. The first problem—which took over 20 years to solve—was to find a way over the Great Dividing Range that separates most of the east coast from the rest of the continent. The first route over this barrier was found by Gregory Blaxland, William Lawson, and William Wentworth, who crossed the Blue Mountains in 1813 and discovered good farming country irrigated by rivers on the western side of the range. In the next 20 years many explorers probed farther and farther west and south from their base at Sydney.

The first and perhaps most famous explorer to penetrate deep into the barren heart of the Australian continent was Charles Sturt. He was born in India in 1795 and joined the British army at the age of 18. In 1826, with the rank of captain, he sailed for New South Wales in charge of a shipload of convicts. He became military secretary to the governor of the colony and in 1828 was appointed leader of an expedition to the interior, and discovered the Darling River. The next year he commanded a second expedition that sailed down the Murrumbidgee River in a whaling boat and followed the course of the Murray River to its outlet at Lake Alexandrina and the sea. On this journey Sturt first experienced the hardships of exploration. At one point he nearly starved to death and was temporarily blinded by the sun's glare.

His most ambitious expedition, which began in 1844, had the specific aim of reaching the center of Australia. He took with him 15 men, 11 horses, 30 bullocks, drays and carts, 200 sheep, and a boat for sailing on the inland sea that Sturt was convinced lay at the heart of the continent.

The party set out from Adelaide on the south coast and then sailed up the Murray and the Darling rivers as far as Laidley's Ponds, near Menindee. From here they struck northward. On January 27, 1845, they arrived at Campbell Creek in the Grey Range—"little imagining," as Sturt reflected later, "that we were destined to remain at that lonely spot for six weary months." There was permanent water in the creek but, try as they might, they could find no other reliable

The lush tranquillity of Kangaroo Island (above), south of Adelaide, seen by the British seaman Matthew Flinders in 1802, contrasts strongly with the aridity of much of the Australian interior.

Two officers from H.M.S. *Beagle* are made to dance for their lives during exploration of the north Australian coast, 1837-43.

source in any direction. So they were forced to establish a depot camp at Campbell Creek and be content with making two- or three-man sorties into the parched desert to the north and northwest. In the first week of February, Sturt set out northward with one companion, Joseph Cowley, and a horse and cart carrying food and 69 gallons of water. On the first day they made 22 miles. Rising at dawn on February 11, they found their water tank was leaking, but they continued north in the hope of finding fresh supplies. By mid-afternoon the temperature had risen to 119°F. in the shade. Sturt wrote: "We were then in one of the most gloomy regions man has ever traversed. The stillness of death reigned around us, no living creature was to be heard; nothing visible inhabited that dreary desert but the ant."

They pressed on, leaving small casks of water at various points to support them on their way back. Then on the 13th, shortage of water and the exhausted condition of their horse forced them to turn back.

By the middle of April there was still no sign of rain at their depot, and most days were spent in idling away the time. Some of the men planted seeds in the dry bed of a neighboring creek, "but the sun burnt them to cinders the moment they appeared above the ground." There had been no rain for four months now, and under the effects of the sun's heat "every screw in our boxes had been drawn, and the horn handles of our instruments, as well as our combs, were split into fine laminae. The lead dropped out of our

Charles Sturt, "father of Australian exploration," discovered the Darling River in 1828 and followed it downstream to its junction with the Murray.

Sturt and his companions carry out survey work during their journey to the heart of Australia, 1844-45.

pencils, our signal rockets were entirely spoiled; our hair, as well as the wool on the sheep, ceased to grow, and our nails had become as brittle as glass." To make matters much worse, Sturt and two of his companions were attacked by scurvy.

April passed and then May. By the middle of June, Sturt wrote, "we had been deserted by every beast of the field and every fowl of the air. We had witnessed migration after migration of the feathered tribes . . . all had taken the same high road to a better and more hospitable region. The vegetable kingdom was at a stand, and there was nothing either to engage the attention or attract the eye. Our animals had laid the ground bare for miles around the camp, and never came towards it but to drink." And day by day the water in the creek sank lower and lower.

Early in July Sturt decided to move. He divided the expedition into two parties. One traveled south, making for Adelaide; its leader, James Poole, already weak with scurvy, died on the third day out from the depot. Sturt and his party traveled west hoping to find a better water hole that would enable them to continue the journey into the interior. They found it to the west of the Grey Range, and throughout August and the first half of September journeyed northwest into increasingly parched and hostile country. Their route took them across what is now Sturt Desert and into the southern half of the terrible Simpson Desert. Here the almost total absence of water and the sickness of Sturt and his companions forced them at last to turn back. At this stage they were little more than one degree south of the Tropic of Capricorn. Another member of the expedition died before they reached Adelaide, and Sturt was permanently weakened by his journey.

One of the great mysteries of Australian exploration is centered on Ludwig Leichhardt, a Prussian who emigrated to New South Wales in 1841. Leichhardt made three important journeys to the interior. In 1844 he set off on a 3000-mile journey that took him from Darling Downs to Port Essington on the northwest coast of Arnhem Land. Two years later he led a party that attempted, without success, to cross the continent from Sydney to Perth, a distance of about 2500 miles. In 1848 he tried again, setting out from Darling Downs with four Europeans, two aborigines, 50 bullocks, and seven horses. He intended first to reach Cooper's Creek, where the expedition would turn north to the Gulf of Carpentaria. They would then make their way to the west coast and so down to Perth. The entire expedition vanished without trace, and though many

For mile upon mile, the parched Sturt Desert offers neither landmark nor shelter from the burning sun. Sturt called it "one of the most gloomy regions man has ever traversed."

search parties were sent out at the time and in later years, we still know nothing for certain about their fate. Leichhardt and his companions were probably drowned by floods at Cooper's Creek, which has been known to inundate areas for many miles around during the rainy season.

Equally tragic was the expedition led by Robert O'Hara Burke and William J. Wills who made the first crossing of the continent from south to north. Burke, the son of an Irish officer in the British army, was a brave man, but he had little experience of the Australian bush. Some thought him egocentric and he seems to have had little idea of how to plan his expedition or to earn the respect and affection of his companions. Burke was 40 at the time. Wills, his second in command, was 26 and an experienced bushman.

The expedition set out from Melbourne in August 1860 and spent two months reaching Menindee on the Darling River, where they made their first depot. Here, two of the party had become so impatient with Burke's

Aborigines silently approach an explorers' camp in the outback. Elusive but seldom hostile unless provoked, the native Australians saved the lives of several explorers by their remarkable ability to find food and water in the desert.

Robert O'Hara Burke (above) and William Wills (below) made the first south to north crossing of Australia in 1860-61. Both, however, died of starvation on the return journey to their base in Melbourne.

leadership that they resigned; a third was dismissed by Burke for insubordination.

From Menindee, Burke, Wills, and six others rode north on camels to Cooper's Creek, where they set up a second depot. Burke decided to leave half of his party here and to take Wills and two others—John King and Charles Gray—with him on the 700-mile trek north to the Gulf of Carpentaria. The plan was to reach the gulf by a direct route and to return as quickly as possible to the creek where they would recuperate. The four left behind were to wait at Cooper's Creek for the second part of the expedition, which was supposed to bring the bulk of the provisions and supplies up from Menindee.

Soon after Burke's party left the creek on December 16 a large number of aborigines ran up to them and invited them to their camp for a dance. When Burke refused, the aborigines became even more insistent until Burke made threatening gestures with his gun. In the course of the next few weeks they met other tribes of natives, including some friendly ones who gave them fried fish. None of the aborigines, however, accepted Burke's invitation to act as guides on the journey north.

By January 7 they had crossed the Tropic of Capricorn and throughout that month progressed steadily northward, rarely free from stinging flies and rats. At the beginning of February the party reached a tributary of the Flinders River (which flows into the Gulf of Carpentaria). Here Burke announced that King and Gray were to remain while he and Wills made the remainder of the journey to the sea. In a few days they had reached impassable marshland adjoining the coast, not far from the present Normanton. They could not see the gulf, although the salt-water marshes indicated its closeness. By this time they were too weak to cut their way through the mangrove swamps, so on February 13 they began their return journey. It was almost six months since they had left Melbourne.

During the first few weeks of their journey south all went well. They were never short of water, as many of the creeks were flooded by heavy rain, and toward the end of March they had recrossed the Tropic of Capricorn. At this stage Gray fell ill and for the first time Wills's diary entries showed signs of discouragement. On the 25th, he found Gray hidden behind a tree where he was eating food stolen from the camp store. Wills "sent him to report himself to Mr. Burke ... and [he] received a good thrashing." This may seem a harsh way of treating a companion, but by this time

Above: An aborigine dance ceremony in north Australia. Burke refused invitations to one of these ceremonies on his way to the Gulf of Carpentaria.

Weak with exhaustion on the way back from the north coast, Wills spent the last days of his life in a *mia-mia* (native hut) like these south of Cooper's Creek.

the party were on short rations and both men and animals were suffering from malnutrition. Gray's condition grew worse during the next few days and eventually he had to be strapped on the back of one of the two remaining camels. On April 17 he died. Burke, Wills, and King scooped a hole in the sand with their hands, buried Gray, and spent the remainder of the day resting—a delay that was to cost the lives of both Burke and Wills.

Four days later they reached their depot at Cooper's Creek but found it deserted. Wills made this bitter comment in his diary: "A note left by Brahe [leader of the support party] communicated the pleasing information that they have started for the Darling; their camels and horses all well and in good condition. We and our camels being just about done up, and scarcely able to reach the depot, have very little chance of overtaking them. . . . Our disappointment at finding the depot deserted may easily be imagined; returning in an exhausted state, after four months of the severest travelling and privation, on legs almost paralysed, so that each of us found it a most trying task only to walk a few yards. . . . The exertion required to get up a slight piece of rising ground, even without any load, induces an indescribable sensation of pain and helplessness, and the general lassitude makes one unfit for anything."

Brahe's party had left Cooper's Creek only a few hours before.

Instead of following Brahe southward, Burke decided to march southwest in the hope of reaching one of the new sheep stations between the Grey and

Flinders ranges to the north of Adelaide. They set out from the depot on April 23, taking with them the meager but welcome provisions left behind by Brahe. By the 26th they were making steady progress, their morale was improving, and, wrote Wills, "I believe that in less than a week we shall be fit to undertake any fatigue whatever."

Then on the 28th there was another disaster. One of their two remaining camels became stuck in quicksands. Realizing the danger of losing half their available transport, they tried for two days to get the camel out, but failed. Finally they killed it and, nearly exhausted by their rescue attempts, continued on foot.

On May 6 Wills wrote: "The rations are rapidly diminishing; our clothing, especially the boots, are all going to pieces . . . the camel is completely done up and can scarcely get along." Next day they met some natives who gave them fish and some bread made from nardoo seeds. A few days later, while searching for aborigines, they came across some sandy flats covered with these seeds, and nearby they found a reliable water hole. They decided to make a camp here in the hope that a search party might pass this way.

On May 27 Wills walked alone to the Cooper's Creek depot to leave instructions for search parties, and returned to Burke and King on June 6. All three men were by now weakening fast. On the 21st Wills

Several relief expeditions were mounted when nothing was heard from Burke and Wills in 1861. One, led by John McKinlay, set out from Adelaide in August 1861 and reached the north coast the following May after finding relics of Burke's party en route. Encounters with alligators (above) and with a tremendous gale (below) were two hazards endured by McKinlay's men and amusingly recorded by an Australian artist of the time.

wrote: "I feel much weaker now, and can scarcely crawl out of the *mia-mia* [native hut]. Unless relief comes in some form or other, I cannot possibly last more than a fortnight."

While Wills lay in the hut, Burke and King spent the next week looking for nardoo seeds or searching vainly for aborigines in the hope of begging food from them. The last entry in Wills's diary is dated June 28: "Nothing now but the greatest good luck can now save any of us; and as for myself, I may live four or five days if the weather continues warm . . . I can only look out, like Mr. Micawber, 'for something to turn up,' but starvation on nardoo is by no means very unpleasant, but for the weakness one feels, and the utter inability to move oneself. . . ."

Wills died a day or two after this. Burke and King, meanwhile, continued to look for aborigines. They marched for most of the day, Burke collapsing from exhaustion several times. Finally, toward the end of the afternoon, Burke could go no farther. King made a camp fire, and they huddled around it to keep warm. When King awoke next morning, Burke was dead.

A few days later King was picked up, starving and half mad, by aborigines who fed and looked after him until, about 10 weeks later, a search party from Melbourne discovered him.

The route which Burke and Wills took to cross the continent could be used only in a season of high rainfall. At any other time lack of water would have stopped them long before they had reached the Gulf of Carpentaria. The discovery of an all-seasons route was made by the most persistent of all the explorers of the interior, John McDouall Stuart, who had been a member of Sturt's expedition to the Simpson Desert in 1844.

Stuart had emigrated to South Australia in 1838, and became a government surveyor. Between 1858 and 1860 he made four journeys from Adelaide, each one taking him farther north. His fourth expedition, which was intended to make the first transcontinental crossing, took him beyond Lake Eyre and on to the true heart of Australia, the Macdonnell Ranges. But Stuart was stopped by near starvation and the difficulties of the terrain to the north of the range.

In October 1861 Stuart set out once more from Adelaide with nine other Europeans. Mounted on horses, the group took the same route to the Macdonnell Ranges, then traveled due north across Sturt Plains to Daly Waters and Roper River. From here Stuart went northwest and in July 1862 reached Van Diemen

Adelaide, seen above in about 1860, was founded in 1836 and was the starting point for many expeditions to the Australian interior.

John McDouall Stuart hoists the British flag (above) at Van Diemen Gulf, near the present city of Darwin, after his transcontinental journey from Adelaide in 1862.

Gulf at the site of the present city of Darwin. His diary of the journey is unexciting but, as befits a surveyor, bristles with geological and botanical information. It is also full of patriotic fervor. When he arrived at the gulf Stuart wrote that he climbed the tallest tree he could find, tied the Union Jack to it, and then called for three cheers for Queen Victoria and three more for the Prince of Wales.

Stuart's route north had been a well chosen one, and it was used for laying the overland telegraph from Adelaide to Darwin in 1872. The opening of the telegraph gave a great boost to exploration in Australia. It cut the great continent in half and the various telegraph stations provided explorers not only with permanent depots from which they could start their journeys, but also with means for communicating with rescue parties if they got into difficulties.

To the east of the telegraph most of the land was known. To the west (except for the south coast explored in 1840 by Edward Eyre) it was almost unknown. The first crossing of the continent from the south to the west coast by way of the interior was made by an expedition headed by Colonel Peter Warburton. An amazingly spry man of 60, he and his large party traveled by camel north from Adelaide to the Macdonnell Ranges. From here they turned west and reached the De Grey River on the west coast in December 1873, nearly 15 months after they had set out.

Australia had now been crossed from south to north and from east to west, but a great many more journeys had to be made before the geography of this vast continent began to be known in any detail. One of the most important of these was made in 1874 by John Forrest, who later became prime minister of Western Australia. He was an exceptionally gifted bushman and, although only 29, showed a mature grasp of the techniques of exploration. His journey, with his brother Alexander, took him northeast from Perth, through the Gibson Desert, on to Alice Springs, and then south to Adelaide.

The last of the great Australian explorers was Ernest Giles. He is known chiefly for his double journey—from South Australia to the west coast at Geraldton, and back again, in 1875-76. But perhaps his most remarkable adventure occurred during his earlier journey into central Australia in 1874. This four-man expedition began to the west of Finke River, near Alice Springs, in April. Terrible heat, extreme shortage of water, and an inadequate diet of horsemeat

Edward John Eyre is seen off by Adelaide townsfolk (above) at the start of his journey to Western Australia in 1840.

Colonel Peter Warburton leads his camel train (above) during the trek from Adelaide to the northwest coast via the Macdonnell Ranges in 1872-73.

forced them to turn back. Before doing so, however, Giles decided to make a quick 100-mile sortie west on horseback with one companion named Gibson (whose brother had died on the Franklin expedition to find the Northwest Passage in 1845).

Giles and Gibson had crossed about 100 miles of the parched area that Giles later named the Gibson Desert when one of their horses collapsed and died. Giles now decided to return to his base camp. He told Gibson to ride the one remaining horse to the camp as quickly as possible and to have an extra horse sent out to him. Gibson departed—but was never seen again. Giles was now alone and on foot in one of the worst regions in all Australia. At times he went without food or water for several days on end. Occasionally he found eucalyptus trees offering a patch of shade, but usually he could not lie down beneath them because of the huge nests of ants which were also seeking refuge from the glare of the sun.

"On what I thought was [April] 27," he wrote later, "I almost gave up the thought of walking any further, for the exertion in this dreadful region, where the *triodia* [prickly thorn bush] was almost as high as myself and as thick as it could grow, was quite overpowering, and being starved, I felt quite light-headed. After sitting down, on every occasion when I tried to get up again, my head would swim round, and I would fall down oblivious for some time. Being in a chronic state of burning thirst, my general plight was dreadful in the extreme. A bare and level sandy waste would have been Paradise to walk over compared with this. My arms, legs and thighs were so punctured with spines, it was agony only to exist; the slightest movement and in went more spines, where they broke off in the clothes and flesh, causing the whole of the body that was punctured to gather into minute pustules. . . ."

Giles finally staggered into his base camp, emaciated and half dead, on May 1, after the grimmest and loneliest feat of endurance in Australian desert exploration.

Even today, many of the worst desert regions of Australia remain little known. About a third of the continent receives less than 10 inches of rainfall a year and is far too arid to support a settled population. This third—mainly in the central and west-central regions —is likely to remain unsettled unless means are found to bring water from beneath the desert in sufficient quantities to irrigate the parched soil and provide grazing for sheep. Until such time, it belongs to the now diminished tribes of aborigines, who alone are able to win a meager living from this hostile land.

John Forrest's party pauses (left) near the source of the Murchison River during the 1874 journey from Western Australia to the telegraph line south of Alice Springs.

6 The Challenge of Mountains

The great mountains of the world have always presented a special challenge to the explorer. They have faced him with a set of difficulties that he has found nowhere else.

The greatest of these difficulties is produced by altitude itself, by the fact that as one goes higher and higher above sea level reduced air pressure makes it more difficult to breathe. Men who first climbed the slopes of the world's mountains were not fully aware of this danger. All they knew was that as they went higher they found it increasingly difficult to breathe, so it was not unnatural to suppose that the snow-covered summits of the world could not support human life.

The snow itself presented other problems, for its consistency varied from one season to the next. Men did not know whether they would find it hard and frozen, or so soft that they would sink into it up to their thighs. Then there were the glaciers—huge rivers of ice—many miles long and hundreds of yards across, which in some places offered the easiest approaches into the mountain recesses. But the glaciers were split by huge fissures, called crevasses, hundreds of feet deep and in which a man could be lost forever. These crevasses, as the first mountain explorers soon learned, changed from year to year, so that it was impossible to find a permanent path through the maze that they formed. There was also the danger from snow glare— the reflection of the sun from the great expanses of snow, so strong that it could blind a man unless he was wearing dark glasses, and blister the skin from his face if he did not wear a protective veil.

Finally, there was the fact that in exploring mountains men had to battle against a force that was not involved in any other kind of exploration—the force of gravity. They had to pull or push themselves strenu-

To many non-climbers, the lure of mountaineering for men like these may seem strange. Yet the desire to tread where no man has been before; to test mental and physical powers to the utmost; to savor the comradeship born of shared danger and excitement have continually attracted men to the great mountains of the world.

ously upward, using much energy, and learning only slowly the special craft of climbing rocks.

These things would have made the mountainous areas of the world among the last to be explored even had it not been for other factors: Mountains support less vegetation, have fewer animals and smaller human populations than any other kind of country except deserts and the polar regions. Explorers of the mountain world could not, therefore, hope to find new regions to settle; they could not hope to find riches or rewards, and they could only rarely hope to discover new "races" of people.

For these reasons, many of the men who went first into the mountain world were not explorers in the usual sense of the word. Some, it is true, climbed peaks merely to find out what lay beyond—for much the same reason that some of the early navigators sailed over the "rim" of the oceans. Far more ventured above the snow line to carry out scientific experiments at heights that they could not otherwise reach. Others went through a spirit of adventure, to test their own physical powers against those of the elements.

They were able to do this because some of the least-known mountain regions are surrounded by well-known populous areas. The high Alps, for instance, although virtually unexplored until the middle of the 18th century, have some of the great cities of Europe only a few miles from their lower slopes. This meant that, while only a few men could sail to new continents, and others required years to explore distant jungles and deserts, far larger numbers were able to take part in the shorter expeditions needed for mountain exploration. The men who first circumnavigated the globe or set out for the polar regions disappeared for years; the Alps could be explored during a long vacation. The first great mountaineering expedition to the Karakorams—Martin Conway's of 1892—was made almost as a passing incident in a very busy life.

Conquest of Mont Blanc

The first mountain explorers of the modern world were Saussure, Paccard, and Balmat. Horace Benedict de Saussure, a Genevese scientist, offered a reward to anyone able to find a way to the top of Mont Blanc (15,782 feet—the highest peak in the Alps), whose summit could be seen from the shores of Lake Geneva. Dr. Michel Paccard and Jacques Balmat, doctor and guide respectively, came from Chamonix, the little village that lies at the foot of Mont Blanc.

Saussure made his offer when he first visited

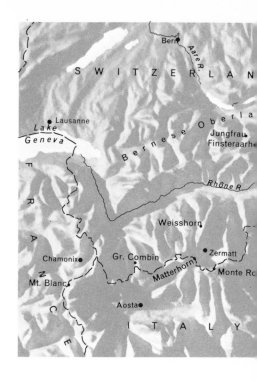

Mountaineers have listed about 180 major Alpine peaks. The map above shows the positions of a few of the highest in the western Alps.

Albert Smith's entertainment *The Ascent of Mont Blanc in 1851* ran for six years in London—proof of the great interest in mountaineering in the mid-19th century.

Chamonix in 1760 as a young man of 20. "From that moment," he later wrote, "Mont Blanc became for me a sort of illness. My eyes could not look at this mountain, which one sees from so many spots in our neighbourhood, without my being seized by a pang."

Yet it was 26 years before Mont Blanc was first climbed. Nothing was known about the approaches to *Mont Maudit*, or "the accursed mountain" as it was called, and only slowly did the local men begin to piece together a route which would take them up across the glaciers and snow fields to the great white summit. It was, in fact, only on the evening of August 8, 1786, that Paccard and Balmat strode out of Chamonix on the journey that was to provide the first important landmark in the story of mountain exploration.

The two men spent the night wrapped in rugs on the rocks of a ridge called the Montagne de la Côte. Then, "at two o'clock, the white line of the dawn appeared, and soon the sun rose without a cloud, brilliant and beautiful, a promise of a glorious day," as Balmat wrote later. They crossed a glacier, "a sea full of great crevasses whose depth could not be measured by the eye," and were soon making for the Grand Plateau, a great snow basin from which the final slopes of the mountain rise. They were buffeted by the wind, more than once forced to their knees, and at one point Paccard's hat hurtled off toward Italy. "We must go into mourning for it," Balmat joked. "You will never see it again, for it has gone to Piedmont, and good luck to it."

They climbed steadily upward all the morning, past midday and on into the early afternoon—by which time they could look back and down on the distant village of Chamonix. "As I rose higher," wrote Balmat, "the air became much less easy to breathe, and I had to stop almost every ten steps and wheeze like one with consumption. I felt as if my lungs were gone and my chest was quite empty. I folded my handkerchief over my mouth which made me a little more comfortable as I breathed through it. The cold got worse and worse, and to go a quarter of a league took an hour." But they refused to admit defeat.

It was now past six in the evening and the two men still plodded upward, heads down, going more and more slowly. The glare of the snow had pained their eyes all day, and with each new step upward their breathing became more difficult. Then, at last, they found themselves standing on the summit: "I was where no living being had ever been before, no eagle nor even a chamois! I had come alone, with no help but my own will and my own strength. Everything

French climbers Jacques Balmat (above) and Dr. Michel Paccard (below) made the first ascent of Mont Blanc, the highest peak in the Alps, in 1786.

Paccard, Balmat, and most other early conquerors of Mont Blanc made their ascents up the mountain's north face, seen above.

Horace de Saussure's party, third to climb Mont Blanc, descends from the summit in 1787. Saussure, 27 years before, had offered a prize to the first men to conquer the peak.

around belonged to me! I was the monarch of Mont Blanc! I was the statue on this unique pedestal!"

So, of course, was Dr. Paccard, who now tried for half an hour to make scientific observations, but he was severely hampered by the cold. It was seven o'clock before the men started to descend, eleven before they got off the ice, and next morning before they staggered into Chamonix. "I was quite unrecognizable," said Balmat. "My eyes were red, my face black, and my lips blue. Every time I laughed or yawned the blood spouted from my lips and cheeks, and I was half blind."

When Saussure heard the news of Paccard's and Balmat's success, and that his reward had at last been won, he left almost immediately for Chamonix, but the weather quickly broke, and it was not until the following year—1787—that he was able to set out for the summit—with a valet and 18 guides. The party carried ladders with which to cross the crevasses but, even so, had to spend two nights on the snows. On the second they were "awakened by the roar of a great avalanche which covered part of the slope we had to follow on the morrow." Although they started at dawn, it was eleven in the morning before they arrived on the summit; and Saussure was so tired that he could hardly enjoy his triumph. "At the moment that I trod the highest point of the snow that crowned the summit I trampled it with a feeling of anger rather than of pleasure," he wrote. "Besides, my object was not only to reach the highest point. I felt bound, also, to make the observations and experiments which alone gave value to my venture, and I was very doubtful of being able to carry out more than a portion of my plans."

In spite of his doubts, Saussure spent three and a half hours on the summit, testing the boiling point of water, the temperature of the snow, the pulse of his guides, and the exact color of the sky when measured against 18 differently shaded pieces of blue paper. His journey was in fact a great success, the outcome of the offer that he had made in Chamonix.

Where Paccard and Balmat had led, others followed. During the succeeding years, men climbed not only Mont Blanc but also many lesser peaks of the Alpine chain—the Finsteraarhorn and the Jungfrau in the Bernese Oberland, Mont Pelvoux in the Dauphiné Alps of southern France, the Piz Bernina in the Bernina Alps, and more than a score of others. These ascents were made by English, French, Swiss, German, and Italian climbers, many of whom were also scientists. Their efforts were so successful that by 1860 only a few major peaks of the Alps remained unclimbed.

The Matterhorn, although 1000 feet lower than Mont Blanc, was for long considered impossible to scale. The first ascent was made by the Englishman Edward Whymper in 1865, after seven unsuccessful attempts.

Whymper, the greatest mountaineer of his time, was only 25 years old when he conquered the Matterhorn. He went on to climb many peaks in North and South America.

Challenge of the Matterhorn

There then appeared on the scene the most famous of all mountaineers. His name was Edward Whymper, and he was a London artist-engraver, just 20 years old. He was sent to the Alps to prepare illustrations for a book to be written by members of the Alpine Club formed in London three years earlier. Whymper was a powerfully built man, immensely active, and during the next five years he succeeded in making first ascents of many Alpine peaks. But, more than any other peak, it was the Matterhorn (14,780 feet) that fascinated him. Rising on the Swiss-Italian frontier above the little village of Zermatt, this huge pyramid of rock had for years been considered utterly inaccessible. This fact, together with the majestic shape of its three steep rock faces, made it for Whymper the greatest challenge in the Alps. Between 1860 and 1865 he made no less than seven unsuccessful attempts to climb the mountain. In some of these he was helped by the Italian guide Jean Antoine Carrel, "the cock of his valley . . . a well-made, resolute-looking fellow, with a certain defiant air which was rather taking."

On other occasions he climbed alone—and once slipped and fell while crossing a narrow ledge. "The knapsack brought my head down first, and I pitched into some rocks about a dozen feet below," he later wrote. "They caught something and tumbled me off the ledge, head over heels, into the gully; the baton was dashed from my hands, and I whirled downward in a series of bounds, each longer than the last; now over ice, now into rocks; striking my head four or five times, each time with increased force. The last bound sent me spinning through the air, in a leap of fifty or sixty feet, from one side of the gully to the other, and I struck the rocks, luckily, with the whole of my left side. They caught my clothes for a moment, and I fell back on to the snow with motion arrested. My head fortunately came the right side up, and a few frantic catches brought me to a halt, in the neck of the gully, and on the verge of the precipice. Baton, hat, and veil skimmed by and disappeared, and the crash of the rocks—which I had started—as they fell on to the glacier, told how narrowly had been the escape from utter destruction. As it was, I fell nearly 200 feet in seven or eight bounds: Ten feet more would have taken me in one gigantic leap of 800 feet on to the glacier below."

Whymper managed to find his way to safety—and a few days later was back on the Matterhorn for yet another unsuccessful attack!

In the summer of 1865, Whymper was once again

in the shadow of the Matterhorn. This time he was, as he later recorded it, "bamboozled and humbugged," for Jean Antoine Carrel, whom he had expected to guide him, was off leading an Italian party to the peak whose ascent would be the most coveted victory in the mountaineer's world.

Whymper, fuming with anger, met Lord Francis Douglas, another young but experienced climber. Together the two men crossed the frontier to Zermatt, intent on scaling the Matterhorn from the Swiss side— a route which had for long been considered utterly impracticable. In Zermatt, Whymper found, by a trick of fate, yet another party preparing for an attempt on the mountain. It consisted of five men: the Rev. Charles Hudson, a brilliant mountaineer, and his inexperienced friend Douglas Hadow, two local guides—the Taugwalders—and another of Whymper's guides, Michel Croz.

The two parties decided to join forces. The following morning they left Zermatt and the same evening they pitched camp high on the mountain.

Early the next day they received a tremendous surprise, for when they turned a rock rib and saw the upper slopes of the mountain at close quarters for the first time, the difficulties seen from Zermatt were revealed as largely a trick of perspective. "Some parts were more and others were less easy," Whymper wrote, "but we were not once brought to a halt by any serious impediment, for when an obstruction was met in front it could always be turned to the right or to the left."

Higher up, the slope steepened but, said Whymper, "the solitary difficult part was of no great extent. We bore away over it at first, nearly horizontally, for a distance of about 400 feet; then ascended directly toward the summit for about 60 feet; and then doubled back to the ridge which descends toward Zermatt. A long stride round a rather awkward corner brought us to snow once more. The last doubt vanished! The Matterhorn was ours! Nothing but 200 feet of easy snow remained to be surmounted."

At 1:40 P.M. on the early afternoon of July 14, 1865, the party stood triumphantly on the summit— looking down with satisfaction on the Italian party, whose members were apparently stopped by difficult rocks hundreds of feet lower down and obviously would not complete their ascent for several hours.

Croz stuck a tent pole in the summit snow, tore off his blue blouse and attached it to the pole as a flag. Whymper sketched, Hudson took notes, and after an hour's rest the party began the descent.

The triumph of Whymper's seven-man Matterhorn party turned swiftly into tragedy soon after they began their descent. One of the leading men fell on a difficult section, the rope snapped, and four of the party plunged 4000 feet to their death.

They climbed down the first few hundred feet and came to the steeper section. All around them was the vast panorama of the Valais Alps; below, the great depths dropping to the glaciers that surround the base of the Matterhorn. All was silent except for the occasional scrape of boot on rock, or the chink of ice ax. They moved slowly and with great care, in awe of the immense void beneath them.

Croz, leading the way, and young Hadow, behind and already tired by the ascent, were both hidden from Whymper by the steepness of the rocks. Suddenly he heard a startled exclamation from Croz. Then he saw the guide and Hadow falling, arms and legs splayed out in an unavailing effort to save themselves.

"In another moment Hudson was dragged from his steps, and Lord F. Douglas immediately after him," Whymper wrote. "All this was the work of a moment. Immediately we heard Croz's exclamation, old Peter and I planted ourselves as firmly as the rocks would permit; the rope was taut between us, and the jerk came on us both as on one man. We held; but the rope broke midway between Taugwalder and Lord Francis Douglas. For a few seconds we saw our unfortunate companions sliding downward on their backs, and spreading out their hands, endeavouring to save themselves. They passed from our sight uninjured, disappeared one by one, and fell from precipice to precipice on to the Matterhorn-gletscher below, a distance of nearly 4000 feet in height. From the moment the rope broke it was impossible to help them."

Whymper and the two Taugwalders, saved by the breaking of the rope, slowly descended to Zermatt, where they stammered out the news that was to shock all Europe—four men killed in a single mountaineering accident.

After the Matterhorn disaster, Whymper gave up most of his climbing in the Alps. But he was only 25, and before he died almost 50 years later, he had traveled in Greenland, climbed in the Andes—that great range stretching 4500 miles from the southernmost tip of Tierra del Fuego to the narrow isthmus of Central America—and had gone more than once to the Canadian Rockies.

Meanwhile, the other great mountain ranges of the world were being explored—the Caucasus stretching along the southern frontier of Russia; the Himalayas and the Karakorams, which form a huge wall enclosing India on the north and northeast; the Southern Alps of New Zealand; and the Rockies and other great ranges of North America.

Geologists studying Alpine glaciers and rock forms helped develop climbing techniques in the mid-19th century. Above: James Forbes, a Scots geologist, measures the depth of a glacier near Mont Blanc.

Below: A primitive mountaineering ladder used in the 1850s.

Early American mountaineers were mainly surveyors who in the 1850s and 1860s were helping to map the West. The picture above shows (from left to right) James Gardiner, Richard Cotter, William Brewer, and Clarence King in 1864. King discovered Mount Whitney and Mount Tyndall, and later was director of the United States Geological Survey.

Below: A survey party in Colorado's San Juan Mountains in 1876.

Surveyors Try their Hand

In North America, where the West was still being opened up in the mid-1800s, the exploration of mountains often formed part of men's day-to-day work. Many of them enjoyed their work—men such as Lieutenant (later General) John Frémont, who as early as 1842 climbed the 13,790-foot peak later named after him. At the time it was thought to be the highest in the Rockies, and he climbed it, as he put it, "beyond the strict order of our instructions." Many of the early mountain explorers of the United States were surveyors, busily mapping the half-known territory that was then being occupied by white men for the first time. Among these was Clarence King, a young Yale graduate who traveled west in 1863 intent on "seeing the whole interior of the Continent."

King, whose book *Mountaineering in the Sierra Nevada* was the first great American mountain classic, had the romantic outlook of the genuine mountaineer. He could never see a distant peak without wanting to climb it and look over onto the far side. Before he settled down to a career as geologist and man of letters, he spent a number of carefree years exploring the ranges of the West with only the most primitive mountaineering equipment.

When he went from New York in 1863, King met W. H. Brewer, an assistant in the Geological Survey of California, joined the organization largely because it offered him a free open-air life, and started on the work that was to make him, only a few years later, director of the newly formed United States Geological Survey.

King discovered and named Mount Whitney and Mount Tyndall, surveyed Yosemite Valley, and was prevented from completing a survey of Arizona only by the attacks of Apaches. Yet he and his most constant companions—James Gardiner, Richard Cotter, and Brewer—were not mountaineers in the European sense of the word. They were their own guides and had little or no knowledge of how to use the rope. And for ice axes they used their geological hammers.

The way in which these surveyors of a century ago first climbed virgin peaks in the Sierra Nevada, in the Colorado Rockies, and summits in Utah, Idaho, and Wyoming, is shown by King's story of his ascent of Mount Tyndall, 14,025 feet high. He tackled this mountain with Richard Cotter after news of a great and unexplored group had been brought into camp by Brewer and his chief topographer, Charles Hoffman.

"Our walking-shoes were in excellent condition," wrote King, "the hobnails firm and new. We laid out

Mount Whitney (above), at the southern end of the Sierra Nevada, was first climbed by three Californian fishermen in 1873.

Map of the western United States showing some of the main peaks climbed in the 1840s to 1870s.

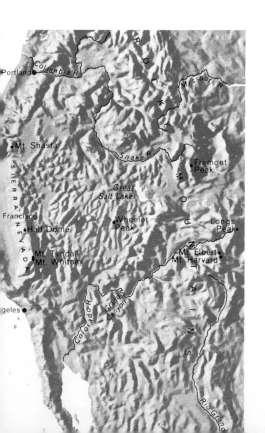

a barometer, a compass, a pocket level, a set of wet and dry thermometers, notebooks, with bread, cooked beans, and venison enough to last a week, rolled them all in blankets, making two knapsack-shaped packs strapped firmly together with loops for the arms, which, by Brewer's estimate, weighed forty pounds apiece."

The packs, soon making their shoulders black and blue, tended to overbalance them, and they were glad to bivouac that night, shortly before the sun went down. "A sudden chill enveloped us," King wrote later. "Stars in a moment crowded through the dark heaven, flashing with a frosty splendor. The snow congealed, the brooks ceased to flow, and, under the powerful sudden leverage of frost, immense blocks were dislodged all along the mountain summits and came thundering down the slopes, booming upon the ice, crashing upon the rocks."

The following day, as they scrambled into a great wilderness of peaks, they were forced to pad the straps of their packs with handkerchiefs and socks, so painful had their loads become. They climbed near-vertical rocks and looked into unknown valleys over which a blue haze hid details, "giving a bottomless distance out of which, like the breath of wind, floated up a faint tremble, vibrating upon the senses, yet never clearly heard." At one point they were forced to lasso a rock high above them and climb hand over hand up the rope. Finally, within sight of their summit, they were faced by a rock wall. Covering it was a huge spire of compacted snow 10 feet wide at the bottom and two feet wide at the top. It was the only possible path to take.

"We climbed the first half of it with comparative ease; after that it was almost vertical, and so thin that we did not dare to cut the footsteps deep enough to make them absolutely safe," wrote King. "There was a constant dread lest our ladder break off, and we be thrown either down the snow-slope or into the bottom of the crevasse. At last, in order to prevent myself from falling over backwards, I was obliged to thrust my hand into the crack between the ice and the wall, and the spire became so narrow that I could do this on both sides; so that the climb was made as upon a tree, cutting mere toe-holes and embracing the whole column of ice in my arms."

At the top of the difficult pitch the ground was easy, and a few seconds later, King and Cotter were looking over the vast wilderness of unexplored California. "I rang my hammer upon the topmost rock," King wrote. "We grasped hands, and I reverently named the grand peak, Mount Tyndall [after John Tyndall, the British mountaineer]."

The enthusiasm for mountaineering that King showed in his accounts, published as 14 articles in the *Atlantic Monthly* during the late 1860s, bore fruit over the following decades. During this time the first of the American climbing clubs—the Appalachian Mountain Club, the Sierra Club, the Mazamas, and finally the American Alpine Club—filled in more and more mountaineering gaps left by the surveyors, the railway builders, the geologists, and other men who pushed west during the last part of the 19th century. Mount Whitney, 14,495 feet high, then the highest peak in the United States, was climbed in 1873 by three fishermen from the nearby Owens Valley. Two years later so much was known of European mountaineering techniques that Half Dome in Yosemite was climbed by local men with the help of both rope and pitons.

Climbing the World's Highest Peaks

While King and his successors were exploring the mountains of the United States, men on the other side of the world had at last begun wondering whether it would be possible to climb the highest mountains of all. These lay in the Himalayas and the Karakorams, the 1500-mile, sickle-shaped group of ranges to the northeast of the subcontinent of India. No less than 50 peaks are 25,000 feet or higher. These huge mountains lie between India and the bleak upland of Tibet, and they have at times formed an effective barrier isolating different civilizations.

The first men to cross these ranges were not explorers in the proper sense of the word. They were Jesuit missionaries such as Father Antonio de Andrade and Brother Manuel Marques, who in 1624 set out from India for Lhasa. Although they never reached Lhasa, they did make their way over the 18,300-foot Mana Pass before founding a mission. There was also Father Ippolito Desideri, who traveled from Srinagar to Tibet in 1714. There were the surveyors who climbed the lower hills as part of their job in mapping India's frontier territories. And there were naturalists such as Sir Joseph Hooker, who in 1847 started out on a three-year expedition through Sikkim that took him deep into the heart of the great range.

Toward the end of the last century came the real mountain explorers, men whose aim it was to see if they could climb the peaks above 20,000 feet, peaks that would take them higher into the rarefied air than man had ever been before. Already, climbers had dis-

British army camp in the Himalayan foothills about 1840. At this time army surveyors were beginning to map the great ranges on India's largely unexplored northern frontier.

In 1892 Martin Conway (below) led the first large mountaineering party to the Karakorams. The picture is by A. D. McCormick, the expedition's artist.

covered how to tackle many of the problems presented
by ice and snow. They had found that studded boots
prevented their feet from slipping on rock or snow,
and that sets of metal spikes—known as crampons—
enabled them to move with greater safety on ice. They
had evolved an ice ax with which they could cut steps
or secure themselves should they slip on hard-packed
snow.

Mountaineers had also devised a number of ingeni-
ous methods of using a rope so that it safeguarded all
members of a party. When crossing glaciers it could
save a man should he slip into a crevasse. On rock
climbs, it could lessen the chances of a dangerous fall.

A lot was already known, therefore, about the purely
technical problems of climbing high mountains when,
early in 1892, the first big mountaineering expedition
set out to climb in the Karakorams. It was led by Martin
Conway, an Englishman of independent means who
had made many famous climbs in the Alps, and who
was later to climb in other great ranges.

One of Conway's aims was to map the huge glaciers
around the 28,250-foot peak known as K2 (or Godwin-
Austen), the second highest mountain in the world.
Another was to study the effects of altitude by climbing
some of the nearby peaks—not necessarily the most
difficult, but those that would take him well above the
heights that other men had attained. Conway's party
was a big one, as were most of those that were to visit
the Himalayas and Karakorams during the next few
decades. With him went A. D. McCormick, a well-

High in the Karakorams, McCormick
drew this fragile rope bridge
across which the party had to carry
sheep, goats, and 103 pieces of
equipment and baggage.

Over 50 mountains in the Himalayas
and Karakorams rise above 25,000
feet. The map below shows a few of
the major peaks in these ranges.

known artist, who was to draw illustrations for a book about the expedition. An officer came along to collect birds, and one of the great Alpine guides, Matthias Zurbriggen from Macugnaga in Italy, joined the group to give technical climbing advice. In addition, there were scores of porters who were needed to carry the baggage, food, cameras, theodolites, and plane tables.

It was a strange, vast world of glacier and snow into which Conway and his companions penetrated, a world where the huge glaciers were up to 40 miles long, where no white man had before penetrated, and where the sheer physical problems of moving the heavy equipment nearly defeated them. "Here," wrote Conway in describing his approach to the Hispar Pass, "was a highway into another world with which man had nothing to do. It might lead into a land of dragons or giants or ghosts. The very thought of man vanished in such surroundings, and there was no sign of animal life. The view was seen like music. Nowhere was there a bright patch of sunshine. The lower half of the glacier was densely blanketed over with stones, grey, brown, or black. The vast snow fields beyond were all a pallid grey like the sky. Nothing glittered. Silence was broken only by a faint hum of moving water. No stone stirred. No avalanche fell. All appeared as still as death, and I sat motionless an hour or more."

Into this immense landscape Conway and his party could move only slowly. At one place they had to carry their flock of sheep and goats (on which they were to live) and 103 separate baggage loads over a single, crazy rope bridge that would support only one man at a time. At another stage they came to a junction of two glaciers and found that each of the separate arms, through whose tangled ice they had to make their way, was more than a mile across. In spite of all their difficulties they surveyed more than 2000 square miles of unknown territory.

At last they turned to the other part of their task—the ascent of the highest peak that looked practicable. "We fought a way up a great ice-fall that impeded access to the highest snow field," Conway said. "We out-weathered another terrible storm. We camped in blasting heat by day and bitter cold by night at the foot of our mountain; then forced the camp yet farther up it and finally essayed the peak. It was a fine climb up a steep snow-slope to a ridge of ice and rock, and along that, over one peak after another, till we found the ridge cut through by a deep depression and the actual mountain rising over 1000 feet above and beyond, for us hopelessly virgin."

Conway's party surveyed and mapped many of the huge glaciers around K2, at 28,250 feet the second highest mountain in the world.

The summit that they reached they named Pioneer Peak, and at 22,600 feet it was the highest mountain in the world that had then been climbed.

Conway was one of the men who climbed for climbing's sake. In so doing he increased man's knowledge of the mountain world. He climbed in Spitsbergen and made the first crossing of that island. In 1898 he went to the Andes, making the first ascent of Illimani (21,184 feet), climbing Aconcagua (23,081 feet), and then sailing south to see the almost totally unknown mountains of Tierra del Fuego at the southernmost tip of South America.

Some of the Andes were already known when Conway visited the range. The "silver bell" of Chimborazo, reaching more than 20,000 feet in Ecuador, had been known to the Western world since the Spanish colonization of South America in the 1600s; in 1745 La Condamine led his Franco-Spanish expedition of scientists to nearly 17,000 feet on its slopes. Alexander von Humboldt visited the mountain in 1802, and Whymper had made the first ascent of it in 1880. Near the other end of the range, the first ascent of the great Aconcagua was made by Edward Fitzgerald's party in 1897, but vast stretches of it were still unknown, unmapped, and unexplored when Conway came the following year.

Like many other mountaineers, he was attracted not only by the adventure of opening up new country and by the personal battle with a mountain, but by the immense splendor of the world seen from great heights. He shows this in his description of his own ascent of Aconcagua, which started in the small hours of a bitterly cold clear night with the heavens blazing with stars. For a number of hours he and his companions climbed the higher rocks, half numbed with the cold even though they were dressed in fur-lined clothes and wore wolf-skin gloves. Then, suddenly, the sun began to rise beyond the mountain.

"It flung its purple shadow like a solid beam to the far horizon of the Pacific, upward of 200 miles away," he later wrote. "A fiery radiance filled all the air outside the shadow and gave to the latter an aspect of solidity. Its outer surface was rainbow-tinted. It was a marvellous effect, one of the most wonderful I have ever beheld. As the sun ascended, the remote point of the shadow withdrew towards us on the water, till it reached the Chilean shore, then swiftly came inland over the foothills, dipped into the Horcones Valley, climbed the slope up which we had come, and finally reached our feet. Turning round and raising our eyes to

The major peaks of the Andes are very uniform in height. The map below shows the main ones between 20,000 feet and 23,000 feet.

the crags aloft, lo! the blinding fires of the Sun God burning upon the crest."

There was still a long way to go, over loose rocks that slipped underfoot. "At last they became bigger and firmer and we could halt for some food," wrote Conway. "A final scramble planted us on the crest of the mountain, and Argentina was at our feet with the cliffs dropping a vertical two miles to the glacier below."

Conway's successful expeditions to the Andes and the Karakorams led to many more during the following two decades. As a result of them, many thousands of square miles of glacier and rock ridge in both ranges were mapped for the first time. Meanwhile, men from many different countries were busy exploring lesser ranges of the world and the isolated mountains and peaks no climber had yet dared approach.

Ernest Shackleton's men, probing deep into the Antarctic during his 1907-09 expedition, climbed 13,300 feet up Mount Erebus and looked down into the boiling crater of an active volcano rising from the snow-shrouded wastes. The Duke of the Abruzzi, in 1897, proudly planted an Italian flag on the summit of Mount St. Elias (18,008 feet), the great peak towering over the Alaskan wilderness. And in 1913 Harry Karstens; Hudson Stuck, Archdeacon of the Yukon; Robert Tatum, a young man training to become a priest; and Walter Harper, 21-year-old dog driver, stood together on the summit of Mount McKinley. Known as "The Great One," it is the highest summit of North America, rising to 20,320 feet. And in Africa, where most of the Ruwenzori, the near-legendary Mountains of the Moon, had by now been climbed, men at last conquered both Kilimanjaro (19,317 feet) and the more difficult Mount Kenya (17,040 feet).

The ascent of Mount Kenya, whose snows were first seen in 1849 by Dr. Ludwig Krapf, a German missionary, was one of the most remarkable mountaineering feats of any era. Krapf's reports of "a gigantic wall, on whose summit I observed two immense towers or horns, as you might call them," was at first disbelieved. "A most delightful mental recognition only, not supported by the evidence of his senses," was one comment from those who found it difficult to believe a tale of snow on the equator.

During the following half century other men confirmed Krapf's story, but it was not until 1899 that Halford Mackinder, a brilliant young English geographer, approached the mountain with the aim of climbing it.

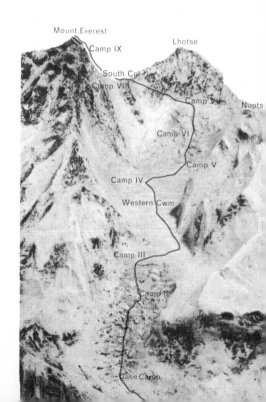

View to the northeast from the top of Everest—a photograph taken by Edmund Hillary after he and Tensing Norkey had reached the summit on May 29, 1953.

The scale model (left) shows the route of the successful ascent of Everest. The route distance from Camp II to the summit is more than seven miles.

From the first, almost everything went wrong with Mackinder's expedition, which included three other scientists and two Alpine guides. The party, with its retinue of nearly 200 porters, was attacked by Masai tribesmen, and poisoned arrows missed Mackinder by only a few inches. Some of his men were ambushed, others tried to desert. Finally he managed to set up a base camp on the mountain, but the following day the group found itself almost completely surrounded by a great bush fire, which had been started by a match carelessly dropped. Realizing that it was hopeless to try to put it out, the group fled, barely escaping with their lives.

Mackinder was to make more than one unsuccessful attempt to work his way up through the glaciers that festoon the upper slopes of the twin peaks forming the mountain. On his last attempt he set off with two guides and bivouacked out as high as he could. "We were up at earliest dawn," he told the Royal Geographical Society on his return, "and away as soon as the sun rose out of the cloud roof to eastward, thawing our hands so that we could grasp the rocks." A steep hanging glacier lay before them, its ice so hard that cutting a way across it took three hours instead of the expected 20 minutes (and earned it the name of the Diamond Glacier). A final rock scramble landed them on the summit, and Mackinder's terse description reminds us of the scientists who were opening up the Alps sixty years earlier: "We reached the higher summit about 12 o'clock. It was entirely devoid of snow. The afternoon cloud had just come up, but the temperature was 40 degrees Fahrenheit, and I counted about five different kinds of lichens." The achievement can best be judged by one fact: Mount Kenya was not climbed again for 30 years.

The Lure of Everest

During the first half of the present century, many of the greatest peaks of the world were climbed for the first time. The blanks on the maps showing mountain ranges were steadily filled in with glaciers and ridges. But in the Himalayas the greatest mountain of all repulsed repeated attempts to scale it for more than three decades.

This mountain, called Everest after the man who had headed the Indian Trigonometrical Survey when it had been found to be the highest summit in the world, was first tackled by mountaineers in 1921. Even then, the party that left England planned to reconnoiter the mountain rather than climb it. Forty years ago the

233

problems of such an ascent were far greater than they are today. Although the position of Mount Everest was known, its immediate approaches were still blank on maps; and the mountaineering problems that its upper slopes presented were completely unknown. Also there was the problem of altitude itself. Whether man could breathe at 29,000 feet without the aid of bottled oxygen was doubtful. The cases for and against using this "artificial aid"—heavy containers that would have to be carried on the back—were argued almost continuously between 1920 and 1939. During this period the first seven assaults—all unsuccessful—were made on Mount Everest. Then, in 1952, the Swiss tried, but again all efforts failed.

In the spring of 1953 a crack British and New Zealand team of mountaineers assembled at the foot of Everest. They were equipped with the best that modern science could provide: ropes made of nylon, high-altitude boots insulated with a synthetic material called tropal, foam-rubber floorings for their tents, concentrated foods, lightweight "walkie-talkie" sets that enabled members of the party at different camps to talk to one another, and lightweight oxygen equipment. Special wind-proof clothes had been devised by manufacturers and then tested in wind tunnels where gale-strength winds were blown around them. Specially designed stoves enabled the climbers to prepare food and drink at high altitudes with the minimum of trouble.

The leader of the 1953 expedition was John Hunt, an officer in the British army who had climbed for many seasons in the Alps and other ranges. Among his companions was Edmund Hillary, a New Zealander, and Tensing Norkey, soon to become the most famous of all Sherpas. These men were the two who were to play the most dramatic parts in the historic climb that was about to start.

Hillary was nearly 34, a tall, big-boned man who had been brought up on his father's bee farm in North Island. He had learned to climb in the Southern Alps of New Zealand. On his first visit to Europe he had climbed five 13,000-foot peaks in the Alps in five days, and had already taken part in a number of Himalayan expeditions when he joined John Hunt.

Tensing Norkey was nearly 40, but he had won the Tiger Medal from the Himalayan Club for his mountain exploits. He had been on Everest several times— with the British expeditions in 1935, 1936, and 1938, and with the two Swiss expeditions in 1952. He had climbed elsewhere in the Himalayas and was an enthu-

Sherpa porters, sure-footed and skilful mountaineers, have become essential to most modern Himalayan expeditions. Above: Sherpas carry crates through "Hellfire Alley" between Base Camp and Camp II.

Below: A heavily loaded Sherpa scales a rope ladder on the Ice Fall leading to the Western Cwm.

siastic mountaineer. In his own right he was an expert climber, quite apart from his ability to manage the rest of the porters who served the expedition.

From the start, almost everything went according to plan, for Hunt had worked out in the greatest detail every move of his campaign. A route was cut up through the Western Cwm across the face of Lhotse to the South Col where a camp was set up on May 21. From here the southern ridge of Everest rises to the summit, and along it the first assault party set out on May 26. It consisted of Charles Evans and Tom Bourdillon—two young men who were faced with the task of making the 3000-foot climb in a single stage.

As they progressed high up the ridge, they found fresh snow that slowed their progress. Then the weather closed in. According to plan, there was a time past which they had agreed not to climb—one o'clock. When the time came they were tantalizingly close to becoming the first men to stand on the "top of the world." They had reached the South Peak of Everest, some 300 feet lower than the summit itself, which lay little more than 1200 feet along the ridge. Reluctantly they turned back.

The following morning, May 27, the wind howled round the little tents perched on the South Col. It continued to blow throughout the day, but by dawn on May 28 conditions seemed to be improving. The second assault party, consisting of Hillary and Tensing, began its preparations.

They planned to spread the final ascent over two

Tents and oxygen equipment at Camp VII on the west face of Lhotse. At an altitude of 24,000 feet, the camp lay about a mile and a half south of the summit of Everest.

Tensing (left) and Hillary, at the Advance Base at the head of Western Cwm, prepare for the final assault.

On the roof of the world, Hillary took this photograph of Tensing triumphantly waving an ax bearing the United Nations, British, Indian, and Nepalese flags. Tensing buried small packets of food on the summit as token gifts to the spirits that, Buddhists believe, have their home on the mountain.

days, and on the afternoon of May 28 they pitched their tent 27,900 feet up on the South Ridge. They wriggled into their sleeping bags, thawed out a tin of apricots, and with their Primus stove roaring prepared a meal of fruit, dates, biscuits, jam, honey, and sardines.

The following morning they crawled from their tent soon after it was light, loaded up food and 30 pounds of oxygen kit, then moved off up the South Ridge. The going was good, and by nine o'clock they had reached the South Summit—four hours earlier than the first assault party.

"At first glance it was certainly impressive and even rather frightening," Hillary wrote of the view that they now had of the 1200 feet of ridge running toward the peak of Everest. "On the right the great contorted cornices, overhanging masses of snow and ice, stuck out like twisted fingers over the 10,000 foot drop of the Kangshung Face. Any move on to the cornices could only bring disaster. From the cornices, the ridge dropped steeply to the left until the snow merged with the great rock face sweeping up from the West Cwm."

They had, Hillary estimated, enough oxygen to last them four and a half hours. Everything, therefore, depended on the state of the snow on the ridge ahead.

"As my ice-axe bit into the first steep slope of the ridge, my highest hopes were realised," he wrote. "The snow was crystalline and firm. Two or three rhythmical blows of the ice-axe produced a step large enough even for our oversized high altitude boots and, the most encouraging feature of all, a firm thrust of the ice-axe would sink it half-way up the shaft, giving a solid and comfortable belay."

They moved one at a time, each man protecting the other against the chance of a slip. After an hour they come to a formidable obstacle, a 40-foot rock step that Hillary was able to climb only by drawing on all his powers. Then Tensing came up, too, safeguarded by the rope.

Then they turned to the snow ridge again, cutting steps, moving into them, cutting again, moving on and up, almost interminably it seemed. Then, without warning, they realized that they could see over to the North Col on the far side of the mountain. There were a few more blows of the ice ax and Hillary and Tensing found themselves standing on the summit of the world.

"My initial feelings were of relief," Hillary wrote, "relief that there were no more steps to be cut—no more ridges to traverse and no more humps to tantalise us with hopes of success. I looked at Tensing and in

spite of the goggles and oxygen mask, all encrusted with icicles that concealed his face, there was no disguising his infectious grin of pure delight as he looked all around him. We shook hands and then Tensing threw his arm round my shoulders and we thumped each other on the back."

The ascent of Everest was an omen that the last major "problems" of the mountain world were about to be solved. Within the following few years men stood on the summits of one after another of the great peaks that had held off the mountaineer for decades. Five weeks after Everest had been climbed, Hermann Buhl, a member of an Austro-German party, reached the top of Nanga Parbat in an amazing solo climb. The next year the Italians conquered K2, and the Austrians climbed Cho Oyu, while in 1955 the British climbed Kangchenjunga, and the French Makalu.

Most of these ascents succeeded because mountaineers were able to use to the full newer and lighter oxygen equipment, lighter and more efficient tents, more efficient materials for clothes and boots, and a whole range of minor items that science had provided. There was also the psychological importance of the fact that men had already reached the highest point in the world. Surely, any peak was now possible.

The mountaineering successes that followed the ascent of Everest have been added to during every year that has passed since then, and have been extended from the Himalayas to the Andes. They have all helped to underline one thing: that by 1953 the exploration of mountains, as distinct from the climbing of them, was coming to an end. In both the Himalayas and the Andes many great virgin peaks still remained—as they do today—even though their approaches were familiar. And in a few rare places, such as the more remote parts of the Andes, there were still small areas that needed real exploration. But with these few exceptions the mountains of the world had been explored.

The conquest of Everest encouraged successful attempts on several other Himalayan peaks once considered inaccessible. Kangchenjunga, third highest mountain in the world and one of the most difficult of all, was climbed in 1955 by a British party (right) led by Charles Evans, who had reached the South Peak of Everest two years before.

7 New Worlds to Conquer

Today, in the mid-20th century, all the oceans have been navigated and charted, most of the jungles and deserts explored, nearly all important mountains climbed, and the polar regions crossed. At first sight it might seem that the great days of exploration are past. In fact, our planet still offers adventurous men the challenge that attracted explorers of long ago. An example of this was the voyage on the raft *Kon-Tiki* that Thor Heyerdahl, the Norwegian anthropologist, made with five companions across 4300 miles of the southeast Pacific in 1947. Their purpose was primarily scientific—to prove that ancient Peruvians could have migrated on just such rafts from South America to Polynesia. The Heyerdahl expedition had all the ingredients of danger, excitement, and scientific purpose that spurred earlier explorers of the Pacific.

It is true, however, that the character of exploration has changed radically in recent years, especially since World War II. The challenge to modern explorers springs mainly from man's quest for scientific knowledge of the world around him—the ocean depths, the earth's structure, and outer space.

Exploring the Ocean Depths

Man's first probings into the depths of the oceans must have come soon after he first ventured across open seas, since it was important for him to know as much as possible about the reefs and rocks that could wreck his vessels. The first record that we have of underwater exploration, however, is that of Alexander the Great, who is claimed to have descended in a diving bell to examine the Mediterranean Sea.

The seafarers of the great age of oceanic exploration—from the 15th to 18th centuries—took routine soundings near the coasts along which they sailed, but

The character of exploration has changed much in recent years. The astronaut depends, to a greater extent than any previous explorer, upon scientists and technicians (right) who are able to control and observe every detail of modern space flights and who can interpret the mass of scientific information sent back from the vehicle during its journey. The space pilot and ground crew contribute equally to man's growing knowledge of the limitless regions beyond his planet.

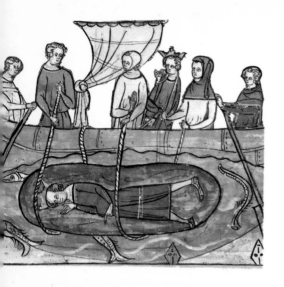

Alexander the Great (above) is supposed to have examined the floor of the Mediterranean in a diving bell about 330 B.C.

The diving cage below is used by aqualung divers for protection in shark-infested seas.

these gave little indication either of the shape of the sea floor or of the great depths found in many parts of the oceans. Magellan was one of the first who attempted to do something more. Between two islands in the Pacific he and his men tied six sounding lines together, estimated that the line went down some 400 fathoms (one fathom being equal to six feet) without touching bottom, and judged from this that they were over the deepest ocean in the world. (We know now that the *average* depth of the oceans is about 3000 fathoms and that of the deepest parts is nearly 6000 fathoms.) Along with other mariners of his time Captain Constantine Phipps took soundings in the Arctic in 1773; but it was only during the middle of the 19th century that men began a systematic exploration of the ocean bottom and of animals living in deep waters.

During the late 1860s the British naturalist Professor Charles Wyville Thomson carried out a series of experiments off the Scottish coasts. Thomson, who discovered abundant life at 600 fathoms and also found that water temperature at specific depths could vary widely, suggested that the oceans might support a much larger animal population than had ever been considered possible.

The laying of the first transatlantic cable between Britain and the United States in 1866 further stimulated the growing interest of scientists in the sea and in marine life. As a result, the most famous of all oceanographic expeditions set out from England in 1872 aboard H.M.S. *Challenger*, a naval steamship of 2300 tons. This round-the-world voyage, which was sponsored by the British Admiralty and the Royal Society, lasted for three and a half years. The *Challenger*'s team of scientists, led by Thomson, made hundreds of depth soundings, recorded water temperatures at many different depths, and collected a huge number of animal, plant, and mineral samples—many from depths of more than 3000 fathoms.

The voyage of the *Challenger* encouraged further oceanographic explorations during the late 19th century by scientists from other countries, many of which added much to our knowledge of the oceans and of marine life. But it is only during the last 35 years or so that we have been able to measure the depths and trace the contours of the ocean floor with speed and accuracy. Until this time, depth soundings had been made by "swinging the lead"—lowering a weight over the side of a ship and measuring the length of the line when the weight touched the sea bed. This method is quite accurate, but takes a long time. In the deepest

H.M.S. *Challenger* was fitted with a well-equipped laboratory (above) for its historic round-the-world oceanographic expedition, 1872-76.

Challenger scientists used the equipment below to collect samples of sea water from depths of more than 3000 fathoms.

parts of the oceans, the weight takes several hours to reach the bottom and longer to be hauled up.

Today, however, the oceanographer has a more accurate and much quicker instrument to measure depths. This is the echo-sounder, which is attached to the hull of a ship and transmits a continuous stream of high-frequency signals. These signals are bounced off the ocean floor and, because the speed at which sound travels through water is known, the time taken for their journey to and from the bottom can be used to determine the depth of water.

Man has also devised methods of collecting samples of animal and plant life by dredging and by drilling into the sediments and the underlying rocks of the sea floor. But in spite of the most modern developments in this field of research, the best way to investigate the ocean depths is for man himself to descend to the bottom and see things with his own eyes. Modern diving suits and aqualungs of the kind used by Commandant Jacques-Yves Cousteau and his colleagues are invaluable for exploring water down to about 50 fathoms. But to probe the black, silent regions on the floor of the oceans, man has had to design strong, watertight containers to protect himself against the tremendous pressure of the water, which at the greatest depths is as much as nine tons to the square inch.

One of the pioneers of deep-sea exploration was the American Dr. William Beebe, who made many dives in the *bathysphere*, a steel sphere, designed by Otis Barton, with walls one and a half inches thick and fitted with a small window of rock crystal. The bathysphere was connected by cable to a surface ship; it could not be maneuvered about nor could it descend to the sea bottom without danger of fouling the cable on rocks. Nevertheless, Beebe reached a record depth of 250 fathoms in 1930 and, four years later, about 510 fathoms—more than half a mile down.

Man's ability to plumb the greatest ocean depths is due mainly to the inventive genius of Professor Auguste Piccard, the Swiss scientist and explorer. In the last few years before World War II Piccard designed a deep-sea vessel capable of diving to the greatest known depths under its own delicately controlled power. Basically his idea was a simple one. The diving chamber—similar to but stronger than Beebe's—was attached to a cigar-shaped steel "float" filled with gasoline and fitted with compartments for storing lead shot. The gasoline, which is lighter than water, made the craft buoyant; moreover, as this liquid cannot easily be compressed, the float could not be crushed by the great pressure of water. With a full load of lead shot, the craft would sink. When the diver wished to return to the surface, all he had to do was jettison a proportion of the shot. Piccard called his invention the *bathyscaphe*, from Greek words meaning "deep boat."

The outbreak of war prevented Piccard from experimenting with his invention. But in 1948 the bathyscaphe (without anyone inside it) descended to a depth of 750 fathoms off Dakar on the west coast of Africa. During the next five years Piccard greatly improved the design of the float, and in 1953 a new bathyscaphe, named *Trieste*, took Piccard and his son Jacques to a depth of 1732 fathoms– nearly two miles—off the Italian coast near the island of Capri. In 1954 seamen of the French navy, using another bathyscaphe based on Piccard's design, dived to 2214 fathoms off Dakar. Then, in the Pacific Ocean in 1960, with the help of the United States Navy, Jacques Piccard and American Lieutenant Donald Walsh descended 5940 fathoms (about seven miles) to the bottom of the Challenger Deep, which lies in the Mariana Trench south of the island of Guam.

Deep dives of this kind are much more than tests of courage and technical ingenuity. Before the *Trieste*'s time oceanographers had to rely on still photographs for their knowledge of the appearance of the deep sea bottom and the animals that live there. Today man himself can descend into the black depths and, with the help of searchlights and cinecameras, can learn much of scientific importance about these hitherto inaccessible regions.

Probing the Earth's Interior

Jules Verne's adventure *A Journey to the Center of the Earth* (first published in 1864) reflects vividly man's age-old speculations about the structure of our planet. The idea that some caves and underground tunnels could lead from the surface to the core of our planet is a fascinating one—but bears no relation to the truth. Nevertheless, Verne's story may have played its part in encouraging the development, in the late 19th century, of the art of cave exploration that has taught us many things about the earth's crust.

The pioneer of cave exploration was E. A. Martel, a Frenchman who was seized with a desire to penetrate the gaping vertical holes of the Causses, the limestone region of central France. Martel designed all his own equipment—rope ladders, collapsible boats for sailing

Of peculiar fascination to the mind of man, caves have for centuries been a rich source of legend and fantasy. Jules Verne's adventure *Journey to the Center of the Earth*, from which the picture of a diamond mine (right) is taken, is among the best of such fantasies. The chief pioneer of cave exploration was the Frenchman E. A. Martel (above) who descended many of the deepest caves in Western Europe during the last decades of the 19th century.

on underground streams, special clothes that did not tear on the sharp rocks, magnesium flares for lighting, and a score of other devices. He made his first descent of the great Gouffre de Padirac on July 9, 1880. Later he went to England, where he made the first-ever descent of Gaping Ghyll, in Yorkshire, the deepest "pothole" in the British Isles; then to the Pyrenees and to Austria.

Martel's work was carried on many years later by another Frenchman, Norbert Carteret, who penetrated many of the deepest and most inaccessible caves in the Pyrenees and elsewhere. They and their successors laid the foundations of modern *speleology*, which has enthusiastic followers all over the world. Among other things, they have shown that even the deepest caves extend little more than 1500 feet below the surface.

The deepest that man has yet managed to burrow underground is about 11,000 feet (over two miles) in a gold mine in South Africa; whereas he has drilled holes to a depth of four to five miles in search of oil. Yet five miles represents the merest scratch on the surface of our planet, for the distance from the crust to the center is about 4000 miles. So it is not surprising that our knowledge of the earth's interior is sketchy.

By studying earthquake waves as they travel through the earth, and by setting off underground explosions that also send out waves, scientists have discovered that our planet is made up of a series of concentric layers of rock. The crust or outer layer varies considerably in thickness but averages about 20 miles. Below the crust is the mantle, which seems to consist of rock in a plastic state and is about 1800 miles thick. Next comes the "liquid" outer core, about 1300 miles thick, inside which there is an inner core about 850 miles thick that acts like a solid. When we use words like "plastic" and "liquid" rock we refer to their behavior, not their composition. The kinds of rocks forming the mantle and core remain a subject of the keenest interest, and it is to discover something about the nature of the mantle that a series of important experiments is being planned.

The object is to bore holes through the earth's crust and to bring up samples of the underlying mantle. On land, the crust may be up to 25 or 30 miles thick, but beneath the oceans the mantle approaches to within three or four miles of the sea floor. So if we allow an additional two or three miles for the depth of water and a further 1500 feet for the sediments on the bottom, it is obviously simpler to try to reach the mantle by drilling at sea. And this is what scientists

are now preparing to do. A Russian team is believed to have made test borings off the Kamchatka Peninsula in eastern Siberia with the aim of drilling a hole 65,000 feet deep. The Americans, meanwhile, have planned their Mohole Project—named after the Mohorovičić Discontinuity (*Moho* for short), the layer at which the crust and mantle rocks meet. They have already made some test borings from their drilling ship *Cuss I*, a converted freight barge of 3000 tons. In the spring of 1961 the ship, with drilling pipe sections massed high on its deck, began tests in 2000 fathoms of water off the Pacific coast of Mexico. By the time you are reading these pages, scientists may already have succeeded in boring through the Earth's crust and brought back samples of mantle rock that may tell us much about the structure and history of the earth.

Exploring the Frontiers of Space

Meanwhile, man has made his first tentative steps toward investigating the limitless regions beyond his planet. The great envelope of atmosphere enclosing the earth consists mainly of a mixture of the gases oxygen (about 21 per cent) and nitrogen (about 78 per cent). Other gases and some water vapor make up the remaining one per cent. These proportions remain fairly constant at all heights, but their quantity diminishes as the altitude increases. Thus the oxygen available at the top of Mont Blanc is less than that at ground level, and the amount at the top of Mount Everest is less still. At a height of about 10 miles, the pressure of oxygen is so low that air-breathing engines fail to work. Higher up still the atmosphere continues to tail off into empty space.

Man is only just beginning to explore this dangerous world, but for the last two centuries or so he has been acquiring information about it by various means. Some of the first men to experience difficulties owing to lack of oxygen were, as we have seen, the early mountaineers. But it was only with the coming of balloon flight that man gained practical experience of the upper atmosphere.

The first successful manned ascent was made in 1783 by Pilâtre de Rozier and the Marquis d'Arlandes, who sailed over part of Paris in a flight lasting 25 minutes. Most early ascents were made by lighting a fire in a carriage below the silk, canvas, or paper balloon; the hot air in the balloon would then cause it to rise. During the 19th century, however, this method was replaced by the use of hydrogen, coal gas, or other lighter-than-air gases.

The first passengers to make a successful journey by balloon were a sheep, a cock, and a duck (above), which in 1783 were sent aloft by the pioneer French balloonists Joseph and Étienne Montgolfier.

Two years later the first crossing of the English Channel by air was made by the Frenchman Jean-Pierre Blanchard and the American Dr. John Jeffries (below), who sailed from Dover to a point near Calais.

One of the most important 19th-century balloonists was James Glaisher, the British meteorologist who between 1862 and 1866 made 28 ascents, many on behalf of the British Association for the Advancement of Science. Glaisher's ascent with a single companion from Wolverhampton, England, on September 5, 1862, set an altitude record that stood for over 30 years; he reached more than 30,000 feet, higher than Mount Everest—an astonishing feat for the time.

Although these early balloonists were at the mercy of the winds, they gained much valuable information about the upper air. Their greatest enemy was the hostile environment at high altitude. No matter how courageous an explorer may be, his frail human body, if unprotected, simply cannot survive in the upper atmosphere. To go higher, man had to devise special protective equipment. The technological breakthrough was provided by the scientist-explorer Professor Piccard.

Piccard was the first of a long line of men who bravely sailed aloft in airtight gondolas slung below balloons. Because the gondolas contained their own atmosphere and could be kept warm, these balloonists could ascend to much greater heights than their predecessors. The first ascent by Piccard, who was trying to discover more about cosmic rays that bombard the earth from outer space, was from Augsberg, Germany, on May 27, 1931. Within half an hour of take off, Piccard had risen 50,000 feet—more than nine miles—and was able to see, in his own words, "640,000 square kilometres of the planet, more than the area of the whole of France." The following year Piccard made an ascent from Zurich, Switzerland, with the scientist Max Cosyns, and reached 52,140 feet—just under 10 miles. Piccard's work showed what could be done, and he was quickly followed by others—a Russian team in 1933 that reached 58,700 feet, and an American team later in the same year that reached 61,220 feet. In 1935 the Americans Albert Stevens and Orvil Anderson reached 72,394 feet, a record that was not broken until 1957, when another American, Captain Joe W. Kittinger, ascended to 95,120 feet. By this time, however, the problems of man's exploration of space had been dramatically altered by rocketry.

The rocket has been of prime importance in man's early probings into space because it has one great advantage over aircraft. Both the engines and wings of conventional aircraft depend on the presence of air —which, as we have seen, becomes progressively

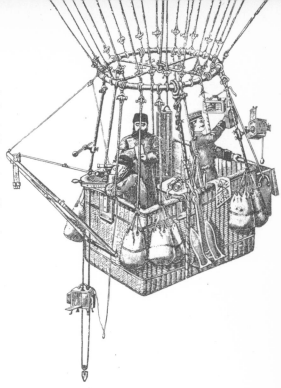

Scientific studies of the earth's atmosphere were made by many balloonists in the late 19th century (above). Lacking oxygen equipment, however, they could not ascend much above three miles without danger.

In 1932 Professor Auguste Piccard (below) ascended to an altitude of almost 10 miles in his spherical gondola containing its own supply of air—a technique now used by all high-altitude balloonists.

rarer the higher one goes. A rocket, however, operates independently of the gases that make up the atmosphere. The explosion of fuel in the rocket's combustion chamber exerts a high pressure within the chamber and so creates thrust, thus pushing the rocket forward through the atmosphere or space.

German scientists were the first to send rockets high into the atmosphere. Following experiments and trials in the 1920s and 1930s, rockets like the V-2 were used during 1944 and 1945 to bombard London and Antwerp. As the Allied armies rolled across Germany in 1945 the Americans and Russians captured stocks of these weapons, as well as many of the scientists who had developed them. Both took men and weapons back to their own countries. And both the United States and the Soviet Union began intensive programs of "space" research and development.

When the possibility of reaching the moon was first seriously discussed soon after the war, the host of scientific and technological problems posed by such a journey seemed overwhelming. Even the most powerful of the rockets developed from the V-2 fell back to earth, and it was realized that it would be necessary to increase their speed to around 25,700 miles an hour—about seven miles a second—before they could escape from the pull of gravity and continue on into outer space. Secondly, how could an astronaut be brought back through the earth's atmosphere at a speed slow enough to prevent him and his spaceship being burned up by friction—as are millions of meteors that rain down toward earth from outer space? Thirdly, there was the problem of guidance, for the slightest error might send the astronaut hurtling forever through space. Finally, there was a host of biological hazards affecting the health and comfort of astronauts in space.

During the last 10 years or so most of these problems have been solved, theoretically in the laboratory and practically in the growing number of space vehicles man has sent aloft. The first and in many ways the most spectacular success came in the autumn of 1957 when the Russians launched the 184-pound Sputnik I and then astonished the world by repeating the feat —this time with Sputnik II, weighing more than half a ton and carrying an animal passenger.

The Americans followed a few months later with Explorer I, and in March 1958 launched one of the most useful of all the early satellites. This was Vanguard I, the first of a series of research vehicles designed to discover information about the earth's

Scientists had theorized about space craft for many years before Sputnik I orbited the Earth in 1957. In 1883 the Russian engineer Konstantin Tsiolkovsky produced this idea for a space vehicle.

Today the exploration of space— and, less happily, the "space race" to which it has led—are part of everyone's lives. On television screens at home and in public places (as in New York's Grand Central station, right) manned orbital flights are watched as they occur. Public commemoration of space triumphs is made with the issue of souvenirs such as these Russian postage stamps (below).

shape and the influence of radiation belts in the upper atmosphere. From 1958 onward both the Russians and the Americans made fresh advances, putting more animals into orbit and solving the problems of retrieving them safely. The Russians also "crash landed" instruments on the moon and sent a satellite around it to photograph the face that is always turned away from the earth.

The question of whether the human frame could stand the great stresses of rocket-powered space flight was answered beyond doubt on April 12, 1961, when the Russian Major Yuri Gagarin orbited the earth in his 4½-ton Vostok I. Some months later, the Americans sent two men on 300-mile journeys to the fringe of space. And in August Major Gherman Titov made 17 orbits of the earth in a 25-hour journey during which he traveled farther than the 240,000 miles that separate our planet from the moon. Since then, the Americans Colonel John Glenn and Lieutenant-Commander Malcolm Scott Carpenter have orbited the earth, and have helped to guide their spacecraft in flight. And in August 1962 Major Pavel Nikolayev and Lieutenant-Colonel Andrian Popovich, aboard Vostok III and Vostok IV, orbited for several days as "neighbors" in space.

So far, the Americans have concentrated on learning about the atmospheric envelope and the radiation belts surrounding the earth. They have specialized in delicate instrumentation while the Russians have concentrated on the problems of producing the giant rockets that must be perfected before man takes his first steps onto another planet. It seems likely that the research program of the one country tends to complement that of the other, and there is no doubt that space science would benefit greatly if co-operation between these two great countries were possible.

Man clearly has the scientific know-how to land astronauts on the moon and to bring them back safely. But the "conquest of space" is a problem of a wholly different order. Even assuming that his space vehicle could travel at the speed of light—186,000 miles a second—an astronaut would take four years to reach the nearest star (apart from the sun) in our galaxy. A journey to the nearest star in the nearest galaxy beyond our own would take about 140,000 years traveling at the speed of light. These almost unimaginable distances help to put the idea of space travel in its true perspective. Yet they cannot lessen man's determination to escape from the confines of earth and to explore at least a part of the limitless regions beyond.

Index

Text Credits

Acknowledgment is made for various quotations appearing in this book:

1 Explorers of Old
The Periplus of Hanno translated by C. Simonides published by Routledge & Kegan Paul Ltd.
The Persian Expedition translated by Rex Warner published by Penguin Books Ltd.
The Invasion of India by Alexander the Great by J. W. McCrindle published by Constable & Co. Ltd.
The Book of Sir Marco Polo by Sir Henry Yule published by the Hakluyt Society

2 Voyages into the Unknown
Columbus's First Voyage by Sir Clements Markham published by the Hakluyt Society
Voyages of Da Gama by E. G. Ravenstein published by the Hakluyt Society
First Voyage round the World by Magellan by Lord Stanley of Alderney published by the Hakluyt Society
Official Admiralty instructions to Captain James Cook

3 Jungles and Forests
Explorations into the Valley of the Amazons by Sir Clements Markham published by the Hakluyt Society
Missionary Travels in South Africa by David Livingstone published by John Murray (Publishers) Ltd.

4 The Polar Regions
Farthest North by Fridtjof Nansen published by Constable & Co. Ltd.
Scott's Last Expedition by R. F. Scott published by John Murray (Publishers) Ltd.: reprinted in U.S.A. by permission of Dodd, Mead & Company
Little America by Richard Byrd published by Putnam & Co. Ltd.: reprinted in U.S.A. by permission of G. P. Putnam's Sons.
A Voyage of Discovery and Research in the Southern and Antarctic Regions by J. C. Ross published by John Murray (Publishers) Ltd.

5 Sand and Sun
Voyages through Russia and over the Caspian Sea into Persia by Anthony Jenkinson published by the Hakluyt Society
Travels in Desert Cathay by Sir Aurel Stein published by Macmillan & Co. Ltd.
The Heart of a Continent by Captain F. E. Younghusband published by John Murray (Publishers) Ltd.
Arabian Days by H. St. J. Philby
Arabia Felix by Bertram Thomas published by Jonathan Cape Ltd.: reprinted in U.S.A. by permission of Charles Scribner's Sons

6 The Challenge of Mountains
Autobiography of a Mountain Climber by Martin Conway published by Jonathan Cape Ltd.
The Ascent of Everest by Sir John Hunt published by Hodder & Stoughton Ltd. based on the original despatches from Sir John Hunt and other members of the Everest Expedition to *The Times*: reprinted in U.S.A. from *The Conquest of Everest* by permission of E. P. Dutton & Co. Inc.

Illustration Credits

By courtesy of the Trustees of the British Museum: 12(T), 19(T), 30/31(T) (photo John Freeman); 16(T), 70(T) (photo Mansell Collection); 21(T), 22, 43, 44(T), 46, 49(T), 50, 52/53(B), 54, 58, 59, 60, 61, 62, 64, 65, 70(B), 76, 77(T), 82(B), 83, 84, 85(B), 86, 90, 92, 94(T), 97(T), 126(B), 172(B), 182(T), 183(T), 190(T), 192(T), 201(T), 221, 222(B), 240(T), 244(T), endpaper
Uni-Dia-Verlag: 12(B)
British Travel & Holidays Association: 16(B)
Mansell Collection: 19(B), 25(B) (photo Alinari); 48(B), 49(B), 72(B), 73(B), 79, 95, 102(T), 111(T), 143(L), 163(B), 195(BP), 196(B), 244(B)
Paul Popper: 21(B), 94(B), 99, 154, 165, 166, 167, 170, 176
Bibliothèque Nationale: 23, 34, 35, 38(T), 42(T), 44/45(B)
Kungl. Vitterhets Historie Och Antikvitets Akademien: 28
Universitets Oldsaksamling: 29(B)
Bodleian Library, Oxford: 30/31(B), 38(B)
Biblioteca Capitular y Colombina: 39
New York Public Library Rare Book Division: 45(T)
Museo Navale di Genova: 48(T)
Illustrations from *The Journal of Christopher Columbus*, Anthony Blond Ltd., Orion Press Ltd., London, 1960, and Clarkson N. Potter, Inc., New York: 52/53(T)
© Relief maps copyright Geographical Projects Limited, London: 63, 220(T), 227(B), 229(B), 231
By courtesy of the Trustees, National Maritime Museum, Greenwich: 68(T), 69, 71, 137(B)

(Greenwich Hospital Collection); 78 (on loan from the Admiralty)
By courtesy of the National Portrait Gallery, London: 68(B), 109(T), 130(T), 198
By courtesy of the Trustees of the British Museum (Natural History): 75, 93
Staatliche Museen zu Berlin: 82 (T)
City of Liverpool Museums: 85(T)
Frick Art Reference Library: 97(B)
Provincial Archives, Victoria, B.C.: 101
Canada House, London: 102(B)
W. & B. Forman, *Benin Art*, Paul Hamlyn Ltd., 1960: 107
Royal Geographical Society: 112(T), 116, 117(B), 157(T), 158, 163(C), 164, 173, 191(B), 196(T), 199, 202(T), 205(T), 232(B)
By kind permission of Richard Stanley: 119(B)
Radio Times Hulton Picture Library: 126(T), 143(R)
The Parker Gallery, London: 128, 140(T)
William Campbell: 132(B), 149
Reproduced from *Farthest North*, London, 1897, by permission of Constable & Co. Ltd.: 144
Robert E. Peary, Jr., and Marie Peary Stafford, Courtesy National Geographic Society: 147(B), 148, 150, 151
Trans-Antarctic Expedition: 161(T), 178(B), 179
Black Star: 161(B)
Royal Norwegian Embassy, London: 163(T)
Scott Polar Research Institute: 168/169, 172(T)
By kind permission of Peter Scott: 172(B)
Richard E. Byrd, *Little America*,

Putnam & Co. Ltd., 1930 (photo Capt. McKinley): 174(B)
Sir Francis Younghusband, *The Heart of a Continent*, John Murray Ltd., London: 184(L)
Henri Cartier-Bresson, Magnum: 184/185
Sven Hedin: 186, 187
By kind permission of the Indian Ministry of Scientific and Cultural Affairs: 190(B), 192(B)
B. Arthaud: 191(T)
Wilfred Thesiger, *Arabian Sands*, Longmans Green Ltd. and Curtis Brown Ltd.: 200
Axel Poignant: 210
Illustrated London News: 220(B)
A. Kern: 222(T)
Swissair, Advertising Division: 223(T)
Ronald W. Clark: 223(B), 224, 226(T)
Francis P. Farquahar: 226(B)
Ernest Benn Ltd.: 228(B), 229(T)
The Mount Everest Foundation: 232/233(T), 234, 235, 236, 237
Ministère de la Marine, Paris: 240(B)
Planet News: 245(B); 247

Artists' Credits

Hans Schwarz: 6, 11, 15, 27, 36/37, 40/41, 56/57, 66/67, 74, 81, 88/89, 100, 120/121, 125, 145, 152/153, 181, 188/189, 204, 211, 219, 230, 239, 242/243
Peter Sullivan: 14, 18(T), 24/25, 33, 51, 55, 67, 72/73, 87, 96, 98, 106, 114, 122, 127, 131(T), 136(B), 146, 147(T), 155(T), 156, 159(T), 171(B), 175(T), 178(T), 182(B), 193, 201(B), 207
John Messenger: 17, 26, 32
Brian Lee: 20, 110(T), 140(B), 141(B)
Shirley Kitson: 47